Securing the
Smart Grid

Securing the Smart Grid

Next Generation Power Grid Security

Tony Flick

Justin Morehouse

Technical Editor
Christophe Veltsos

AMSTERDAM • BOSTON • HEIDELBERG • LONDON
NEW YORK • OXFORD • PARIS • SAN DIEGO
SAN FRANCISCO • SINGAPORE • SYDNEY • TOKYO
Syngress is an imprint of Elsevier

SYNGRESS

Acquiring Editor: Rachel Roumeliotis
Development Editor: Matthew Cater
Project Manager: Julie Ochs
Designer: Alisa Andreola

Syngress is an imprint of Elsevier
30 Corporate Drive, Suite 400, Burlington, MA 01803, USA

Library of Congress Cataloging-in-Publication Data
Flick, Tony.
  Securing the smart grid : next generation power grid security / Tony Flick, Justin Morehouse ;
technical editor, Christophe Veltsos.
    p. cm.
  Includes bibliographical references and index.
  ISBN 978-1-59749-570-7 (pbk. : alk. paper)
  1. Electric power systems–Security measures. I. Morehouse, Justin. II. Veltsos, Christophe. III. Title.
TK1025.F58 2011
  333.793'2–dc22   2010029873

British Library Cataloguing-in-Publication Data
A catalogue record for this book is available from the British Library.

For information on all Syngress publications
visit our website at *www.syngress.com*

Printed in the United States of America

10 11 12 13 14   10 9 8 7 6 5 4 3 2 1

Typeset by: diacriTech, Chennai, India

Contents

Acknowledgments (Tony Flick)... xiii

Acknowledgments (Justin Morehouse)....................................... xv

About the Authors... xvii

About the Technical Editor.. xix

Introduction.. xxi

CHAPTER 1   Smart Grid: What Is It?..................................... 1

A Brief History of Electrical Grids..................................... 1

    What Is an Electric Grid?... 1

    Grid Topologies... 2

    Modernizing the Electric Grids.................................... 4

What Is Automatic Meter Reading (AMR)?.................................. 6

    AMR Technologies.. 6

    AMR Network Topologies.. 8

Future Infrastructure.. 8

    Justifications for Smart Grids.................................... 8

What Is a Smart Grid?.. 10

    Components... 10

What Is AMI?.. 13

International Initiatives.. 14

    Australia.. 14

    Canada... 14

    China.. 15

    Europe... 15

Why Do We Need to Secure the Smart Grid?.............................. 15

    Smart Grid versus Security....................................... 16

    Mapping Smart Grid Goals to Security............................. 16

Summary... 18

Endnotes.. 18

CHAPTER 2   Threats and Impacts: Consumers............................ 19

Consumer Threats.. 19

Naturally Occurring Threats... 20

    Weather and Other Natural Disasters.............................. 21

Individual and Organizational Threats................................. 22

    Smart Thieves and Stalkers....................................... 22

    Hackers.. 23

    Terrorism.. 25

    Government.. 26

    Utility Companies.. 27

Impacts on Consumers...................................... 28
    Privacy... 29
Impacts on Availability..................................... 30
    Personal Availability................................. 30
    Mobility.. 31
    Emergency Services................................... 31
Financial Impacts.. 31
Likelihood of Attack....................................... 32
Summary.. 32
Endnotes... 32

CHAPTER 3   **Threats and Impacts: Utility Companies and Beyond**.......... **35**
Confidentiality... 36
    Consumer Privacy..................................... 36
    Proprietary Information............................... 37
Integrity.. 38
    Service Fraud... 38
    Sensor Data Manipulation.............................. 39
Availability... 40
    Consumer Targets..................................... 40
    Organizational Targets................................ 41
    Vertical Targets...................................... 42
    Market Manipulation.................................. 43
    National Security Target............................... 44
Summary.. 47
Endnotes... 48

CHAPTER 4   **Federal Effort to Secure Smart Grids**........................ **49**
U.S. Federal Government................................... 49
    Energy and Independence Security Act of 2007.......... 50
    American Recovery and Reinvestment Act of 2009...... 50
DOE.. 53
    Legacy Electric Grid Technologies..................... 54
    Current Smart Grid Technologies...................... 55
    Lack of Deployment Equals Lack of Risk............... 56
FERC... 56
    Mandatory Reliability Standards....................... 57
    Smart Grid Policy..................................... 57
NIST.. 57
    NIST SP 1108.. 58
    Smart Grid Cyber Security Strategy and Requirements... 62

DHS NIPP.. 66
    Sector-Specific Plans.................................... 67
Other Applicable Laws...................................... 67
    The Identity Theft Enforcement
    and Restitution Act of 2008............................ 67
    Electronic Communications Privacy Act of 1986......... 68
    Breach Notification Laws.............................. 69
    Personal Information Protection
    and Electronic Documents Act.......................... 69
Sponsoring Security.. 70
Bureaucracy and Politics in Smart Grid Security............ 70
Summary.. 70
Endnotes... 71

CHAPTER 5 **State and Local Security Initiatives**......................... **73**
State Government... 73
    State Laws... 73
State Regulatory Bodies.................................... 75
    National Association of Regulatory Utility
    Commissioners... 76
    Colorado PUC.. 78
    PUC of Texas.. 79
    Planning for the Future............................... 80
State Courts... 81
    Colorado Court of Appeals............................. 81
    Implications.. 81
Promoting Security Education............................... 82
Politics and the Smart Grid................................ 83
Summary.. 83
Endnotes... 84

CHAPTER 6 **Public and Private Companies**............................. **85**
Industry Plans for Self-Policing........................... 85
    NERC Critical Infrastructure Protection
    Standards... 86
Compliance Versus Security................................ 104
How Technology Vendors Can Fill the Gaps.................. 105
How Utility Companies Can Fill the Gaps.................. 106
Summary.. 106
Endnotes... 106

CHAPTER 7 **Attacking the Utility Companies**............................ **109**

Motivation.. 109

Vulnerability Assessment versus Penetration Test....... 110

Other Aspects of a Security Assessment................ 111

Network Attacks... 112

Methodologies.. 114

System Attacks.. 119

SCADA... 119

Legacy Systems...................................... 120

Application Attacks.. 121

Life-Imitating Art.................................... 121

Attacking Utility Company Web Applications.......... 122

Attacking Compiled Code Applications................ 134

Wireless Attacks.. 135

Wireless Clients..................................... 137

Wi-Fi... 138

Bluetooth... 138

Cellular... 138

Social Engineering Attacks................................ 138

Selecting Targets.................................... 139

Physical Attacks.. 139

Attacking with a Friend.............................. 139

Putting It All Together.................................... 140

Summary.. 141

Endnotes... 141

CHAPTER 8 **Securing the Utility Companies**........................... **143**

Smart Grid Security Program.............................. 143

ISO/IEC 27000....................................... 144

Top 12 Technical Practices to Secure the Smart Grid........ 153

Threat Modeling..................................... 153

Segmentation.. 154

Default Deny Firewall Rules.......................... 155

Code and Command Signing.......................... 155

Honeypots... 156

Encryption.. 156

Vulnerability Management............................ 156

Penetration Testing.................................. 157

Source Code Review................................. 157

Configuration Hardening............................. 158

Strong Authentication................................. 158
Logging and Monitoring............................. 158
Summary... 159
Endnotes... 159

CHAPTER 9 Third-Party Services.. **161**
Service Providers....................................... 161
Billing.. 161
Consumer Interfaces................................. 162
Device Support....................................... 166
Attacking Consumers.................................. 167
Functionality Undermines Security.................... 167
Microsoft Hohm and Google PowerMeter............. 167
Smart Devices Gone Wild............................ 169
Attacking Service Providers........................... 170
Securing Third-Party Access to the Smart Grid.............. 171
Trust... 171
Data Access.. 172
Network Access...................................... 173
Secure Transport.................................... 174
Assessing the Third Party............................ 175
Securing the Third Party............................. 176
Summary... 177
Endnotes... 177

CHAPTER 10 Mobile Applications and Devices.......................... **179**
Why Mobile Applications?............................. 179
Platforms... 180
Trust.. 180
Trusting Strangers.................................... 181
Attacks... 182
Why Attack the Handset?............................. 183
SMS.. 183
E-mail.. 183
Malicious Web Sites.................................. 184
Physical.. 184
Securing Mobile Devices................................ 186
Traditional Security Controls.......................... 187
Secure Syncing...................................... 187
Disk Encryption...................................... 187
Screen Lock.. 188

Wiping the Device....................................190
Recovery..190
Forensics...190
Education...191
Secure Mobile Applications................................191
Mobile Application Security Controls..................191
Encryption..192
Summary..192
Endnotes...192

CHAPTER 11 **Social Networking and the Smart Grid**......................**195**
The Smart Grid Gets Social................................195
Twitter...195
Facebook..199
Social Networking Threats.................................203
Information Disclosure...............................204
Smart Grid Social Networking Security Checklist...........207
Before You Begin....................................207
Basic Controls......................................207
Summary..209
Endnotes...210

CHAPTER 12 **Attacking Smart Meters**.................................**211**
Open Source Security Testing Methodology
Manual (OSSTMM).......................................211
Information Security.................................213
Process Security Testing............................214
Internet Technology Security Testing................215
Communication Security Testing......................223
Wireless Security Testing...........................223
Physical Security Testing...........................225
NIST Special Publication 800-42: Guideline on
Network Security Testing..................................226
Security Testing Techniques.........................226
Summary..231
Endnotes...231

CHAPTER 13 **Attacking Smart Devices**................................**233**
Selecting a Target Smart Device...........................233
Attacking a Smart Device..................................235
Network Surveying...................................236

Port Scanning...238
Services Identification and System Identification........239
Vulnerability Research and Verification...............241
Internet Application Testing..........................245
Password Cracking....................................251
Denial-of-Service Testing............................254
Exploit Testing......................................255
Summary..256
Endnotes...256

CHAPTER 14 What's Next?...**257**
Timeline...257
What Should Consumers Expect?............................258
Smart Devices..259
Smart Meters...261
Home Area Network....................................266
Electric Vehicles....................................267
Personal Power Plant.................................268
Privacy..268
What Should Smart Grid Technology Vendors Expect?......269
What Should Utility Companies Expect?....................270
Reducing Energy Demand to Reduce Costs
and Security...270
Diagnosing Problems Faster...........................271
Beyond Electricity...................................272
Curiosity Attacks....................................273
What Should Security Professionals Expect
and What Do They Predict?................................273
Security versus Functionality........................273
Security Devices.....................................275
Visions of Gloom and Doom............................275
Smart Grid Community.....................................276
Conferences..276
Agencies and Groups..................................276
Blogs, News Web Sites, and RSS Feeds.................278
Summary..279
Endnotes...279

Index...**283**

Acknowledgments (Tony Flick)

I want to thank my parents for pushing me into the computer science field, buying many computers along the way, and not getting too angry when I would secure their new computer by breaking it. After all, I was only following in my Dad's footsteps after he secured the dustbuster. My dad taught me many things in life and worked hard to give me a good life. From working midnight shifts to keep the streets safe and still finding the time to coach the teams I played on, I can only hope to be half the dad that you were to me someday. Although not the most conventional method, playing cards (euchre and poker were the best) with your collection of pennies, nickels, and dimes at the age of three made math classes enjoyable and easy throughout life. The other parents and teachers often asked me if my parents used flash cards or hired tutors to improve my math skills. I would just think back to the fun I had playing cards, while subconsciously learning the fundamentals of math. Mom, I know you were a little worried when you came home one day and heard me yell, "hit me!" during a poker game at the age of three. But after all, I did eventually get a degree in math.

Mom, you introduced me to computers when you brought home the computer that could only display green characters on the monitor. Playing video games and learning how to initially type with you on that old computer only grew my fascination with electronics, which drove me to the field of computer science and eventually security. I also want to thank you for working hard to give me a better life. I know it was not always easy, but I am eternally grateful for the opportunities you gave me in life.

My brother Matt, thank you for helping significantly with the application security portions of this book, letting me bounce ideas off of you, and providing a ton of great ideas that were used in the book. I am thankful that you always took the time out of your busy schedule to help me with homework and computer-based projects, and to play hours-upon-hours of video games.

I also want to thank my sister for having the patience to review my reports in college and teaching me how to write professionally. Even though I was playing video games with your future husband while you reviewed those reports, I did actually pay attention to your comments and learned from your gentle editing jokes. Hopefully, you can read this book to Brooke and Samantha; it is good to teach security at a young age.

Over the past eight months, I locked myself in my office or hotel room on week-nights and weekends to write this book. I want to thank everyone who supported me during this time and allowed me to shut the world out in order to finish. I can only hope to repay the debt I owe to those who brought me food when I was hungry and convinced me that taking a break to grab a drink, or two, with friends and loved ones could only improve the book.

Thank you Rachel Roumeliotis and Matthew Cater at Syngress for giving us the opportunity to write this book and guiding us along this journey. Christophe Veltsos, thank you for providing advice and suggestions that greatly enhanced the content of this book. Finally, thank you to my coauthor, Justin Morehouse, for working late nights and weekends to write this book.

Acknowledgments
(Justin Morehouse)

I would like to thank my wife, Lisa, the love of my life, for the support, patience, and understanding she showed me throughout the writing process. Without her, much of what I have accomplished and the person I have become today simply would not be. I am grateful to my parents, John and Susan, for always supporting me in whatever endeavors I pursue and teaching me that I am capable of almost anything if I put my mind to it.

Thank you to Rinaldi Rampen, Jeff LoSapio, and Mike Volk for recognizing in me the ability to become someone more than just another consultant and showing me that I could turn my passion into a career. Thank you to Steve Dunkle for reminding me that there is more in this world than just my career. Thank you to the Becks, Ryan, Melissa, and the Joels for your enduring support and understanding.

Thank you to Rachel Roumeliotis, Matthew Cater, and Christophe Veltsos for the support and vision you provided me with while authoring this book. Thank you to Matt Flick, Jeff Yestrumskas, Rich Robertson, and Shawn Moyer for picking up my random calls or responding to my countless e-mails. Finally, thank you to my coauthor, Tony Flick, for battling through these last couple of months to see this book to press.

About the Authors

Tony Flick (CISSP) has been working in the information security field for more than seven years and is currently a principal with FYRM Associates. Tony's background is in network and application security, assessments, compliance, and emerging technologies. In the energy industry, Tony has performed network and application penetration testing, written and reviewed security policies and procedures, and provided guidance for utility companies and related technology vendors. He graduated from the University of Maryland, College Park, with a Bachelor of Science in Computer Science and a Bachelor of Science in Mathematics. Tony has spoken at Black Hat, DEF CON, ShmooCon, ISSA, and OWASP meetings on Smart Grid and application security concepts. Additionally, Tony has been recognized as a security subject matter expert and utilized by numerous media outlets including the Associated Press (AP), *SC* magazine, Dark Reading, and eWeek.

Justin Morehouse (CISSP, CISM, MCSE) has been working in the information security field for over eight years, primarily focusing on the areas of attack and penetration. He has performed over 200 security assessments for Fortune 1000 companies and Federal government agencies and is currently the assessment lead at one of the nation's largest retailers. Justin has developed numerous tools including PassiveRecon and GuestStealer, and has spoken at DEF CON, EntNet, ISSA, ISACA, OWASP and ShmooCon conferences. He graduated with a bachelor's degree from The George Washington University and a master's degree in Information Assurance from Norwich University. Justin is currently an adjunct professor at DeVry University and leads the OWASP Tampa Chapter.

About the Technical Editor

Dr. Christophe Veltsos (CISSP, CISA, CIPP) is a faculty member in the Department of Information Systems & Technology at Minnesota State University, Mankato, where he regularly teaches Information Security and Information Warfare classes. Christophe has presented at the local, regional, and national level, including at major security conferences like RSA.

Beyond the classroom, Christophe is also very active in the security community, engaging with community groups and business leaders as well as IT and security professionals. In 2007, he was elected president of the Mankato chapter of the Information Systems Security Association (ISSA). In 2008, he made numerous contributions to the SANS NewsBites newsletter as an advisory board member. In 2009, he joined and has contributed to the work of the privacy subgroup of the NIST Smart Grid Interoperability Panel Cyber Security Working Group (SGIP-CSWG), formerly known as the NIST Cyber-Security Coordination Task Group (NIST-CSCTG).

Christophe holds a PhD from the University of Louisiana at Lafayette and is a member of many information security and privacy related organizations including ISSA, ISACA, (ISC)^2, and IAPP. Both faculty and practitioner, Christophe maintains the DrInfoSec.com blog.

Introduction

INFORMATION IN THIS CHAPTER

- Book Overview and Key Learning Points
- Book Audience
- How This Book Is Organized
- Conclusion

BOOK OVERVIEW AND KEY LEARNING POINTS

This book provides you 14 chapters of content exploring the strengths and weaknesses of the smart grid. By examining components of the smart grid in detail, you will obtain a strong understanding of how the confidentiality, integrity, and availability of these components can be both compromised and secured.

Discussing both the smart grid's strengths and weaknesses will help you understand threats and attacks, and hopefully prevent insecure deployments of smart grid technologies. In this book, you will also learn controls that will allow consumers, device manufacturers, and utility companies to minimize the risk associated with the smart grid. Each chapter aims to provide you with information that can be used to not only secure current implementations, but future ones as well.

BOOK AUDIENCE

This book will prove to be a valuable resource for anyone who is responsible for the network or application security of smart grid deployments. It will also provide value to those who are tasked with auditing smart grid deployments, as well as consumers utilizing smart grid devices. System engineers, application developers, and system integrators will find value in learning the strengths and weaknesses of the smart grid, and utilize this knowledge to secure current and future deployments.

Executive-level management will gain an appreciation for the complex issues presented by implementing smart grid technologies, as both a provider of these technologies, as well as a consumer. This book will reinforce the value of funding and supporting security initiatives that help protect the smart grid deployments that will soon touch nearly every home, business, and organizations.

HOW THIS BOOK IS ORGANIZED

This book is divided into 14 chapters, each diving deep into specific subject matter. Due to the nature of the subject matter, it is highly recommended that you read this book starting with Chapter 1, "Smart Grid: What is it?" and finishing with

Chapter 14, "What's Next?" Later chapters reference material from previous chapters, building on the concepts, attacks, threats, and technologies already discussed.

Chapter 1: Smart Grid: What Is It?

In this chapter you will learn about the history of electrical grids, ranging from Tesla and Edison to automatic meter reading (AMR). This chapter also discusses the infrastructure that will comprise the smart grid, including automatic metering infrastructure (AMI). Finally, you will learn about international initiatives and review why the smart grid needs to be secured.

Chapter 2: Threats and Impacts: Consumers

This chapter explores potential threats and impacts to the smart grid, and in particular, how they may affect consumers. One of the major goals of the smart grid is to provide more information to consumers, so that they can make informed decisions regarding their energy consumption. By providing information on the threats that consumers will face, readers will learn why they should seek to minimize the risks associated with the smart grid. This chapter furthers the awareness of these threats so that utility companies, technology vendors, and consumers can try to avoid devastating impacts of a successful attack.

Chapter 3: Threats and Impacts: Utility Companies and Beyond

This chapter reviews similar information to Chapter 2, "Threats and Impacts: Consumers," but applies them specifically to utility companies and other organizations. This chapter discusses the threats and impact to such organizations, categorized by the impact to the CIA Triad: Confidentiality, Integrity, and Availability. In this chapter, you will learn how the smart grid will forever change the way that organizations manage risk and the potential impact of successful attacks. The threats and impacts discussed in this chapter are based in reality and are often overlooked when discussing the benefits of the smart grid. This chapter does not aim to spread fear, uncertainty, and doubt, but rather bring to light the potential impact of smart grid deployments so that protective measures can be implemented to prevent such attacks before it is too late.

Chapter 4: Federal Effort to Secure Smart Grids

Many countries consider the security of their electric grids to be a matter of national security and as a result, these governments are funding initiatives and enacting laws to ensure security is considered in smart grids. This chapter explains to readers the different roles that Federal agencies are performing and discusses the different smart grid security standards, guidelines, and best practices being developed by Federal agencies. This chapter also informs the readers of how the Federal government is planning to help utility companies and technology vendors secure the smart grid.

Chapter 5: State and Local Security Initiatives

This chapter focuses on the efforts of state and local governments and organizations. Similar to Chapter 4, "Federal Effort to Secure Smart Grids," this chapter discusses how government agencies are impacting the security of smart grids. Additionally, this chapter examines how the judicial system may use the massive amount of information that is collected in the smart grid. Finally, this chapter discusses the role that state and local agencies will need to perform to educate consumers on how to securely interact with the smart grid.

Chapter 6: Public and Private Companies

This chapter discusses how public and private companies can help secure the smart grid. First, this chapter discusses industry plans for self-policing, such as NERC's Critical Infrastructure Protection standards. Second, you will learn how compliance with such regulations does not equate to securing the smart grid. Finally, this chapter reviews how technology vendors can fill the gaps between compliance and security.

Chapter 7: Attacking the Utility Companies

This chapter addresses the numerous different attack vectors that utility companies should be prepared for. Penetration testing and vulnerability assessments are an integral part of any organization's security program. However, limiting testing to only certain attack vectors can give an organization a false sense of security. Whether you work for a utility company or a third party that performs security assessments, this chapter will help you perform a comprehensive security assessment of utility companies.

Chapter 8: Securing the Utility Companies

In this chapter, you will learn how to build or mature information security programs tailored for utility companies. By taking a detailed look at standards and best practices such as the ISO 27000 series and the ISF's Standard of Good Practice, you will understand the components necessary to implement a functional and effective Information Security program. This chapter also contains the authors' top 12 technical security practices that should be implemented to help secure smart grid deployments. If you work for a utility company, then this chapter is for you!

Chapter 9: Third-Party Services

This chapter examines the trust relationship between utility companies and third parties. In this chapter, you will learn why relaxing security controls for partners can introduce significant risk to your organization. This chapter explores the roles that third-party service providers can perform and how they can potentially be attacked. Additionally, this chapter discusses the risks that utility companies pose to third-party service providers. If the company you work for utilizes third parties or partners with a utility company, then this chapter will help you secure your organization from getting attacked through a trusted partner.

Chapter 10: Mobile Applications and Devices

In this chapter, the use of mobile applications and devices within the smart grid is analyzed. You will learn how utility companies intend to utilize mobile devices and applications to help achieve the goals of the smart grid. This chapter details attacks against mobile devices and mobile applications designed to allow consumers and utility workers to interact with the smart grid. Finally, this chapter will describe how to secure mobile devices, as well as mobile applications.

Chapter 11: Social Networking and the Smart Grid

This chapter discusses the integration of smart devices and social networking sites such as Facebook and Twitter. You will learn the reasons why smart device manufacturers, as well as consumers, are excited about the merger of these two technologies. This chapter then discusses the threats associated with providing energy-consumption data to the masses, as well as includes the authors' Smart Grid Social Networking Security Check List. This check list aims to provide those who plan to utilize social networking sites to capture and potentially distribute energy-consumption data, with a check list of controls to help secure their implementations.

Chapter 12: Attacking Smart Meters

In this chapter, you will learn how to systematically attack smart meters using one of two common security-testing frameworks. First, you will learn how to utilize ISECOM's *Open Source Security Testing Methodology Manual* (OSSTMM) to attack smart meters. This chapter includes discussion of the tools used to attack smart meters, as well as provides resources for you to obtain and utilize the same tools. Following the OSSTMM review, you will learn how to similarly apply NIST's Special Publication 800-42: Guideline on Network Security Testing to Attacking Smart Meters. This chapter will provide you with the information necessary to attack smart meters, as well as understand how they may be attacked.

Chapter 13: Attacking Smart Devices

Where Chapter 12, "Attacking Smart Meters," reviewed the testing methodologies that can be used when attacking smart meters, this chapter shows you how to actually attack a smart device. First, this chapter discusses the process of selecting a target smart device. Then, you will learn how to utilize specific tools to perform network and application layer attacks against the selected smart device. This review is performed utilizing the common security-testing frameworks previously covered in Chapter 12, "Attacking Smart Meters." This chapter is technical and very hands on, so it is recommended that you read Chapter 12, "Attacking Smart Meters," before reading this chapter.

Chapter 14: What's Next?

This chapter wraps up the book by preparing you for what is coming next with the smart grid. In this chapter, you will learn what to expect as a consumer, technology vendor, or utility company. This chapter then discusses what to expect if you are a security professional who works with the smart grid, as well as what some security professionals predict. Finally, this chapter describes how you can get involved in the smart grid community and stay current with the latest developments, as the smart grid becomes a reality.

CONCLUSION

Writing this book has been a rewarding experience for both of us, and we hope that you will enjoy it. This book reviews current and theoretical threats and attacks against today's smart grid and smart devices. As the smart grid evolves, so with these threats and weaknesses. However, the fundamental controls that we discuss in this book should transcend and provide you with a solid foundation for securing today's and tomorrow's smart grid deployments.

Smart Grid: What Is It?

INFORMATION IN THIS CHAPTER

- A Brief History of Electrical Grids
- What Is Automatic Meter Reading (AMR)?
- Future Infrastructure
- What Is a Smart Grid?
- What Is AMI?
- International Initiatives
- Why Do We Need to Secure the Smart Grid?

Over the past several years, the promise of smart grids and their benefits has been widely publicized. Bringing updated technologies to power generation, transmission, and consumption, smart grids are touted to revolutionize our economy, environment, and national security. Corporations large and small foresaw the emerging markets for smart grid technologies and rushed to be the first to deliver. More often than not, security has taken a backseat to the rush to implement. This book will take a look at the potential consequences of designing and implementing smart grid technologies without integrating security. We will also offer recommendations on how to address these consequences so that the promise of smart grids can be fulfilled … securely.

A BRIEF HISTORY OF ELECTRICAL GRIDS

Technologies related to electric grids have roots dating back to the late nineteenth century. Thomas Edison's, as shown in Figure 1.1, direct current (DC) and Nikola Tesla's, as shown in Figure 1.2, alternating current (AC) continue to be utilized to this day. Today, electricity is transmitted using AC, while DC has special applications, usually within residential and commercial buildings.

What Is an Electric Grid?

Electric grids perform three major functions: power generation, transmission, and distribution. Power generation is the first step in delivering electricity and is

FIGURE 1.1

Thomas Edison.

FIGURE 1.2

Nikola Tesla.

performed at power station (coal, nuclear, geothermal, hydro, and so on). Power transmission is the second step in delivering electricity and involves the transfer of electricity from the power stations to power companies' distribution systems. Finally, power distribution completes the electric grids' functions by delivering power to consumers. The major difference between power transmission and power distribution is that power transmission utilizes infrastructure that can handle high voltage (110+ kV), whereas power distribution utilizes infrastructure that can handle medium (<50 kV) and low (<1 kV) voltage.

Grid Topologies

In its simplest form, an electric grid is a network. The use of the term "grid" can refer to a complete infrastructure that encompasses power generation, transmission, and distribution, or it can refer to a subset of a larger infrastructure.

Distribution networks are less complicated than that of transmission networks, as transmission networks are often interconnected with other regional transmission networks to provide greater redundancy. At first glance, this interconnection appears to provide greater reliability in feeding distribution networks, but many factors come into play in ensuring continuous power to end consumers.

Transmission networks must effectively manage both power generation and consumption as a power failure, or spike in consumption in one area may result in adverse affects in another area of the network. The United States established the North American Electric Reliability Corporation (NERC – www.nerc.com) to ensure the reliability of the bulk power system in North America. This nonprofit organization's area of responsibility includes the contiguous United States, Canada, and part of the Baja peninsula in Mexico.

There are two primary topologies in use in the United States for power distribution. The most common topology is the radial grid, as shown in Figure 1.3. In a radial grid, electricity is distributed from a substation in a pattern that resembles a tree with many branches and leaves. As the electricity is carried across the power lines, its strength is reduced until it reaches its final destination. The other primary topology utilized for power distribution is mesh grid, as shown in Figure 1.4. Mesh grids provide greater reliability than radial grids because in a radial grid, each branch and leaf receives power from a single source (the tree), whereas in a mesh grid, power can be provided through other sources (other branches and leaves). Radial grids do provide limited redundancy, in that a second substation in close proximity can feed into the grid, but this assumes that the secondary substation is not suffering from the same condition as the primary.

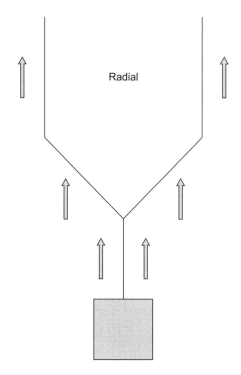

FIGURE 1.3

Radial grid.

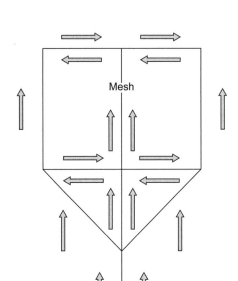

FIGURE 1.4

Mesh grid.

The looped topology, utilized primarily in Europe, is a mix between the radial and mesh topologies. A looped topology, as shown in Figure 1.5, is much like a radial topology, except that each branch and leaf has two separate paths from the substation. Where the radial topology is vulnerable to single points of failure, the looped topology provides greater reliability. The goal of the looped topology is to be able to withstand a disruption in the grid, regardless of where it may occur. Much like the mesh topology, the looped topology is costlier than the radial topology, as each end of the loop must meet the requirements for power and voltage drops.

Modernizing the Electric Grids

Currently, the electrical infrastructure in the United States is not up to the task of powering America's future. According to Carol Browner, director of the White House Office of Energy and Climate Change, "We [the United States] have a very antiquated (electric grid) system in our country...The current system is

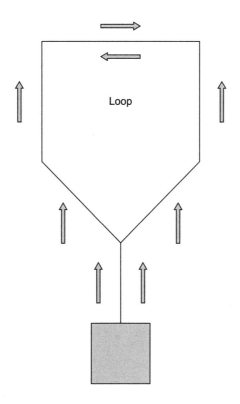

FIGURE 1.5

Loop topology.

outdated, it's dilapidated."[1] Across all three functions of an electrical grid, significant improvements can be made to increase the reliability and efficiency of power generation, transmission, and distribution.

Deregulation is often touted as a means to modernizing today's electrical grids. Deregulation encompasses moving from today's regulated landscape where often larger power companies are granted monopoly status and control power generation, transmission, and distribution for a geographic area to a deregulated landscape where the free markets would dictate all three functions of the electrical grids. In a deregulated landscape, power generation, transmission, and distribution could be handled by separate companies, all working to provide more efficient, reliable, and cost-effective solutions.

Many other ideas exist to modernize today's electrical grids. The most prominent of which is the smart grid. Recent initiatives championed by the Obama Administration, including $3.4 billion awarded for projects such as smart meter implementations, grid infrastructure advancement, and manufacturing smart appliances[2] will soon be a reality.

WHAT IS AUTOMATIC METER READING (AMR)?

Evolving from Tesla's design, the automatic meter reading (AMR) infrastructure introduced automation to the electric grid in 1977 (read more at www.metretekfl. com). Through a combination of technologies, including wired and wireless networks, AMR's most significant advancement resulted in electric companies being able to remotely read meters. Once AMR was implemented, the electric companies could more easily obtain meter readings in near real time, and provide customers with consumption-based bills. Previously, the electric companies relied on estimates when billing customers. With better, timelier information, electric companies were able to improve energy production through tighter control during peak and low demand periods.

AMR Technologies

To support the advancements of the AMR infrastructure, several technologies are utilized. For data collection, utility employees leverage handhelds and notebook computers. For data transport, wired and wireless networks are deployed to remotely read meter data.

Handhelds

Supporting utility employees' efforts to quickly and efficiently obtain meter readings, handheld devices, much like your common Personal Digital Assistant (PDA), as shown in Figure 1.6, are utilized. These devices read meter data in one of two ways. First, the electric worker can utilize "touch" technology to read a meter by simply touching the meter with a probe. This probe stores the meter data to the handheld for later retrieval and processing. Second, the handheld device may instead be fitted with a wireless receiver that reads the data transmitted by the meter, again with the data stored for later retrieval and processing.

Notebook Computers

Utility employees also utilize traditional mobile computers in meter reading. Rather than physically visiting each meter, as with the handheld devices, a mobile computer can be installed inside of an electric worker's vehicle to wirelessly read meters. Usually these deployments involve a combination of technologies, including a wireless technology, software, and the necessary hardware (GPS, antennas, and so on).

Wireless Networks

For data transport, a broad range of wireless technologies are utilized by the electric companies to read meter data. Radio Frequency (RF), Wi-Fi, Bluetooth, and even cellular technologies are currently in use. A majority of AMR devices utilize RF wireless technologies, with narrow band, direct-sequence spread spectrum (DSSS), and frequency-hopping spread spectrum (FHSS) being the most

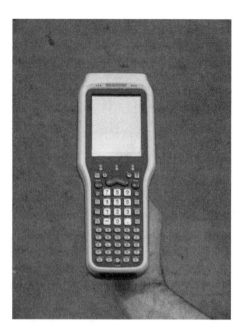

FIGURE 1.6

A wireless handheld device.

common. Less common technologies such as Zigbee and Wavenis have found their way into AMR deployments. When wireless communications are utilized, device makers either license frequencies from government agencies such as the Federal Communications Commission (FCC) or use unlicensed frequencies.

When Wi-Fi is chosen as the technology for remote data transport, traditionally the meters are not themselves Wi-Fi enabled, rather a management station that they report to (through RF) utilizes Wi-Fi to communicate its aggregated data to the electric company. This is the deployment model utilized by the city of Corpus Christi in Texas. In this deployment, the power meters mostly rely on the use of batteries and thus utilizing Wi-Fi was impractical because of its relatively high power consumption, when compared with RF. The power consumption requirements of Wi-Fi technology remain a barrier to its inclusion in AMR deployments.

Power Line Communication (PLC)

Power line communication (PLC) provides a completely remote solution for reading meter data. Data from meters is transmitted across the existing power line infrastructure to the local substation. From the local substation, data is then transported to the electric companies for processing and analysis. This type of dedicated infrastructure from the meter to the electric company is commonly referred to as a "fixed" network.

Hybrid Models

Although some AMR deployments may rely on a single technology for each part of its deployment, others utilize a hybrid model where multiple technologies are used. For example, data transport may primarily rely on PLC, but RF may be utilized if the PLC is unavailable. Other hybrid models may rely on RF to send data to aggregation points and then utilize PLC or Wi-Fi to transport data to the electric company.

AMR Network Topologies

Utilizing one or a combination of the aforementioned technologies, electric companies create a network from which meter information is obtained. These networks take on one of several topologies, including the following:

- Star network – A star network topology is implemented when meters transmit data to a central location. This central location can be a repeater, which then forwards the data to the electric companies, or it can simply act as data storage. A star network topology can utilize wireless technologies, PLC, or both.
- Mesh network – A mesh network topology is implemented when the meters themselves both transmit and receive data from other meters. Meters act much like the repeaters in a star network, and eventually data reaches the electric companies or a data storage device.

What Does It All Mean?

Looking at all of the parts that make up an AMR infrastructure, it is easy to see that security needs to be included from the design phase. With such a wide range of technologies possessing the ability to impact the confidentiality, availability, and integrity of data being transmitted across the AMR infrastructure, it is imperative to evaluate the security posture of each individual technology, as well as its interactions with other technologies.

FUTURE INFRASTRUCTURE

As described in "A Brief History of Electrical Grids" section of this chapter, the current electric power infrastructure was designed to utilize existing technology and handle the requirements defined during the nineteenth and twentieth centuries. The increasing demands on an aging infrastructure can only be met by the fine-grain control and insight into consumer demand that the smart grid promises to deliver.

Justifications for Smart Grids

The proposed smart grids seek to remediate these issues, as well as numerous others. The major justifications for smart grids tend to fall into three categories: economic, environmental, and reliability. The United States Department of Energy (DOE) defines the goals of a smart grid as[3] follows:

- Ensuring its reliability to degrees never before possible
- Maintaining its affordability
- Reinforcing our global competitiveness
- Fully accommodating renewable and traditional energy sources
- Potentially reducing our carbon footprint
- Introducing advancements and efficiencies yet to be envisioned.

Waste

Electricity must be consumed as soon as it is produced and consumers have grown accustom to the on-demand availability of electricity. Currently, this combination requires utility companies to generate enough supply to meet the electrical demand at any given moment. Because the exact demand is unknown, utility companies generate more electricity than is needed to compensate for the unexpected rise in consumption and achieve this level of service. This system of supply and demand results in waste when demand is overestimated and rolling blackouts when demand is underestimated.

Reliability

In addition to waste, the reliability of the electric grid can be disrupted by numerous factors. Specifically, a drop in voltage from a power supply can cause brownouts, whereas environmental factors ranging from falling trees to thunderstorms and hurricanes can cause blackouts. Although these reliability problems tend to occur on a local scale, they can lead to more widespread problems that affect larger areas. Table 1.1 describes the different categories of power outages.

Renewable Energy Sources

Traditional power generation relies on an inexhaustible supply of energy resources that has no negative effects on the world. In such a scenario, centralized power

Table 1.1 Power outage categories[4]	
Category	**Description**
Dropout	A loss of power that has a short duration, on a timescale of seconds, and is usually fixed quickly.
Brownout	The electrical power supply encounters a partial drop in voltage, or temporary reduction in electric power. In the case of a three-phase electric power supply, when a phase is absent, at reduced voltage, or incorrectly phased.
Blackout	An affected area experiences a complete loss of electrical power, ranging from several hours to several weeks.
Load shedding	An electric company either reduces or completely shuts off the available power to sections of the grid. Sometimes referred to as rolling brownouts and rolling blackouts.

generation that relies on an endless supply of the traditional energy resources would excel. However, limited resources and concerns over environmental impact are driving the movement for clean and renewable energy sources, such as wind and solar. Unfortunately, these types of clean, renewable resources have problems of their own including localization and continuity. For example, a solar power plant could generate large amounts of electricity if located in Florida; however, the output would be negligible if located in Antarctica. Additionally, current solar power plants all but cease to generate power during the night or during severe weather such as thunderstorms and hurricanes, which would drive the need for alternate sources of energy to meet demand. As a result, the current electric grid simply does not properly accommodate renewable energy sources.

WHAT IS A SMART GRID?

A smart grid is not a single device, application, system, network, or even idea. There is no single, authoritative definition for the question: What is a smart grid? However, the definitions from the various authoritative organizations, such as DOE, NERC, and SmartGrids Technology Platform (www.smartgrids.eu/), follow a common theme: Smart grids utilize communication technology and information to optimally transmit and distribute electricity from suppliers to consumers. Figure 1.7 illustrates the basic concepts of a smart grid. Additionally, smart grid is not a static concept. It will continue to evolve as the existing technologies evolve and new technologies are developed. The type, configuration, and implementation of these technologies and the access to and transmission and use of relevant information are of primary concern in securing smart grids and for this book.

Components

To achieve the desired goals of reliable, efficient, and clean energy distribution, smart grids employ a combination of different technologies. According to DOE, the following technologies are considered Key Technology Areas[3]:

- Integrated two-way communication
- Advanced components
- Advanced control methods
- Sensing and measurement technologies
- Improved interfaces and decision support
- Applications of smart grid technology.

Integrated Two-Way Communication

Two-way communication enables operators to monitor and interact with components of the smart grid in real time. This type of communication improves the operator's ability to manage grid operations. For example, in the current grid, operators are unaware of blackouts until customers notify them, typically by way of

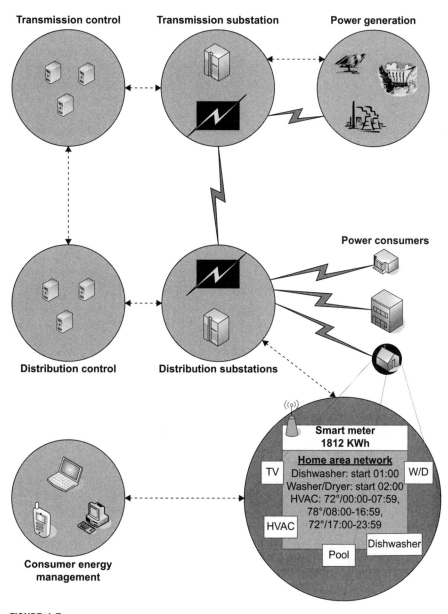

FIGURE 1.7

Basic smart grid diagram.

telephone calls to a customer support center. In a smart grid, operators are able to detect and manage the problem without any notification from customers, resulting in faster problem resolution and decreased operational costs. In order to achieve this capability, the components of smart grids require two-way communication abilities. Different smart grid implementations will employ different technologies, but they will all require an underlying network for data transport. Current smart grids utilize the networking technologies that are also used in AMR deployments, as previously discussed in the "AMR Network Topologies" section of this chapter.

Advanced Components

Advanced components include the areas of superconductivity, fault tolerance, excess electricity storage, smart devices, and diagnostics equipment. This technology actively determines the electrical behavior of the grid.[3] For example, the excess electricity that is created during the day by solar power plants could be stored in electrical storage devices and used during the night when the solar power plant is unable to generate electricity. So-called smart devices can provide useful consumption feedback to both the consumer and the energy providers to enable better energy management. Although the above-mentioned list may appear to be a dispersed variety of technological devices, this Key Technology Area involves smart grid components that will provide unique advantages over technology of the current grid.

Advanced Control Methods

Utilizing the two-way communication component described in the "Integrated Two-Way Communication" section of this chapter, the advanced control methods allow operators (human or machine) to manage the various smart grid components. Specifically, the advanced control methods enable advanced data collection, as well as diagnostics and appropriate maintenance. For example, an operator could identify a problem with a component and apply a patch remotely, thus saving time and costs associated with sending crews to the location of the problem.

Sensing and Measurement Technologies

New sensing and measurement technologies support smart grid stability, health, and security functionality. The most common of these technologies is the smart meter. Figure 1.8 displays a current smart meter. A smart meter monitors usage statistics and reports the usage details to the utility company, consumers, and third-party service providers. Depending on the smart meter and supporting infrastructure, the smart meter can be used for other administrative functions, such as power outage notification and remotely disabling service.

Improved Interfaces and Decision Support

Humans and machines understand different languages and, as a result, important information can be lost in translation. Due to its nature, a smart grid will collect data too complex and immense for a human to comprehend in a short time frame. The human machine interface (HMI) must be able to simplify the data and

FIGURE 1.8

Example smart meter.

resulting analysis in an efficient manner to enable operators and managers to make decisions quickly. HMI can be described as how users interact with a machine. According to the International Engineering Consortium (IEC – www.iec.org), the success of a system often relies on how effective the HMI is in gaining the user's acceptance of the system.[5]

Applications of Smart Grid Technology

An informed consumer is an intelligent consumer. This is the theoretical reason behind the drive to provide consumers with real-time usage data. Applications will provide consumers with real-time usage statistics and pricing, as well as recommendations for reducing their utility bill, such as running the dishwasher late at night during nonpeak hours as opposed to the afternoon when residents return from work or school. The applications seek to provide this information in a ubiquitous manner ensuring the consumer always knows exactly how much electricity they are using and how much that electricity costs.

TIP

Security should not be sacrificed for functionality. Utility companies and third-party application service providers should ensure the confidentiality of this information.

WHAT IS AMI?

Advanced metering infrastructure (AMI) allows utility companies to remotely measure, collect, and analyze usage statistics from smart meters. AMI is similar to AMR; however, AMI provides a significant upgrade over AMR: two-way communication with the meter. The information gathered by the smart meter drives the demand-response smart grid and enables the majority of smart grid applications. The underlying network in an AMI implementation connects the meters with business systems and ultimately provides this information to customers, utility companies, and service providers.

> **WARNING**
>
> An easy approach to providing business partners with this information is to grant them access to a database in your internal network; however, this approach could leave your environment at risk. The principle of least privilege should always be applied, including with your "trusted" business partners.

INTERNATIONAL INITIATIVES

Although the main focus for smart grid deployments is on the United States, other areas around the globe are making headway in implementing smart grid technologies. Spanning the globe, countries including Australia, Canada, and China have established smart grid deployments, projects, and initiatives. Along with the United States, Europe is leading the march toward smart grid technologies, with several large deployments and initiatives.

Australia

In 2009, the Australian government promised to reserve $100 million for the development of smart grid technologies through the Nation Energy Efficiency Initiative. The goal of Australia's smart grid is to deliver a more efficient, robust, and consumer-friendly electric network.[6] Coined as the "Smart Grid, Smart City" initiative, Australia aims to implement a smart grid that utilizes advanced communications, sensors, and meters with existing transmission and distribution networks in an attempt to automate, monitor, and regulate the bidirectional flow of power.

The Smart Grid, Smart City initiative will select one proposal and implement its design into a single community that is serviced by a single power company. Australia is hoping to showcase not only modernized transmission and distribution networks in the demonstration community, but also modernized consumer applications and devices. The project is currently slated for proposal assessment and announcement in late 2010.

Canada

In 2006, as part of the Energy Conservation Responsibility Act, Ontario's government mandated that all consumers be provided with smart meters by 2010. Hydro One, a power company owned by the government of Ontario, is currently deploying smart meters to 1.3 million consumers within the Province of Ontario. This deployment is utilizing smart meters from Trilliant (www.trilliantinc.com/), a Redwood City, California based company and was named the "Best AMR Initiative in North America" by the Utility Planning Network in October of 2007.

China

On May 21, 2009, China publicized its desire to implement smart grid technologies through the "Strengthened Smart Grid" initiative. This initiative is broken down into three distinct phases: Planning and Testing, Construction and Development, and Upgrading. From 2009 through 2010, the Planning and Testing phase of the Strengthened Smart Grid will focus on developing plans, technologies, standards, and performing trials. The Construction and Development phase will occur from 2011 through 2015 and will include infrastructure construction, operational framework development, device manufacturing, and deployment. The final stage, Upgrading, will occur from 2016 to 2020 and will simply complete the initiative.[7]

Europe

In 2005, the European Union (EU) created the European Technology Platform for the Electricity Networks of the Future. Alternatively known as the SmartGrids Platform, this European Commission was founded by the European Commission Directorate General for Research and is charged with advancing the EU's electricity networks.

The SmartGrids Platform developed a shared vision that Europe's smart grid technologies of tomorrow will be[8]

- Flexible – Address the needs of consumers while adapting to changing environments.
- Accessible – Provide universal access to all users to ensure they can utilize renewable power.
- Reliable – Assure security and consistency that meet future demands while withstanding hazards and uncertainty.
- Economic – Provide value through innovation and efficient energy management through competition and regulation.

The SmartGrids Platform's goal for achieving this vision is 2020. A recommended read is the "European SmartGrids Technology Platform: Vision and Strategy for Europe's Electricity Networks of the Future," published in 2006.

WHY DO WE NEED TO SECURE THE SMART GRID?

At this point, smart grids may seem like the panacea for the world's energy problems. They promise increased efficiency, reliability, and a more economical means of distributing and transmitting power. These improvements rely on new technologies and new levels of interconnectivity built into the electrical grid, as well as cooperation among different organizations and analysis of massive amounts of data. However, with every new technology and with easier access to energy data and devices come new attack vectors that can be exploited.

Smart Grid versus Security

When most people hear the terms "new technology," "interconnectivity," "data sharing," and "business partners," the immediate thought is of new functionality and benefits. Alternatively, security professionals immediately consider the new risks that these new functionalities and benefits have introduced to the environment. Security professionals commonly rely on the principle of least privilege to secure data and resources, which restricts access. As a result, security departments sometimes conflict with business units and security controls can sometimes conflict with new functionality; however, properly implemented security controls should not impede proper functionality. The purpose of a security control is to enable the functionality to operate correctly and protect against abuse and misuse. Ideally, security professionals would work with business units to ensure the new functionality operates in a secure manner, while striving to maintain the original intended purpose.

> **NOTE**
> The principle of least privilege requires that a user be given no more privileges than necessary to perform his/her job function.[9] By limiting access to only the required users, the risk introduced is reduced to an acceptable and manageable level.

Completely secure applications, networks, or environments do not exist and smart grids will not be an exception. Marketing schemes that advertise "Hacker Proof" systems are simply marketing schemes and have never held up in the real world. Although each of the identified smart grid components introduces much needed functional or operational improvements, they also introduce new vulnerabilities and additional risk into the electrical grid. If not properly managed, attackers will exploit these vulnerabilities for various, common motives including curiosity, profit, notoriety, activism, and warfare.

Mapping Smart Grid Goals to Security

One of the often-mentioned goals of smart grids is to increase the security of the electric grid. This may make security seem like an additional feature; however, security will need to be integrated into smart grids to be effective. Confidentiality, integrity, and availability (CIA) are the core principles of information security that must be applied to ensure the smart grid goals are achieved.

Reliability

As explained in the "Justifications for Smart Grids" section of this chapter, one of the intended improvements of smart grids over the traditional grid is reliability. Reliability can be mapped to the information security principles of availability and integrity. Security is responsible for preventing all forms of denial of service (DoS), which includes both human initiated and environmental attacks. With the proper security controls, smart grids are able to either prevent or minimize the negative impact of DoS; thus, increasing the reliability of the grid.

Data analysis will play a major role in smart grids and the accuracy, or integrity, of the data is vital. Appropriate security controls are required to ensure collected data has not been tampered with. For example, smart meters will be sending consumption statistics to the utility company for billing and operational purposes. A security mechanism, such as hashing, could be used in this example to enable the utility company to validate the consumption data and ensure their customers are accurately billed.

Affordability

For smart grids to be successful, their benefits can not significantly increase costs for utility companies, and ultimately consumers. The implementation and operational costs of smart grids must not affect the affordability. Although the exact amount is unknown, recent estimates put the cost of electricity theft at $6 billion per year.[10] Meter tampering is one of the largest methods for electricity theft in the current grid, and similarly, smart meters used in smart grids are expected to be targeted. Appropriate security controls will be required to ensure the integrity of smart meters, as well as each component in the smart grid. Although eliminating fraud and electricity theft is unrealistic, reducing the amount will result in significant savings for the utility companies. As a result, allowing utility companies to charge customers cheaper rates.

Accommodating Renewable Energy Sources

Renewable energy sources are intended to play a major role in the future electric grid. Electricity theft is a concern that utility companies have faced for decades; however, a new related concern will be with consumers, fraudulently, selling electricity to the grid. If a customer installs solar panels on their roof, they will have the ability to sell excess electricity to the grid; however, utility companies will need to ensure that they are not paying for spoofed electricity. Similar to the affordability goal, the integrity of smart grid components will be vital to accommodating renewable energy sources in an effective manner.

Reducing Our Carbon Footprint

One proposed method to reduce our carbon footprint is to reduce our energy consumption. Utilizing the data collected through components of the smart grid, utility companies and third parties will provide consumers with real-time usage statistics to help consumers modify their habits to reduce their energy usage. Due to privacy concerns, the confidentiality of this information must be maintained through proper security controls, such as encryption.

SUMMARY

The centuries old debate between Thomas Edison, Nikola Tesla, and George Westinghouse continues. Both AC and DC are utilized today, and the current centralized power generation model, George Westinghouse's vision, has been called into question. Smart grids will support more distributed power generation options that utilize localized renewable resources.

Before the 1990s, the majority of software applications were developed for internal use only and were not prepared for unrestricted access through Internet connectivity. Similarly, the electric grid was not designed with modern interconnected networks in mind and will encounter significant new risks. Security can either be viewed as an obstacle to the progress of smart grids or as an enabler to allow nations to meet their ambitious smart grid goals.

Endnotes

1. CBN.com. Obama pledges $3.4B to upgrade power grid [document on the Internet]. Christian Broadcasting Network; www.cbn.com/cbnnews/politics/2009/October/Obama-Pledges-34B-to-Upgrade-Power-Grid; 2009 [accessed 15.11.09].
2. M2M Magazine. Smart grid stimulus funds awarded [document on the Internet]. Specialty Publishing Co; www.m2mmag.com/news/articles/article.aspx?ID=8028; 2009 [accessed 06.11.06].
3. The U.S. Department of Energy. Technology providers [document on the Internet]. www.oe.energy.gov/DocumentsandMedia/TechnologyProviders.pdf; 2009.
4. Energy Vortex. Energy dictionary [document on the Internet]. www.energyvortex.com/energydictionary/blackout__brownout__brown_power__rolling_blackout.html; [accessed 06.11.09].
5. International Engineering Consortium. IEC: on-line education: WPF: the human-machine interface (HMI) [document on the Internet]. www.iec.org/online/tutorials/hmi/topic01.asp; 2007 [accessed 17.11.09].
6. National Energy Efficiency Initiative. Smart grid, smart city [document on the Internet]. Department of the Environment, Water, Heritage and the Arts; www.environment.gov.au/smartgrid; 2009 [accessed 29.10.2009].
7. Li J. From strong to smart: the Chinese smart grid and its relation with the globe [document on the Internet]. www.aepfm.org/ufiles/pdf/Smart%20Grid%20-%20AEPN%20Sept.pdf; 2009.
8. European smartgrids technology platform: vision and strategy for Europe's electricity networks of the future [document on the Internet]. European Commission; http://ec.europa.eu/research/energy/pdf/smartgrids_en.pdf; 2006.
9. Ferraiolo DF, Cugini JA, Kuhn DR. National Institute of Standards and Technology. Role-based access control (RBAC): features and motivations [document on the Internet]. http://hissa.nist.gov/rbac/newpaper/rbac.html; 1995.
10. Energy Association of Pennsylvania. How safe is your utility from theft of service? [document on the Internet]. 2007 [accessed 06.11.09]. www.energypa.org/EEP%20Fall%2007_Energy%20Theft%20-%20EAPA%20TF%20Presentation%209%2007.pdf.

Threats and Impacts: Consumers

INFORMATION IN THIS CHAPTER

- Consumer Threats
- Naturally Occurring Threats
- Individual and Organizational Threats
- Impacts on Consumers
- Impacts on Availability
- Financial Impacts
- Likelihood of Attack

Either directly or indirectly, consumers will be affected by the threats to smart grids. Consumers can be a threat to utility companies; however, they can also be victims. One of the goals of smart grids discussed in Chapter 1, "Smart Grid: What is it?," is providing consumers with more information regarding their energy usage and rates for the electricity they consume. In order to protect consumers from the threats discussed in this chapter, consumers will also need to be informed about these threats, the potential attack vectors, and the protections needed to defend against them. Responsibility for educating consumers will most likely become a hotly debated topic, but a combined effort from government, corporate, and consumer advocacy organizations will most likely develop.

When discussing threats to information technology systems, the easy solution is to just blame hackers. But hackers only represent a small portion of the threats that information technology systems, and ultimately smart grids, have faced in the past and will face in the future. This chapter will describe the different types of threats that smart grids will encounter from the perspective of the consumer.

CONSUMER THREATS

Consumers facing threats from modern technology is nothing new. Although not entirely the same, consumers have faced similar threats from using personal computers, cellular phones, and the current electrical grid. As the dependency on technology grows, so does the dependency on electricity to power the technology. When you take away a single piece of technology from a consumer, such as a laptop or cell phone, the consumer might get angry but will easily adapt. Consumers can easily replace cell phones, but when access to electricity is taken away, consumers would find themselves without access to all of the technology they had grown reliant on. As such, smart grid threats will impact consumers in a variety of different ways ranging from privacy to emergency life support situations.

NATURALLY OCCURRING THREATS

According to the NERC Disturbance Analysis Working Group (DAWG), utilities in the United States and Canada reported 104 disturbances to the bulk electric system during the first three quarters of 2009.[1] As illustrated in Figure 2.1, natural threats, such as severe weather and natural disasters, caused more than 50 percent of these disturbances.

Ranging from small storms to natural disasters, smart grids will face natural threats that can significantly impact consumers. Redundancy can be built into most

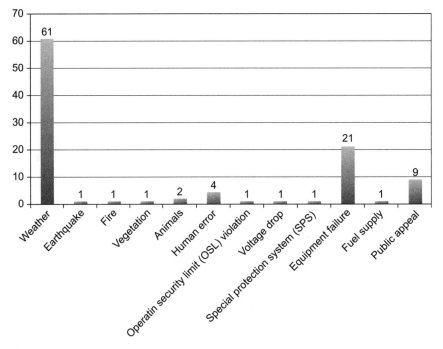

FIGURE 2.1

Breakdown of major causes for disturbances in the United States and Canada in the first three quarters of 2009.[1]

areas of smart grids, but there will still be single points of failure for consumers. Under the current vision, smart grids will be able to route power from a number of different sources. Power lines will still be required to deliver electricity to the consumer's home or office building, but if the single power line connected to the consumer's house is disconnected, the number of different routes in the grid will not matter to that consumer. For example, if a strong wind causes a tree in a consumer's yard to fall onto the power line, the consumer would lose power.

Weather and Other Natural Disasters

In the example from the previous section regarding a falling tree, a utility company should be able to fix the power line and restore power to the consumer within a short amount of time due to the threat being limited to one consumer. However, this will not always be the case. In 2005, Hurricane Katrina caused power outages, which lasted for weeks, to more than 1.7 million people.[2] Additionally, the number of tropical cyclones forming in the Atlantic Ocean rose in previous years, as shown in Figure 2.2. "The average number of named storms since 1995 has been 13, compared to 8.6 during the preceding 25 years during which time the multi-decadal signal was

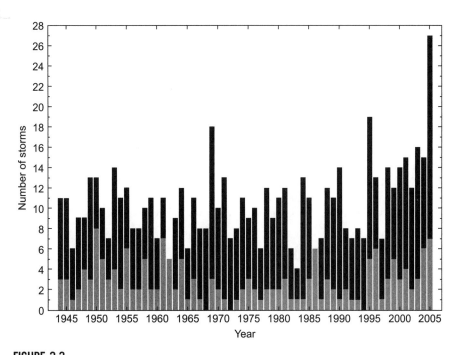

FIGURE 2.2

Number of named storms in the Atlantic Ocean from 1944 through 2005.[2]

in an inactive phase. An average of 7.7 hurricanes and 3.6 major hurricanes since 1995 compares to 5 hurricanes and 1.5 major hurricanes from 1970–1994."[2] The number of significant storms per year will fluctuate, but for the foreseeable future, storms that produce strong winds and other damaging effects will remain a threat to electric grids.

Hurricanes will affect consumers who live and work near the coastline, but every geographical region is under threat to some type of natural disaster or severe weather. For example, consumers in the state of Iowa may not be affected by hurricanes, but tornadoes, blizzards, and floods could affect them. Similarly, consumers in Southern California may not be affected by blizzards, but earthquakes and wildfires can greatly impact the distribution of electricity.

NOTE

Completely eliminating the damage from severe weather or natural disasters is simply not feasible in the near future. Because we cannot stop severe weather from happening, incident response programs will continue to be critical in responding to destructive natural phenomenon.

INDIVIDUAL AND ORGANIZATIONAL THREATS

Advanced metering infrastructure (AMI) and other components of smart grids will allow operators to remotely administer devices in consumer homes. Additionally, smart devices within consumer's home area networks (HAN) will allow consumers and potentially utility companies to remotely control electricity usage. For example, some utility companies will offer a credit to customers in exchange for the ability to turn off the customer's air conditioner or heater during peak demand times. Numerous motives will drive people and organizations to abuse these smart grid functionalities, as well as much other functionality. From angry neighbors to terrorist organizations, the possibility of gaining control of AMI components, HAN devices, and these functionalities will lead to attacks against smart grids and ultimately the consumers utilizing smart grids for electricity.

Smart Thieves and Stalkers

The vision of the smart grid promises to empower consumers with information regarding their energy consumption. Consumers will be able to monitor their energy consumption in quasi-real time, such as hourly, whereas consumers are currently informed of their usage on a monthly basis. One of the desired results is to enable consumers to modify their behaviors in order to reduce their electricity bill. With access to this kind of reconnaissance information, however, others could use it to enable their malicious acts.

This level of information will greatly aid a thief in burglarizing consumers. For example, Alice's utility company uses a social networking site, such as Twitter, to provide real-time energy usage statistics to their customers. Bob, a thief, decides Alice is going to be his next target and begins to monitor Alice's energy usage through her utility company's tweets. Over the course of the first month, Bob notices that Alice uses about 100 W/h, or 2.4 kW/day. He also notes that she uses significantly more electricity between 7:00 A.M. and 8:00 A.M., and then notices a significant drop-off until around 4:00 P.M. Bob uses his powers of deduction to determine that Alice wakes up and leaves for work sometime between 7:00 A.M. and 8:00 A.M., and does not return home until sometime between 4:00 P.M. and 5:00 P.M. Additionally, Bob has noticed that Alice's hourly electricity usage for the last three days has been significantly lower and has not had the normal peaks of her daily usage. Bob now deduces that Alice has not been home for the past three days and is most likely traveling away from home. Thus, Bob now has a window of opportunity to burglarize Alice's home. Taking this concept one step further, a thief could exploit access to consumers' information to identify the best targets, determine daily and weekly activities, and determine when he/she could use washing machines, driers, dishwashers, and other noisy devices as a cover for malicious activities.

A stalker could also benefit greatly by accessing a target's smart grid information. Suppose Alice typically entertains friends and family with dinner parties at her home on Saturday evenings, requiring higher energy usage between the hours of 6:00 P.M. and 10:00 P.M. Recently, Alice's house has tweeted higher energy usage only between 6:00 P.M. and 7:30 P.M. before dropping back down to a standard level, and then increasing again during the 11:00 P.M. to midnight hour. Even more interesting is that now Alice plugs in her electric vehicle to charge during the predawn Sunday morning hours every nondinner party Saturday. With similar powers of deduction, Stalker Steve may deduce that Alice has started a romantic relationship and has been driving to various destinations. If Steve can access more detailed electricity usage information, he may be able to calculate exactly how far Alice has been driving by comparing vehicle recharge energy amounts (dinner party Saturdays versus others). Stalker Steve could then begin to determine Alice's favorite dining locations, dating habits, and ultimately map out Alice's life.

Hackers

The motives for hacking smart grids will cover a broad range. The following list describes the common motives of hackers that can be applied to any environment:

- Intellectual challenge
- Self-expression and peer recognition
- Testing computer security
- Mischief or curiosity
- Monetary gain
- Power
- Vengeance and vindictiveness
- Attacking the "system" or terrorism[3]

These motives will still be relevant with smart grids and can impact consumers in new ways.

Nonmalicious Motives

Not every hacker has malicious intent when hacking into a system. Some hackers are driven by the intellectual challenge of bypassing the security of a system and curiosity of knowing how a device works. To these hackers, the security and operation of the system is a puzzle to be cracked. Smart grid components, such as smart meters and smart devices, will extend into consumers homes and may connect to their home network. Easy physical access to these devices will further entice people to hack components of the smart grid. Other motives, such as self-expression and peer recognition, will drive hackers to use smart grids as a means for obtaining personal gratification or for egotistical purposes. Although these hackers may not have malicious intentions, their actions can inadvertently cause negative impacts against consumers.

Testing Computer Security

Robust information security programs include regular security testing to identify vulnerabilities that could impact the security posture of an environment. The intent of this testing is to improve the overall security posture, and smart grid security programs should also include security testing. Professional security testers, or ethical hackers, take precautions to prevent negative impact during testing; however, risk does exist in performing this testing. In 2007, the Department of Homeland Security leaked a video of a security test where security testers were able to hack into a power plant's generator. The security testers successfully exploited a vulnerability, now commonly known as the Aurora vulnerability, using only digital means and caused the generator to self-destruct in a cloud of black smoke.[4] This test was performed in a lab and thus, there was no negative impact to consumers from the disabled power generator. However, if the test was performed in a production environment, consumers would have most likely experienced a power outage.

> **TIP**
>
> When performing security testing, it is essential to define the rules of engagement to reduce the risk of performing the test. Both the organization and the security testers before the execution of testing should agree to and sign the rules of engagement. For more information and a rules of engagement template, please review Appendix B in NIST Special Publication 800–115: "Technical Guide to Information Security Testing and Assessment," which can be found at http://csrc.nist.gov/publications/nistpubs/800-115/SP800-115.pdf.

Personal Gain – Monetary Gain and Power

Some hackers will attempt to exploit smart grids for both money and power. Hackers have a wide variety of tools and methods at their disposal to either directly extort money from or wield power over consumers. One such method would be to use a specific subset of malware known as ransomware, also known as extortive malware. "Malware, also known as malicious code and malicious software, refers to a program that is inserted into a system, usually covertly, with the intent of compromising the confidentiality, integrity, or availability of the victim's data, applications, or operating system (OS) or of otherwise annoying or disrupting the victim."[5] Malware usually consists of the following categories:

- Viruses
- Worms
- Trojan horses
- Malicious mobile code
- Blended attacks (combination of the different types)[5]

Ransomware refers to the specific type of malware that holds a system or data hostage in order to extort a ransom from the owner or user. Typically, ransomware will disable a specific service, lock the user out of the system, prevent access to critical data, or be a combination of these. For example, the Gpcode virus encrypts user files and then demands the user to send money to the hacker to decrypt the files.[6] Another example would be the RansomSMS-AH virus that blocks Internet access in order to force users into sending a systems management server (SMS) text message to a premium rate SMS phone number, which generates revenue for the hacker.[7]

In order to extort money from consumers, hackers could adapt these techniques to smart grid components. Specifically, hackers could obtain control of the consumer's smart meter and disrupt the consumer's access to power. The hacker could then send a ransom note through traditional mail to demand a monetary sum to restore the consumer's power to normal power levels.

Vengeance and Vindictiveness

Feuds between neighbors and other acquaintances could escalate to smart grid attacks. For a simple scenario, Alice believes her neighbor Bob turns up the volume on his television too loudly. Despite asking Bob to turn down the volume several times, Bob continues to watch television at an annoying level. So, Alice decides to abuse the remote disconnect feature in the smart meter installed in Bob's home to turn off his power, thus lowering the volume completely on his television.

With the current electric grid, the easiest attack vector from personal vendettas is a physical attack. If Alice is determined to turn off Bob's power, she could forcefully disconnect the power line to his house. In a smart grid, this attack would still work; however, Alice could potentially achieve the same impact without leaving the comfort of her own home in a smart grid environment. If Alice takes certain precautions, she could even carry out this attack without leaving physical fingerprints on Bob's smart grid equipment or electronic fingerprints on the systems and networks involved.

Terrorism

For various political reasons, the world has had trouble coming to a consensus for defining the term *terrorism*. One commonly used reference is a United Nations panel that stated "any action constitutes terrorism if it is intended to cause death or serious bodily harm to civilians or non-combatants with the purpose of intimidating a population or compelling a government or an international organization to do or abstain from doing any act."[8] There are different motives behind terrorism, and organizations use varying labels that mostly have common themes. An example terrorism category breakdown includes national separatist, religious fundamentalist, new religious, and social revolutionary.[9] Regardless of motive or category, smart grids will be considerable targets for terrorists. By attacking electric grids, terrorists could affect massive amounts of people and, as a result, create massive attention for their cause. Although digital threats to smart grids will be a primary concern, violent acts such as bombings will of course remain a viable attack vector.

Digital attacks against smart grids may not be the primary goal of a terrorist attack, rather a means to some other end. During and immediately following the September 11, 2001 attacks at the World Trade Center, Pentagon, and rural Pennsylvania, American citizens had access to information sources on television, radio, and the Internet. An attack in the future may begin with a broad shutdown of consumers' access to electricity and therefore disable access to warnings and updates about the primary objective, which may include explosives or other physical attacks.

Eco-terrorism

According to the categories described in the Terrorism section, eco-terrorists would be classified as social revolutionaries. Part of the smart grid vision is to enable the electric grid to better handle clean, renewable sources of energy; however, traditional types of energy sources that are considered harmful to the environment will still be used. In order to further their cause, eco-terrorists could attack smart grids to either decrease or completely eliminate energy usage by consumers.

Government

Government is both a consumer and a threat to consumers. From traffic lights to research labs, government agencies consume large amounts of energy and can be just as susceptible as individuals to the threats described in this chapter. However, governments may also be a threat to consumers. Warfare and law enforcement will cause governments to become threats to consumers.

Warfare

Crippling a nation's critical infrastructure can hinder a nation's ability to operate and as such, smart grids will be targets during war. Traditional weapons of war, such as bombs, will still be effective in disrupting the distribution and transmission of power to consumers when smart grids are deployed. Although, the risk from cyberwarfare will most likely increase when smart grids are more common. The current electric grid is already susceptible to cyber attacks, and the increasing reliance on technology will only increase the risk in smart grids. When asked about reports that the current electric grid had been infiltrated by foreign spies,

U.S. Homeland Security Secretary Janet Napolitano stated, "The vulnerability is something [we] have known about for years,"[10] and also stated, "We acknowledge that... in this world, in an increasingly cyber world, these are increasing risks."[10]

Illegal Activity

Electricity has many uses and not all of those uses are considered legal in every country. For example, the production and use of marijuana is currently illegal in a majority of the United States, as well as many other countries around the world. One method for producing marijuana is in so-called grow-ops, which can involve the indoor cultivation of cannabis. Due to its growth requirements for light, the power consumption of buildings utilized for indoor grow-ops is significantly higher than other comparable buildings. As a result, some utility companies will work with law enforcement agencies to locate potential grow-ops. Because smart grids will produce significantly more accurate usage data, it will be more easy to locate and shut down illegal activity through consumer usage statistics. Although most people will not sympathize with the operators of grow-ops, or other illegal activity, those operators of illegal activity will consider the smart grid a significant threat to their activities. Government agencies will be able use data collected from smart grids to locate and imprison those operators.

Utility Companies

Utility companies, or more precisely agents of utility companies, will be threats to consumers through intentional or unintentional actions. From accidents to insider threats, utility company agents may continue to be a cause of power disruptions, privacy leaks, improper billing, and more.

Accidental Threats

As depicted in Figure 2.1 in the "Naturally Occurring Threats" section of this chapter, human error caused four disturbances in the United States and Canada in the first three quarters of 2009. Additionally, human error caused approximately 10 percent of the disturbances during 2006 and 2007.[11] Although increased automation will decrease the number of incidents caused by human error, operators, and maintenance, employees will be required to interact with the smart grid. Increased training at regular and frequent intervals should decrease the risk of accidents; however, accidents will always remain a threat to the operation and maintenance of smart grids.

Patch Management

Most (if not all) organizations have struggled with patch management and, as evidenced by the continued threat of worms, viruses, and trojans, many organizations still do. Deploying patches or upgrades for operating systems, firmware, and applications to every system in an enterprise does not always go smoothly. Typically, the patches will not install correctly on at least some of the target systems. This can result in several different outcomes. The most likely scenario is that the system continues to operate without the patch or upgrade being applied, and will be found later during an audit or security assessment (or hacker). However, situations can arise where the unsuccessful application of a patch or upgrade causes the system to cease operating correctly. For example, an unsuccessful firmware update to a smart meter could cause the consumer to receive an erroneous bill or shutoff electricity to their house. With smart meters and other smart devices deployed at consumer facilities and connected to the Internet, patch management poses a threat to electricity consumers unlike anything experienced with the current electric grid.

Intentional Attacks

Utility company employees intentionally attacking consumers may seem counterintuitive, but various situations could arise that lead employees to attack consumers. Angry employees lashing out in the workplace is not a new concept. Negative performance reviews, inadequate compensation, impending layoffs, and arguments with management are common reasons for employees to lash out at their employers, which could indirectly cause negative impact to consumers. There will also be situations that cause employees to directly attack consumers. For example, Alice calls the utility company's support phone line to discuss the previous month's bill. Bob, an account support technician, receives the call from Alice and attempts to explain the bill. However, Alice is angry over the rate charged during peak usage times and angrily yells at Bob. As a result, Bob decides to get revenge by remotely disconnecting Alice's power.

> **TIP**
>
> Implementing the principle of least privilege and potentially separation of duties could have prevented Bob from disconnecting Alice. If Bob is only responsible for correcting billing errors, he should not have the ability to disconnect Alice's power.

Load Shedding

When demand is greater than supply, utility companies may resort to load shedding techniques. As a result, utility companies will either reduce or completely shut off the availability of power to some consumers. Utility companies will use load shedding to ensure that priority consumers, such as emergency services, still have power. However, those consumers who are not prioritized will lose power, which could negatively impact their lives.

IMPACTS ON CONSUMERS

When speaking to nontechnical management, security professionals cannot just use vulnerability terms such as buffer overflow to convey why they need additional money to remediate identified vulnerability. Typically, management is more interested in the impact on business operations. For most situations, the impact of vulnerabilities will vary and can only be estimated. For example, an attacker could exploit a buffer overflow in a smart meter to obtain complete control of the smart meter. The attacker may use this vulnerability to shut off electricity to a single house, or they could exploit this vulnerability to shut off power to an emergency service, which would have a higher impact. As a result, security professionals are sometimes criticized for fear mongering when doomsday situations are described as the impact. Similar to other environments, the impact of a successful attack against smart grids will range from annoyance to life or death situations.

Privacy

In AMI implementations, smart meters will autonomously collect massive amounts of data and transport the data to the utility company, the consumer, and third-party service providers. The data will include personally identifiable information (PII) that could compromise the privacy of consumers.

According to a Privacy Impact Analysis (PIA) performed for NIST, "The data items collected from the Distributed Energy Resources (DERs) and smart meters will reveal different types of information about residential consumers and activities."[12] Detailed energy usage information will enable persons and organizations to profile a consumer's habits. Privacy experts, including the Future of Privacy Forum (FPF – www.futureofprivacy.org), have voiced concern over the data being collected on consumers in smart grids. As shown in Figure 2.3, analysts can determine what device is operating by analyzing the current power load.

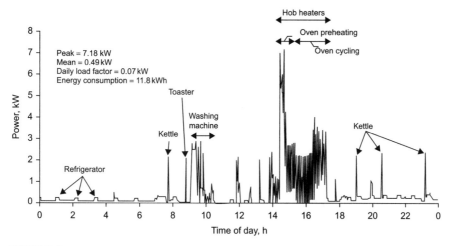

FIGURE 2.3

Device load signatures.[13]

> **WARNING**
>
> When using third-party services, such as social networking sites, to provide information to consumers, the privacy of this information is reliant on that third-party. Even though most social networking sites have some privacy controls, they should not be trusted to maintain the privacy of sensitive information. Most privacy controls in social networking sites have been successfully attacked in the past, and they still remain vulnerable. From a functionality and marketing standpoint, using popular social networking sites to deliver energy usage information to consumers appears to be a good idea. However, this process will present significant risk to the privacy of this information.

Many consumers will not realize the potential impact introduced by collecting and analyzing this type of information. They will not correlate this information with a realistic threat. However, threats such as the ones described previously in the "Smart Thieves and Stalkers" section of this chapter will exploit consumer personally identifiable information to burglarize, stalk, and perform many other malicious acts against consumers.

Although hackers will discover numerous ways to utilize the PII for malicious reasons, companies could also attempt to utilize the PII for more legitimate reasons. Specifically, advertising companies would highly value this personal information. Search engines that utilize targeted ads to generate revenue could be considered an analogous example. For example, when you perform a search on the history of microwaves, advertisements for stores selling microwaves will show up in your browser. Similarly, a utility company sells anonymous, or what they believe to be anonymous, usage information to an advertising company for a particular zip code. The advertising company analyzes the electricity usage to profile the consumers in that geographical region. The advertising company could then sell these results to local businesses who want to do targeted advertising. Although not as dangerous as smart thieves, this example represents a privacy concern among some consumers.

IMPACTS ON AVAILABILITY

Smart grids will introduce new features and benefits to the electric grid, but the main purpose of smart grids will remain making power available to consumers. As such, the majority of the threats described in the "Consumer Threats" sections of this chapter affect the availability of power. The impact will range from altering the thermostat on heaters and air conditioners to limiting emergency services.

Personal Availability

There has been debate on whether the utility company or the government would be able to arbitrarily control consumer power consumption. Ultimately, this will depend on where you are consuming power. The functionality for a utility company or governing authority to remotely control consumer energy consumption does exist and will be installed in consumers' homes and businesses, as is the case in Great Britain.[14]

Mobility

One of the current technological problems is efficient storage of excess electricity that can be used during peak demand times. However, the wide-spread adoption of electric cars could solve this problem. Electric cars will need to be connected to the power grid to recharge their batteries. If the smart grid experienced a higher demand than the current power generation could supply, then the utility company could collect power from the connected electric cars batteries to obtain the extra electricity. Although this may satisfy the needs of the utility company, the consumers who rely on electric cars could remain immobile for a significant amount of time to recharge their cars.

Emergency Services

Most critical emergency services, such as life support medical systems, rely on a stable flow of electricity to operate. Although privacy and temperature control may not seem critical to some consumers, the functioning status of emergency services usually do. Hospitals, emergency response teams, police, and firefighters save lives on a daily basis, and they all rely on electricity to perform their duties. Emergency services normally have their own generators and other backups in the case of power outages; however, these backup plans usually have a fairly short operational time. In the event of a prolonged power outage, the operational abilities of these emergency services will be severely limited. This is especially significant in the case of hospitals that house critically ill patients who are kept alive by electrically powered medical devices.

FINANCIAL IMPACTS

The threats described in this chapter could have significant financial impact on consumers. Corrupt data from smart meters could result in inaccurate billing that causes consumers to overpay for their electrical consumption. Many consumers may not notice that they are overpaying; however, some consumers will attempt to have their electricity bill corrected. If the utility company has detected a malfunctioning smart meter, the utility company will most likely be willing to adjust the bill. Conversely, the utility company may be overconfident with the touted features of a smart grid and refuse to believe they are gathering corrupt data; thus, forcing the consumers to pay their overpriced bill.

The loss of power could also impact businesses' ability to operate, which could escalate to crashing stock markets. In August, 2003, parts of the Northeastern and Midwestern United States, as well as Southeastern Canada experienced a power outage. The blackout affected an estimated 50 million people and lasted for up to four days in the United States and up to one week in Canada. In the United States and Canada, the estimated financial loss in sales and manufacturing goods was between $4 billion and $10 billion, respectively.[15]

LIKELIHOOD OF ATTACK

According to an Idaho National Laboratory (IDL) Critical Infrastructure Protection/Resilience Center report performed for the U.S. Department of Energy, vulnerabilities in smart grid technologies may not currently present significant risk to the national security risk. However, the reason is that smart grid technologies are not widely deployed yet.[16] Similarly, the current risk presented to consumers is relatively low because most consumers are not connected to a smart grid. The vulnerabilities in smart grid technologies are relatively trivial to exploit and have significant impact to consumers. As the technology becomes more widespread, the risk to consumers will increase significantly.

SUMMARY

Consumers will continue to rely heavily on the electrical grid to support all facets of their daily lives. Consumers connected to smart grids will continue to face traditional threats, such as natural disasters and warfare, to the availability of electricity that consumers depend on. However, the additional network connectivity supporting smart grids will increase the risk of cyber threats affecting consumers. To prevent or reduce the negative impact from threats, consumers will almost completely rely on utility companies and governing authorities for security. However, consumers will be partly responsible for ensuring their own security through practices, such as choosing strong passwords and scrutinizing the privacy policies of their utility company.

Endnotes

1. North American Electric Reliability Corporation. 2009 First-third quarter NERC DAWG number of disturbances by region [document on the Internet]. North American Electric Reliability Corporation; www.nerc.com/files/NERC_DAWG_Disturbances_2009_Jan-Sept_Updated.pdf; 2009 [accessed 31.12.09].
2. National Climatic Data Center. Climate of 2005 summary of Hurricane Katrina [document on the Internet]. www.ncdc.noaa.gov/oa/climate/research/2005/katrina.html; 2005 [accessed 2.12.2009].
3. Grabosky P, Smith R. Crime in the digital age. Sydney: Federation Press; 1998. p. 52–53.
4. CNN. Staged cyber attack reveals vulnerability in power grid [document on the Internet]. www.cnn.com/2007/US/09/26/power.at.risk/index.html#cnnSTCText; 2007 [accessed 2.12.2009].

5. Mell P, Kent K, Nusbaum J. National Institute of Standards and Technology. Guide to Malware incident prevention and handling [document on the Internet]. http://csrc.nist.gov/publications/nistpubs/800-83/SP800-83.pdf; 2005 [accessed 2.12.2009].

6. Kaspersky Lab. Virus.Win32.Gpcode.ae [document on the Internet]. www.viruslist.com/en/viruses/encyclopedia?virusid=123334; 2006 [accessed 2.12.2009].

7. Leyden J. The Register. Russian ransomware blocks net access [document on the Internet]. www.theregister.co.uk/2009/12/01/ransomware_turns_off_net_access; 2009 [accessed 4.12.2009].

8. United Nations General Assembly. In larger freedom: towards development, security and human rights for all [documents on the Internet]. http://daccess-ods.un.org/access.nsf/Get?Open&DS=A/59/2005&Lang=E; 2005 [accessed 4.12.2009].

9. Hudson RA. Federal Research Division, Library of Congress. The sociology and psychology of terrorism: who becomes a terrorist and why? [document on the Internet]. www.loc.gov/rr/frd/pdf-files/Soc_Psych_of_Terrorism.pdf; 1999 [accessed 4.12.2009].

10. Shiels M. Spies ''infiltrate US power grid' [document on the Internet]. BBC; http://news.bbc.co.uk/2/hi/technology/7990997.stm; 2009 [accessed 4.12.2009].

11. North American Electric Reliability Corporation. Annual Report 2008 [document on the Internet]. North American Electric Reliability Corporation; www.nerc.com/files/2008-Annual-Report.pdf; 2009 [accessed 1.1.2009].

12. National Institute of Standards and Technology. Draft smart grid cyber security strategy and requirements [document on the Internet]. The Cyber Security Coordination Task Group; http://csrc.nist.gov/publications/drafts/nistir-7628/draft-nistir-7628.pdf; 2009 [accessed 1.1.2009].

13. Wood G, Newborough M. Dynamic energy-consumption indicators for domestic appliances: environment, behaviour and design. Energy Buildings 2003;35(8):822.

14. Department of Energy and Climate Change. Towards a smarter future: Government response to the consultation on electricity and gas smart metering [document on the Internet]. http://decc.gov.uk/Media/viewfile.ashx?FilePath=Consultations%5CSmart%20Metering%20for%20Electricity%20and%20Gas%5C1_20091202094543_e_@@_ResponseElectricityGasConsultation.pdf&filetype=4; 2009 [accessed 4.12.2009].

15. U.S.-Canada Power System Outage Task Force. Final Report on the August 14, 2003 blackout in the United States and Canada: causes and recommendations [document on the Internet]. https://reports.energy.gov/BlackoutFinal-Web.pdf; 2004 [accessed 4.12.2009].

16. U.S. Department of Energy Office of Electricity Delivery and Energy Reliability. Study of security attributes of smart grid systems – current cyber security issues [document on the Internet]. INL Critical Infrastructure Protection/Resilience Center; www.inl.gov/scada/publications/d/securing_the_smart_grid_current_issues.pdf; 2009 [accessed 4.12.2009].

Threats and Impacts: Utility Companies and Beyond

INFORMATION IN THIS CHAPTER

- Confidentiality
- Integrity
- Availability

We discussed the threats and their impact to consumers in the last chapter, but now let us focus on those that are relevant to utility companies, businesses, and governments. Some of these threats are similar, some are unique, but attacks against utility companies, businesses, and governments will have a broader impact than attacks against consumers.

The threats are broken down into the components of the CIA triad, depicted in Figure 3.1 below: confidentiality, integrity, and availability. The impact of these threats is presented in a hypothetical scenario format. However, these threats and their impact could very easily become reality. In some cases, they already have.

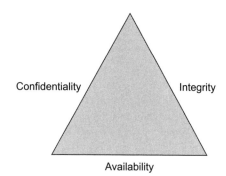

FIGURE 3.1

The CIA triad.

CONFIDENTIALITY

Confidentiality is attained when information is protected from unauthorized disclosure. A loss of confidentiality has the greatest effect on consumers. However, the aggregation of personal information about consumers by the utility companies makes them a significantly larger target to hackers.

Consumer Privacy

Utility companies collect and store customer information such as name, address, social security number, and consumption data; all information you and I expect to remain confidential. Breaching this confidentiality to access such information is the goal of many hackers, as highlighted in Verizon Business' 2009 Data Breach Investigations Report, "... criminals have had to overhaul their processes and differentiate their products in order to maintain profitability. In 2008, this was accomplished by targeting points of data concentration or aggregation..."[1]

However, hackers may not be the only ones who want this information. With the adoption of smart grid technologies, consumers will more frequently interact with their utility companies through Internet accessible Web applications. These applications will allow consumers to monitor and control their power consumption, and even control their smart devices. Law enforcement could utilize this information to support investigations, much like mobile phone data, such as global positioning satellite (GPS), is used today.

NOTE

Security and Privacy blogger Christopher Soghoian published findings on December 1, 2009 that Sprint, a United States based wireless carrier, provided law enforcement agencies customer GPS location data between 2008 and 2009. Over a 13-month span, Sprint provided customer GPS location data more than eight million times to different law enforcement agencies through a special Web portal.[2]

PII

As discussed in the previous chapter, smart grids present a host of threats to consumers. While we previously discussed targeted threats and impacts, compromising the confidentiality of consumer data housed by the utility companies presents a far greater reward than compromising the confidentiality of single consumer.

Scenario

- **Threat** – Hackers are able to compromise consumer databases operated by the HackMe utility company.
- **Attack vector** – A Structured Query Language (SQL) Injection vulnerability within the HackMe Web site utilized by consumers to manage their accounts, monitor their usage, and make payments.

- **Impact** – Hackers obtain the personally identifiable information (PII) of 500,000 HackMe customers. This information includes customer names, addresses, birth dates, social security numbers, and account numbers. For those customers who utilize automatic or online bill payment, Hackers also obtain customers' credit card numbers and bank account information. The hackers sell this information on the black market, and HackMe's customers are left to deal with repercussions. Government agencies, regulatory bodies, and customers become enraged that this information was compromised and the utility company is fined for not protecting the information properly.

> **NOTE**
>
> SQL Injection is an attack that consists of inserting a malicious Structured Query Language (SQL) query into data that is passed from the application client to the backend database server. Such attacks can allow an attacker to manipulate data within application databases. Often, these databases include sensitive information such as usernames, passwords, credit card information, social security numbers, and more. You can learn more about SQL Injection at www.owasp.org/index.php/SQL_Injection or Justin Clarke's *SQL Injection Attacks and Defense* (ISBN: 978-1-59749-424-3).

Consumption Data

We previously covered, in the "Illegal Activity" section of the previous chapter, how law enforcement agencies may utilize consumption information to determine if utility companies' customers are producing illegal substances. However, alternate uses by law enforcement include using similar information to determine the location of suspects during crimes.

Scenario

- **Threat** – Consumers become disenfranchised with smart grid technologies after the repeated use of consumption information in the prosecution of criminals.
- **Attack vector** – Law enforcement reviews suspects' historical consumption information to determine the likelihood that they were located at their residence during the time of crime.
- **Impact** – Customer backlash at the alleged misuse of consumption information forces utility companies to modify their smart grid deployments. These modifications pose a significant financial burden to the utility companies, and the public backlash slows the adoption of smart grid technologies.

Proprietary Information

Utility companies possess valuable information beyond that of their customers' PII. Proprietary information, such as trade secrets, will be targeted by hackers who believe they can sell the information to competing organizations, governments, or terrorist groups.

Scenario

- **Threat** – A foreign government, frustrated by the sanctions imposed by the United Nations, utilizes its own hackers to compromise an American utility company and obtain trade secrets. These trade secrets will allow the foreign government to significantly increase its power-generating capabilities despite the imposed sanctions.
- **Attack vector** – An exploit is placed on the utility companies' Web site that leverages vulnerability in an unpatched version of a popular Web browser. When a utility company employee visits the Web site, the vulnerability is exploited, and malware is installed on their system. This malware allows the foreign government's hackers to gain access to the utility company's internal network and ultimately steal trade secrets on power generation.
- **Impact** – The foreign government is able to increase power generation despite the United Nations imposed sanctions. The utility company losses their competitive advantage as the trade secrets are eventually made public on the Internet. The utility company sees its profits drop significantly as their competitors reduce the gap that was once created by the trade secrets.

INTEGRITY

Integrity is attained when information is protected from unauthorized modification. A loss of integrity has the greatest effect on the utility companies, which is manifested in fraud and service theft.

Service Fraud

Regardless of the deployment architecture chosen by a particular utility company, their customers will have access to the smart meters deployed in their homes and businesses. While tamper-resistant mechanisms should be employed, countermeasures will undoubtedly be published on the Internet.

Once information on how to hack smart meters makes its way onto the Internet, the masses, ranging from hackers to curious consumers, will possess the knowledge on how to defraud their utility company. Some will steal services, while others will be as bold as to collect money from the utility companies by fooling the system to believe that the dwelling generated electricity for the grid instead of consuming it.

Service Theft

The most predictable threat to the utility companies as a result of smart meter tampering is service theft through under-reporting. Given the current state of the economy, significantly lower utility bills may sound too attractive to resist to the average consumer.

Scenario

- **Threat** – Consumers hack their smart meters to modify the usage information being sent to the utility company.
- **Attack vector** – A vulnerable network device driver within the customers' smart meter allows remote code execution when properly exploited. Customers download and install custom software off of the Internet that exploits the vulnerability and loads custom firmware onto the smart meter.
- **Impact** – Customer is able to under-report their usage to the utility company. Thus, the customer obtains a lower bill while the utility company unknowingly subsidizes their customer.

Net Metering

The most profitable threat for consumers as a result of smart meter tampering is manipulation of net metering data. Net metering allows consumers to provide the utility companies with power generated by the consumers utilizing technologies, including wind and solar. In turn, the utility companies either provide the consumer with an account credit, or issue a check for the amount of energy provided by the consumer to the utility company.

Scenario

- **Threat** – Consumers hack their smart meters to modify the power generation information being sent to the utility company.
- **Attack vector** – An easily guessed password on an administrative interface (Secure Shell [SSH]) of the customer's smart meter allows complete access to the device, including the net metering data. The customer modifies the data using a tool they downloaded from the Internet.
- **Impact** – Customer is able to over-report the amount of power being provided to the utility company. Thus, the customer obtains a larger credit or even a check from the utility company, while they unknowingly are paying their customer for nothing.

> **NOTE**
>
> Within Section 1251 of the Energy Policy Act of 2005, the U.S. Congress mandated that all public electric utilities must make net metering available to their customers.[3]

Sensor Data Manipulation

Smart meters will include sensors that will allow the utility companies to perform myriad tasks ranging from post mortem forensic analysis to power system restoration, to distribution network monitoring, restoration, and self healing. However, if the integrity of the sensor data is compromised, the result will be disastrous.

Scenario

- **Threat** – Brett, a self-taught hacker, is curious about how the "whole smart grid thing works." Being in high school, Brett lives with his parents, whose house was recently fitted with a smart meter. Brett spends hours upon hours playing with the smart meter and eventually is able to create a program that would send false sensor data for his entire neighborhood.
- **Attack vector** – The sensor data is sent from the smart meters to the utility company in an unencrypted format. Brett uses this insecure configuration to capture, manipulate, and successfully transmit false sensor data to the utility company. He is also able to capture network traffic for his neighbor's smart meters and obtains their Internet Protocol (IP) addresses. Using his custom written program, Brett sends false sensor information to the utility company, indicating that Brett's entire neighborhood is without power.
- **Impact** – The utility company, unsure of how a single neighborhood can lose power, sends a crew out to investigate. Upon arrival at the neighborhood in question, the crew reports that there is no outage. The utility company underestimates the criticality of the issue and simply chalks its up to a system malfunction. Brett, amused by the situation, performs similar attacks over the next two years, ultimately costing the utility company thousands of dollars in wasted man hours.

AVAILABILITY

Availability is attained when the service provided by the utility companies is protected from unauthorized interruption. A loss of availability has a significant impact on utility companies and those that rely on their services. This includes consumers, organizations, businesses, and governments.

Consumer Targets

Consumers will be the targets of attacks on the availability of the power to their houses. These attacks will most likely come from script kiddies or people the victims know. Despite the relatively innocuous intent of the attackers, the impact of their exploits will wreak havoc on their victims.

NOTE

Script kiddies is a term for hackers who rely on the tools of others to attack computers and network devices. It is a derogatory term that generally suggests unskilled adolescent attackers whose motivation is notoriety.

Scenario

- **Threat** – Carla's ex-boyfriend, Andy, wants revenge for Carla breaking up with him. Andy is able to attack Carla's smart meter to create a blackout localized to Carla's townhouse.
- **Attack vector** – Carla's default wireless router configuration allows Andy to easily access her wireless network and connect to the Web front end of her smart meter. Once access to the smart meter was obtained, Andy changed its default password, and shutdown power to Carla's townhouse.
- **Impact** – Carla is left without power and is unable to connect to her smart meter to re-enable power as her wireless network is down and she no longer knows the password to the unit.

TIP

Ever wondered what the default password was for a device you own? Or a device someone else owns? Phenoelit-US.org maintains a comprehensive and up-to-date list of default vendor passwords at www.phenoelit-us.org/dpl/dpl.html.

Organizational Targets

Much like consumers, organizations will be the targets of attacks on the availability of the power to their locations. These attacks will come from script kiddies, professional hackers, or people the organizations know. However, unlike the attacks on consumers, the intent of the attackers will most certainly be malicious and may result in extortion.

Utility Companies

The most obvious organization targeted by those attacking the new smart grid is the utility companies. The utility companies will represent the "holy grail" of targets to attackers. Script kiddies will try and compromise the utility companies for notoriety, while professional hackers may be sponsored and have more malicious drivers. We will cover these drivers shortly.

Scenario

- **Threat** – A historical script kiddie, Mike, wants the credibility and notoriety he thinks he deserves. He contacts one of the largest hacking crews and asks how he can join. They respond by saying that he must hack one of the country's largest utility companies and cause a power outage that makes the evening news.
- **Attack vector** – Mike, yearning for membership in the exclusive hacking crew, studies the smart grid infrastructure and targets his local utility company. Exploiting the weak physical security of his utility company's local management station, Mike is able to plug directly into the management station and gain access to an internal utility company network. From here, Mike

performs a denial-of-service (DoS) attack against all of the management stations on the local subnet.

- **Impact** – All of the management stations in Mike's town are impacted by his DoS attack. As Mike properly planned his attack, the units were down during the period in which the utility company polls for usage data. Subsequently, the utility company's billing process is delayed and an announcement is made through local media outlets informing customers of the delay. No mention of the attack is made; however, Mike demonstrates the attack for the hacking crew and is offered membership.

Other Organizations

Much like consumers, organizations, other than the utility companies, will be the target of availability attacks. Attackers will most likely be script kiddies or people the organizations have a relationship with, such as a former employee or a customer. The motivation behind such attacks will most likely be revenge or extortion.

Scenario

- **Threat** – Victor, a former employee of the local gas station, wants revenge for his recent firing. Victor, who is computer savvy and was formerly responsible for paying the gas station's bills, is able to cut off the power to his former employer.
- **Attack vector** – The gas station utilized the local utility company's online account management Web application to pay its bills. This Web application also allows users to close their accounts without any additional verification. Victor simply logs on to the Web application from his home, using the same login and password that he used while he was an employee of the gas station, and requests the account to be closed.
- **Impact** – The gas station's account is closed within a week. As a result, the power to the local gas station is shutoff on a holiday weekend. The gas station is forced to operate on its backup system, but quickly drains the system as a result of the high demand for gas. The utility company cannot send anyone out until the following Tuesday, as a result of the holiday weekend. The local gas company is forced to shutdown midday on Sunday, losing sales on one of its busiest days of the year. Additionally, the utility company will lose revenue from not supplying the gas station and will need to spend time remediating the situation.

Vertical Targets

In the previous section, we walked through scenarios that attacked specific organizations. These attacks were the result of disgruntled employees or ambitious script kiddies seeking revenge or notoriety. However, a different class of attackers, with different motivation will target specific industries in order to achieve their objectives. The impact of these attacks will be significantly greater than those targeting specific organizations.

Activists

Many organizations are in business despite the best efforts of activists. A typical example of this is fur coat manufacturers. Animal rights organizations have historically done everything in their power to prevent these manufacturers from operating their business. The adoption of smart grid technologies presents an additional avenue for these activists to attack the manufacturers.

Scenario

- **Threat** – Lisa, an animal lover her whole life, is also a computer science major. During an animal rights protest on her university's campus, she is recruited by activists to attack the manufacturing operations of three of the most prolific fur coat brands during the period leading up to the holiday shopping season.
- **Attack vector** – Using a targeted phishing e-mail, Lisa is able to install malware on the computers of each of the targeted manufacturers. This malware captures logins and passwords to all sites that are used by the accounting department and sends them to Lisa. Once Lisa obtains the logins and passwords to the utility company's Web applications used by the manufacturers, she simply requests an account suspension for each manufacturer during the period of peak manufacturing. Lisa also changes the account information and secret questions to prevent the manufacturers from easily reactivating their accounts.
- **Impact** – The manufacturers experience power outages during their peak manufacturing periods. They contact the utility companies to inquire about the outage and learn of the suspension. Despite their documented information, they cannot successfully authenticate themselves with the utility companies and are forced to provide supplemental information in order to reactivate service. Once service is finally restored, the manufacturers have lost a total of three days of production, which significantly impacts their ability to meet order requests.

Market Manipulation

Financial gain continues to be the single greatest driver behind computer attacks. With the adoption of smart grid technologies, attackers will exploit weaknesses for financial gain. Extortion is the easiest example of how attackers can obtain financial gain: by withholding organizations power service until a ransom is paid. However, more sophisticated, and potentially more lucrative, attacks are possible.

Financial

Sophisticated movie plots depict hackers as financially motivated individuals who bring specialized skills to a team that includes nontechnical members. Unfortunately, these plots will not remain bound to the silver screen for much longer. Hackers, teaming with those who understand financial markets, can easily exploit the adoption of smart grid technologies to gain significant amounts of money in a short period of time.

Scenario

- **Threat** – Dan, a longtime ethical hacker at a financial institution, is let go because of corporate downsizing. He is approached by fellow coworkers in the commodities division about an opportunity to make a lot of fast money. Without any promising job prospects, Dan agrees to help his former coworker in exchange for a significant cut of the take.
- **Attack vector** – Using a combination of his technical knowledge and the market knowledge provided by his former colleagues, Dan performs a DoS attack against several of the country's largest utility companies during the peak of winter. Dan utilized a remote file-inclusion vulnerability in a common software package deployed as part of the utility companies' Web applications. This vulnerability allowed Dan to discontinue all power-generating activities at the utility companies for several hours.
- **Impact** – Dan's former coworkers strategically purchased a significant amount of heating oil before Dan's attack on the utility companies. In the panic that ensued within the commodities market as a result of the DoS attack, the price of heating oil skyrocketed, increasing by 25 percent. Dan's coworkers promptly sold their holdings at the peak of the panic, and made enough money to retire comfortably.

National Security Target

With the announcement in October of 2009 that the United States issued 100 grants, totaling $3.4 billion for smart grid technologies, it is clear that President Obama sees smart grid technology as a priority.[4] As a presidential priority, smart grid technologies will undoubtedly make their way into America's next generation electric infrastructure. Additionally, the high priority given to smart grid technologies will also increase the scrutiny of its security, by friends and enemies alike.

Domestic

Domestic terrorism is a reality that Americans have learned to live with ever since they watched the horror of the attacks on the Alfred P. Murrah Federal Building in Oklahoma City, Oklahoma, on April 19, 1995. The adoption of smart grid technologies will provide domestic terrorists with a readily available target.

Scenario

- **Threat** – Kyle, a former private in the armed forces, has become disgruntled with his country's alleged occupation of a foreign country. During his tenure in the armed forces, Kyle learned how to attack enemy infrastructure, including those that support utility companies.
- **Attack vector** – Leveraging an outdated version of a Web server running an Internet facing government Web site, Kyle is able to ultimately gain access to a sensitive network that controls regional power distribution for the east coast of the United States. Kyle obtains this access by exploiting the outdated Web

server and weak configurations within the numerous subnets located between the sensitive network and the Internet facing the Web server.

- **Impact** – Kyle is able to shut down power generation to the Northeastern states of the United States. Panic ensues as federal, state, and local authorities scramble to identify the cause of the blackout. Riots and looting occur, as the blackout extends into the evening. All told, the Northeast is without power for hours, and damages as a result of rioting and looting total into the billions.

> **WARNING**
>
> Before you assess a company or government's security posture, make sure you are familiar with all applicable laws. Laws and their subsequent punishments vary by locality. You can read more about individual state's laws at www.ncsl.org/default.aspx?tabid=13494. Similarly, you can review federal laws at http://definitions.uslegal.com/c/computer-hacking/.

International

As much as the images of the Oklahoma City Bombing of 1995, as shown in Figure 3.2, resonate in the minds of Americans, the world has never been the same since the attacks of September 11, 2001. Terrorists targeted the world's financial center and successfully destroyed the Twin Towers in New York City. The adoption of smart grid technologies will create a similar center for the United States' power distribution. This center will become a target of significance to international terrorist groups like Al-Qaeda.

Scenario

- **Threat** – Thierry, a professional hacker for hire, has been approached by Al-Qaeda to attack the United States' power grid. As a professional hacker, Thierry is financially motivated, and despite his reservations of dealing with a terrorist organization like Al-Qaeda, he simply cannot resist the money offered.
- **Attack vector** – Utilizing social engineering attacks that leverage malicious e-mail attachments, Thierry is able to create a worm that infects a majority of the United States' major utility companies. Thierry's worm has command and control capability, which allows him to gain further access into each organization's internal infrastructure. By the time Thierry executes his attack, he has administrative access to 75 percent of the largest utility companies' distribution networks.
- **Impact** – Thierry is ultimately able to shut down power generation at 75 percent of America's utility companies simultaneously. Much like the attack previously conducted by Kyle, the domestic terrorist, panic ensues as federal, state, and local authorities scramble to identify the cause of the blackout. However, this time the scope is nationwide. The blackout encompasses 90 percent of the United States and lasts for three days until the worm can be eradicated. The damage, both financially and psychologically, is devastating to the United States and its final toll is incalculable.

FIGURE 3.2

Oklahoma City bombing of 1995.

Source: DefenseImagery.mil[5]

Precursor to War

The threats described in the previous sections of this chapter have demonstrated the potential impact attacks can have on an organization, an industry, and nation. The impact of these attacks is primarily financial and psychological. These tolls, while not inconsequential to the longevity of a nation, are minimal in comparison to the effect similar attacks could have on a nation as a precursor to a military attack.

Scenario

- **Threat** – Country X, tired of the sanction placed on it by the United Nations, has decided to declare war on the United States. Although Country X does not possess the technology or arsenal to directly attack the United States, they have planted sleeper cells within the United States that will carry out suicide attacks when given the signal. In order to maximize the impact, Country X has targeted the smart grid technologies deployed by the United States in order to create confusion and prevent communications with their citizens, first responders, and government agencies.
- **Attack vector** – Leveraging previously unreported vulnerabilities in the operating systems and network services utilized by the United States' smart grid infrastructure, Country X is able to shut down all of America's power distribution networks simultaneously. The attacks are easily performed because of the prevalence of vulnerable systems and devices. Little to nothing was previously known about the exploited vulnerabilities.
- **Impact** – With the nationwide blackout affecting almost all Americans, mass chaos ensues. Shortly after the blackout, Country X's sleeper cells execute their suicide attacks amplifying the chaos and sinking the American people into a depression. Countless Americans lose their lives as a result of the attacks, and many more are lost as a result of the chaos that was amplified by the blackout. Much like the previously mentioned terrorist attack, the damage is devastating to the United States, and its final toll is incalculable.

SUMMARY

The benefits of smart grid technologies to the utility companies are significant. However, the risks associated with these technologies, both to the utility companies themselves, and to those that rely on them, are equally significant. Traditional threats such as service theft and fraud are likely to become the mainstream. Worse, such attacks are likely to be quickly documented and disseminated on nefarious Web sites, thereby allowing others to launch similar attacks in other areas.

Other threats, such as availability attacks, will have an increased impact as distribution networks become increasingly interconnected. The utility companies will be looked upon as the first level of defense against these threats. However, in order to defend such attacks, a coordinated effort between governments, industries, and consumers must work effectively and efficiently. Otherwise, a "fire sale," as depicted in the movie *Live Free or Die Hard*, could become a reality.

> **NOTE**
>
> A "fire sale" is a term that refers to the complete compromise of a country's infrastructure, including power distribution. The compromise is obtained primarily through the use of computer hacking.

Endnotes

1. Verizon Business. 2009 Data breach investigations report [document on the Internet]. www.verizonbusiness.com/resources/security/reports/2009_databreach_rp.pdf; 2009 [accessed 8.1.2010].
2. Soghoian C. 8 Million Reasons for Real Surveillance Oversight [document on the Internet]. http://paranoia.dubfire.net/2009/12/8-million-reasons-for-real-surveillance.html; 2009 [accessed 12.12.2009].
3. United States Congress. Energy policy act of 2005. [document on the Internet]. www.epa.gov/oust/fedlaws/publ_109-058.pdf; 2005 [accessed 25.11.2009].
4. Carey J. Obama's smart-grid game plan [document on the Internet]. Business Week; www.businessweek.com/technology/content/oct2009/tc20091027_594339.htm; 2009 [accessed 26.11.2009].
5. Chasteen, Staff Sgt. Preston. F-3203-SPT-95-000022-XX-0198 [image on the Internet]. DefenseImagery.mil; www.defenseimagery.mil/imagery.html#a=search&s=april%2019% 201995&n=90&guid=0f7e0c201d7cae42d9ebfbfefc5d1984645d12d7; 1995 [accessed 8.1.2010].

Federal Effort to Secure Smart Grids

INFORMATION IN THIS CHAPTER

- U.S. Federal Government
- DOE
- FERC
- NIST
- DHS NIPP
- Other Applicable Laws
- Sponsoring Security
- Bureaucracy and Politics in Smart Grid Security

Securing the electric grid is a matter of national security, and thus, the federal government will play a significant role in directing the security efforts. Utility companies and smart grid vendors will be looking to the federal government for guidance on how to properly secure their smart grid deployments. Fortunately, several federal government agencies have developed, and are currently developing more, security guidelines and best practices. This chapter will discuss the roles of several of the federal government agencies, as well as their respective initiatives.

U.S. FEDERAL GOVERNMENT

The U.S. federal government began actively regulating the energy industries in the 1920s, with the passing of the Federal Power Act of 1920. For the next 50 years, the energy industry was regulated by a fragmented regulatory framework.[1] In 1977, the Department of Energy Organization Act established the Department of Energy (DOE) to organize the fragmented regulatory process and create a national energy plan.[1] The Federal Energy Regulatory Commission (FERC) was also established in 1977 as an independent regulator within DOE. These agencies will play a critical role in developing the national policy for the smart grid. Additionally, several recent laws were passed that directly affect the development of smart grids, including the following:

- Energy and Independence Security Act of 2007
- American Recovery and Reinvestment Act of 2009.

Energy and Independence Security Act of 2007

U.S. Congress passed the Energy and Independence Security Act (EISA) of 2007, and President Bush signed the act into law on December 19, 2007, which became Public Law 110–140.[2] The text of the law is available from the U.S. Government and Printing Office at http://frwebgate.access.gpo.gov/cgi-bin/getdoc.cgi?dbname =110_cong_public_laws&docid=f:publ140.110.pdf.

Specifically, Title XIII of EISA of 2007 specified that the federal government's official policy is to support the modernization of the electric grid, or in other words support a smart grid. Additionally, Title XIII establishes the Smart Grid Advisory Committee and the Smart Grid Task Force,[2] as well as assigned roles, responsibilities, and accountability to these groups, federal government agencies, and organizations. The Smart Grid Advisory Committee's mission statement is to advise federal government officials on the status of smart grid–related activities.[2] The Smart Grid Task Force's mission statement is to ensure awareness, coordination and integration of federal government smart grid related activities.[2] The Smart Grid Advisory Committee and Smart Grid Task Force will be represented by several federal government agencies including[3]:

- DOE
- FERC
- Department of Commerce
- Environmental Protection Agency
- Department of Homeland Security (DHS)
- Department of Agriculture
- Department of Defense (DOD).

The output of the Smart Grid Advisory Committee and Smart Grid Task Force should be monitored closely as their work will greatly influence the smart grid policies in this country.

American Recovery and Reinvestment Act of 2009

The American Recovery and Reinvestment Act (ARRA) of 2009 was enacted on February 17, 2009, which became Public Law 111-5.[4] The text of the law is available from the U.S. Government and Printing Office at www.gpo.gov/fdsys/pkg/ PLAW-111publ5/content-detail.html.

At a high level, ARRA was created to stimulate the U.S. economy and contains many provisions that are unrelated to the energy industry. However, ARRA does specifically set up $32.7 billion in grants for energy-related programs.[4] See Table 4.1 for a complete breakdown of the funding allocation. As can be seen in Table 4.1, a significant amount of money is designated for smart grid projects. However, this is not without its own controversy. When $4.5 billion is marked for smart grid projects, utilities and smart grid vendors take notice and rush to obtain that funding while it lasts. As a result, developing the technologies and

Table 4.1 Breakdown of funding in ARRA for energy programs[5]

Program	Funds ($)
Energy efficiency, renewable energy industry, and transportation industry	*16.7 billion*
Weatherization Assistance Program	5 billion
State Energy Program	3.1 billion
Energy Efficiency and Conservation Block Grants	2.73 billion
Advanced Battery Manufacturing Grants	2.0 billion
Biomass Program	800 million
Retrofit ramp-ups in energy efficiency	454 million
Geothermal Technologies Program	400 million
Transportation electrification	400 million
Energy-efficient building technologies	346 million
Energy Efficient Appliance Rebates/ENERGY STAR®	300 million
Alternative-Fueled-Vehicles Pilot Grant Program	300 million
Industrial Technologies Program	256 million
Solar Technologies Program	115 million
Vehicle Technologies Program	110 million
National laboratory facilities	104 million
Facility improvements at National Renewable Energy Lab	100 million
Wind energy projects	93 million
Information and communications technology	50 million
Fuel cell markets	41.9 million
Modernizing existing U.S. hydropower infrastructure	32 million
Massachusetts Wind Technology Testing Center	25 million
Community renewable energy deployment	22 million
Small Business Clean Energy Innovation Projects	18 million
Nuclear waste cleanup	*6 billion*
Hanford River Site Recovery Act Project	1.6 billion
Savannah River Site Recovery Act Project	1.4 billion
Oak Ridge National Lab Recovery Act Project	775 million
Idaho National Lab Recovery Act Project	468 million
Office of River Protection Recovery Act Project	326 million
Los Alamos National Lab Recovery Act Project	212 million
Liquid waste tank infrastructure	200 million
Carlsbad Field Office Recovery Act Project	172 million
Portsmouth Recovery Act Project	118 million
Moab Recovery Act Project	108 million
Argonne National Lab Recovery Act Project	98 million
Paducah Recovery Act Project	79 million
West Valley Recovery Act Project	474 million
Title X Uranium/Thorium Reimbursement Program	69 million

(Continued)

Table 4.1 Breakdown of funding in ARRA for energy programs[5]—cont'd

Program	Funds ($)
Energy Technology Engineering Center ARRA Project	54 million
Separations Process Research Unit ARRA Project	52 million
Nevada Test Site Recovery Act Project	44 million
Brookhaven National Lab Recovery Act Project	42 million
Mound Operable Unit 1 Recovery Act Project	20 million
Stanford Linear Accelerator Center Recovery Act Project	8 million
Hanford River Site Recovery Act Project	1.6 billion
Electric grid modernization	*4.5 billion*
Smart Grid Investment Grant Program	3.5 billion
Energy storage demonstration	700 million
Workforce development	100 million
Interconnection transmission planning and analysis	80 million
Enhancing State/Local Governments Energy Assurance	55 million
State assistance on electricity policies	50 million
Program direction	29 million
Interoperability standards and framework	10 million
Carbon capture and sequestration	*3.4 billion*
Industrial carbon capture and storage applications	1.5 billion
Fossil Energy Research and Development Programs	1 billion
Clean Coal Power Initiative Round III	800 million
Geologic sequestration site characterization	49 million
Geologic sequestration training and research	20 million
Program direction	10 million
Scientific innovation	*2.0 billion*
Advanced Research (ARPA-E)	400 million
Energy frontier research centers	277 million
Basic energy services	247 million
High energy physics	216 million
Science laboratories infrastructure	198 million
Biological and environmental research	155 million
Advanced scientific computing research	154 million
Nuclear physics	143 million
Energy Sciences Fellowships and Early Career Awards	97 million
Fusion energy sciences	83 million
Small business innovation research	58 million

deploying them may be rushed in order to obtain funding from ARRA. When technology is rushed, mistakes and the risk of security vulnerabilities increase significantly.

Several other acts have been introduced that may soon become law, such as the Grid Reliability and Infrastructure Defense Act,[6] but the political process usually modifies these acts significantly and there is a chance these acts will never become law. However, these acts should be monitored in the case they become law, which could dramatically change your organization's regulatory requirements.

DOE

As part of the Smart Grid Investment Grant Program (SGIG), which was funded by ARRA of 2009, DOE sought proposals to award the roughly $4.5 billion for smart grid-related projects. There are many requirements spelled out in the Funding Opportunity Announcement (FOA). For the purposes of this book though, the FOA specifically includes a section entitled "Cyber Security" that requires applicants to address their technical approach to cyber security, as well as discussing security throughout the document.[7] The application deadline has already passed, but the cyber security requirements should still be reviewed because it provides a glimpse into DOE's policies and processes for smart grid security. There will most likely be further funding opportunities from DOE that will have similar cyber security requirements. The FOA can be obtained from www.energy.gov/media/xDE-FOA-00000.36.pdf.

The final section of Title XIII, Section 1309: DOE Study of Security Attributes of Smart Grid Systems, assigns DOE the responsibility of reporting on how smart grid deployments will affect the security of the electric grid.[2] While many government agencies will be playing a part in the development of smart grids, DOE was specifically assigned the responsibility for monitoring and reporting on the security of smart grids. The report is required to provide recommendations on the following items:

1. How smart grid systems can help in making the Nation's electricity system less vulnerable to disruptions due to intentional acts against the system.
2. How smart grid systems can help in restoring the integrity of the Nation's electricity system subsequent to disruptions.
3. How smart grid systems can facilitate nationwide, interoperable emergency communications and control of the Nation's electricity system during times of localized, regional, or nationwide emergency.
4. What risks must be taken into account that smart grid systems may, if not carefully created and managed, create vulnerability to security threats of any sort, and how such risks may be mitigated.[2]

In April 2009, Idaho National Laboratory (INL) created a document titled *Study of Security Attributes of Smart Grid Systems – Current Cyber Security Issues*, which can be obtained from www.inl.gov/scada/publications/d/securing_the_smart_grid_current_issues.pdf. The purpose of the document was to provide information for the report to congress required by Section 1309 of Title XIII of EISA.[8] However, the document was not intended to be a comprehensive report that provided recommendations for each of the four requirements. Instead, the document was created to support the full report, being prepared by Pacific Northwest National Laboratory (PNNL), by focusing on the cyber security of the current electric grid.[8]

The INL document discusses the security posture of the current electric grid by discussing the risk in two categories:

- Legacy electric grid technologies
- Current smart grid technologies.[8]

Legacy Electric Grid Technologies

To state the obvious, implementing a smart grid will not happen in one day. Additionally, it would be too costly and logistically infeasible to build a mirror electric grid in order to make the switch in one day. Smart grids will be implemented by continually introducing smart grid technology to the current electric grid. Until the electric grid has fully converted to a smart grid, the risk presented by legacy technology will continue to present risk to the electric grid. As examples of legacy grid technologies, the INL document uses:

- Supervisory control and data acquisition (SCADA)
- Substations
- Communication networks.[8]

SCADA systems are used extensively to remotely control and monitor the transmission and distribution of power in electric grids.[8] These systems are often directly connected to the Internet and managed remotely. Vulnerabilities in SCADA systems and protocols have been known and well documented for many years, in addition to vulnerabilities that have not been disclosed to the public yet.[8]

TOOLS

Common vulnerability scanners, such as Nessus and OpenVAS, include checks for some of the known SCADA vulnerabilities, which can help your organization identify and remediate these vulnerabilities before they are exploited for malicious purposes.

Grid substations usually house transmission and distribution devices, as well as automation and communication devices used to monitor and control those devices. The INL document states that the level of automation in substations is increasing and more importantly states that the "level of automation is indirectly related security because increased automation implies increased computer-controlled electronics and software."[8] Increasing the level of automation will certainly reduce the number of incidents caused by human errors and mistakes, but like the INL document implied, the increase in computer-controlled electronics and software increases the potential for security vulnerabilities.

Utility companies have utilized communication networks for many years to support their operations. The mediums and protocols used to support these communication networks are commonly used among most industries and include the following:

- Frame relay networks
- Asynchronous transfer mode (ATM)
- Public switched telephone network (PSTN)
- Internet
- Wireless technologies
- TCP/IP
- HTTP
- FTP.[8]

The vulnerabilities affecting these methods and protocols have been well documented over the years, and they will be utilized as attack vectors.[8] Most of these mediums and protocols will also be utilized by smart grid technologies, so the risk presented by these mediums and protocols will still remain.

> **WARNING**
>
> Smart grid technologies will be integrated with legacy technologies and thus, there will be no logical separation between legacy grid technologies and new smart grid technologies. As a result, exploiting a vulnerability in a legacy system could lead to the compromise of the new smart grid technologies.

Current Smart Grid Technologies

In addition to the risk from vulnerabilities in legacy technologies, the electric grids will face risk stemming from vulnerabilities in the new smart grid technologies. The INL document specifically describes the current state of security for three technologies used in smart grids:

- AMI security
- Wireless network security
- NASPI security.[8]

Advanced Metering Infrastructure (AMI) Security

AMI is probably the most commonly known technology in smart grids. Smart meters and their supporting infrastructure have been discussed widely by the media and vulnerabilities that have already been identified in these technologies are well documented. The INL document cited research by Travis Goodspeed and Matthew Carpenter as evidence of existing vulnerabilities and makes the statement that AMI security is currently insufficient.[8] The repercussions of this diagnosis could be broad and opens up the question of accountability. Who is responsible for AMI security?

The smart meter technology vendors are an easy target because they are the ones who developed the insecure devices. However, the utility companies should also take responsibility for not requiring a higher level of security from their partners. Chapter 9, "Third-Party Services," discusses in more detail the security implications and recommendations for dealing with technology vendors and third parties.

Wireless Network Security

Numerous wireless technologies will be used in smart grid deployments to facilitate the constant communication between the different smart grid entities. Wireless technologies have been plagued by security vulnerabilities in the past and this will most likely continue with wireless technologies used in smart grids. As a result, the INL document recommends that more research needs to be performed on the particular wireless networks that will be used in smart grids.[8] Chapter 7, "Attacking the Utility Companies," and Chapter 12, "Attacking Smart Meters," contain more information on the wireless security issues of smart grids.

NASPI Security

Smart grids will utilize phasor measurement units (PMU) to monitor the power grid for disturbances. The North American SynchroPhasor Initiative (NASPI) seeks to build a new communications network in order to provide real-time monitoring of the PMUs.[8] Because PMUs have not been widely deployed, the INL document states that the NASPI network is not yet critical.[8] However, this network should still be viewed as a potential attack vector, and the risk will increase as more PMUs are deployed. Even though PMUs are not widely deployed yet, planning the cyber security approach for the supporting communications network should still begin.

Lack of Deployment Equals Lack of Risk

One of the more interesting statements in the INL document states that the current risk to national security posed by vulnerabilities in smart grid technologies is not significant. Unfortunately, the reason is not due to the strong security built into the smart grid technologies. Rather, it is due to the currently small level of smart grid technologies deployed.[8] Until smart grid technology becomes more prevalent, the risk of an attack is not considered significant.

Overall, the INL document implied that the security of most smart grid technologies is insufficient. Using the numerous vulnerabilities that have already been identified and a lack of security standards as reasoning, the INL document clearly makes the case that more needs to be done to secure the power grid.

FERC

The Federal Energy Regulatory Commission (FERC – www.ferc.gov) was founded in 1977, at the same time as DOE, and combined the functions of several agencies such as the Federal Power Commission.[1] FERC is an independent U.S.

federal agency that regulates the interstate transmission of natural gas, oil, and electricity, as well as natural gas and hydropower projects.[9]

Mandatory Reliability Standards

Under the Energy Policy Act of 2005, FERC obtained the authority to mandate reliability standards and impose penalties for noncompliance. As a result, FERC designated the North American Reliability Corporation (NERC) as the Electric Reliability Organization and tasked NERC to create the reliability standards. Additionally, FERC authorized NERC to enforce these reliability standards through severe financial penalties. For more information on this topic, and how to avoid the severe financial penalties, see Chapter 6, "Public and Private Companies," which covers NERC and their Critical Infrastructure Protection standards thoroughly.

Smart Grid Policy

On July 16, 2009, FERC issued a new policy statement intended to accelerate the development of a national smart grid. Although the policy covers a wide range of topics, the security policy statement focuses on the development of cyber security standards. The new FERC policy can be viewed at www.ferc.gov/whats-new/comm-meet/2009/071609/E-3.pdf.

> **NOTE**
>
> Section 1 under the Development of Key Standards section is entitled "System Security." This should send another clear signal to the industry that security is a top priority and that failure to comply with security standards will result in harsh penalties.

NIST

Section 1305 of EISA assigns NIST the responsibility of coordinating the development of a smart grid interoperability framework. In response, NIST developed the following three-phase plan to create the standards:

1. Further engage utilities, equipment suppliers, consumers, standards developers and other stakeholders to achieve consensus on Smart Grid standards. This process will include a stakeholders' summit scheduled for May 19–20, 2009 in Washington, D.C. By early fall, the process will deliver:
   * the Smart Grid architecture;
   * priorities for interoperability and cybersecurity standards, and an initial set of standards to support implementation; and
   * plans to meet remaining standards needs.
2. Launch a formal partnership to facilitate development of additional standards to address remaining gaps and integrate new technologies.

3. Develop a plan for testing and certification to ensure that Smart Grid equipment and systems conform to standards for security and interoperability.[10]

NIST SP 1108

The NIST Framework and Roadmap for Smart Grid Interoperability Standards (NIST SP 1108) is the result of the first phase and can be reviewed at http://nist. gov/public_affairs/releases/upload/smartgrid_interoperability_final.pdf. Security is a major component of NIST SP 1108; however, there are several other areas of focus within this document that are outside the scope of this book. This section of the chapter will focus on the security aspects of NIST SP 1108, although reading the entirety of NIST SP 1108 is highly recommended.

In Section 2.3.1, the smart grid architectures are discussed. Defining the architecture of a smart grid will be critical in determining how to properly integrate security into the smart grid. However, different areas of the electric grid have diverse requirements that a single architecture would be unable to handle. As a result, the nation's smart grid will utilize multiple architecture designs and will not rely on a single architecture. So instead of attempting to define a single, unifying smart grid architecture, NIST has defined a list of desired architecture attributes that every architecture should incorporate:

1. Support a broad range of technology options—both legacy and new. (Architectures should be flexible enough to incorporate evolving technologies. They also must support interfacing with legacy applications and devices in a standard way, avoiding as much additional capital investment and/or customization as possible.)
2. Employ well-defined interfaces that are useful across industries and include appropriate security.
3. Are developed with modern system-modeling tools and techniques that are used to manage the documentation and complexity of the Smart Grid.
4. Architectural elements are appropriate for the applications that reside within the architecture. (The architectures must support development of massively scaled, well-managed, and secure networks with life spans appropriate for the type of associated network, which range from 5 years to 30 years depending on the type of network.)
5. Support third-party products that are interoperable and can be integrated into the management and cyber security infrastructures.
6. Achieve appropriate balance between top-down and bottom-up approaches to system design.
7. Are based on proven enterprise architecture, software, and systems design methodologies.[11]

Although important, these seven attributes are fairly generic and do not provide specific guidance for utility companies or smart grid vendors. Phase three of NIST's approach, which is to develop a plan for testing and certifying smart grid systems and equipment, may fill in some of the details for these attributes, such as which enterprise architecture, software, and systems design methodologies are considered to be "proven." However, each organization should be prepared to defend how their particular architecture design incorporates these seven attributes.

Smart Grid Information Networks

Section 3.3 of NIST SP 1108 discusses the information networks that will support the national smart grid. The national smart grid will contain numerous networks that belong to many different organizations and individuals. In order to facilitate the connectivity required of a national smart grid, each of these networks will need to adhere to a strict set of interoperability requirements. NIST's vision of these networks is depicted in Figure 4.1.

Looking at Figure 4.1, an obvious placement of a firewall might be in between Network A and Network B. But is that the only location for a firewall? There are many components in each network, such as operations and markets. Each component may be supported by one or many different subnetworks that have multiple owners. Trust relationships between the different components (and networks) that reduce security control effectiveness could allow a threat in one component to spread across components and even networks. Thus, if the entire electric grid is interconnected, a single vulnerability in one network could affect the security posture of the entire smart grid. Chapter 9, "Third-Party Services," discusses trust relationships in more detail.

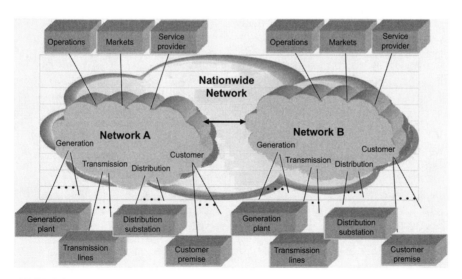

FIGURE 4.1

NIST's depiction of smart grid networks for information exchange.[11]

Reprinted courtesy of the National Institute of Standards and Technology, Technology Administration,
U.S. Department of Commerce. Not copyrightable in the United States

Included Cyber Security Standards

Sections 4.3 and 4.4 of NIST SP 1108 list 75 existing standards, specifications, guidelines, and requirements that are relevant to the smart grid. Many functional areas are covered by these standards and NIST divided them into different categories. The documents listed in the cyber security sections are listed below in Table 4.2.

Out of the 13 cyber security documents listed in Table 4.2, experienced security professionals should already be familiar with at least four of these documents:

- NIST SP 800-53
- NIST SP 800-82
- ISO 27000
- NIST FIPS 140-2.

Table 4.2 Cyber security standards, specifications, guidelines, and requirements[11]

Document	URL
Security Profile for Advanced Metering Infrastructure, v1.0	http://osgug.ucaiug.org/utilisec/amisec/Shared%20Documents/AMI%20Security%20Profile%20(ASAP-SG)/AMI%20Security%20Profile%20-%20v1_0.pdf
DHS Catalog of Control Systems Security: Recommendations for Standards Developers	www.us-cert.gov/control_systems/pdf/FINAL-Catalog_of_Recommendations_Rev4_101309.pdf
DHS Cyber Security Procurement Language for Control Systems	www.us-cert.gov/control_systems/pdf/FINAL-Procurement_Language_Rev4_100809.pdf
International Electrotechnical Commission (IEC) 62351 Parts 1–8	http://webstore.iec.ch/webstore/webstore.nsf/artnum/037996!opendocument
IEEE 1686-2007	https://sbwsweb.ieee.org/ecustomercme_enu/start.swe?SWECmd=GotoView&SWEView=Catalog+View+(eSales)_Standards_IEEE&mem_type=Customer&SWEHo=sbwsweb.ieee.org&SWETS=1192713657
NERC CIP 002-009	www.nerc.com/page.php?cid=2|20
NIST SP 800-53	http://csrc.nist.gov/publications/drafts/800-82/draft_sp800-82-fpd.pdf
NIST SP 800-82	http://csrc.nist.gov/publications/nistpubs/800-53-Rev3/sp800-53-rev3-final-errata.pdf
ISA SP99	www.isa.org/MSTemplate.cfm?MicrositeID=988&CommitteeID=6821
ISO27000	www.27000.org/
NIST FIPS 140-2	http://csrc.nist.gov/publications/fips/fips140-2/fips1402.pdf
OASIS WS-Security	www.oasis-open.org/specs/index.php#wssv1.1
OASIS Suite of Security Standards	www.oasis-open.org/committees/tc_home.php?wg_abbrev=wss

These documents apply to a broad range of industries; however, security professionals who are new to the energy industry will most likely need to familiarize themselves with the rest of the 13 documents. Additionally, only the NERC CIP is mandatory for a utility to comply with. The other documents contain recommendations for security controls that organizations should analyze to determine whether they apply to their environment.

Priority Action Plans

The documents listed in Section 4 of NIST SP 1108 do not represent a comprehensive list of standards, specifications, guidelines, and requirements. There are gaps in the required standards that need to be addressed and NIST has created Priority Action Plans (PAP) to address these gaps. Section 5 of NIST SP 1108 details the 15 existing PAPs; however, more PAPs will be created as the smart grid evolves.[11] When new technology is introduced, new standards, specifications, guidelines, and requirements will need to be created, and a PAP will be issued to create these documents. Thus, your organization should regularly check NIST's smart grid Web site (www.nist.gov/smartgrid) to view any additional PAPs that result in additional standards, specifications, guidelines, and requirements.

The biggest takeaway from the PAPs is the recognition that the smart grid will constantly be changing. New technology will be introduced and new threats will surface. As such, utility companies and smart grid technology vendors must be able to upgrade their devices and implementations to meet the ever-changing challenges.

Other Concerns

Section 7.3 of NIST SP 1108 discusses two potential issues that could affect the availability of the smart grid: electromagnetic disturbances and electromagnetic interference.[11] Electromagnetic disturbances include threats such as electromagnetic pulses (EMP) and geomagnetically induced currents caused by solar storms.[11] These disturbances could cause DoS conditions in the smart grid that interrupt the communication networks, as well as the transmission and distribution of electricity. As a result, the Smart Grid Interoperability Group (SGIP) will be conducting further analysis of applicable protection standards and propose revisions to make the standards relevant to smart grid-directed threats.[11]

An EMP is a burst of electromagnetic energy or radiation, which has the potential to produce electrical voltage surges that can damage electronics. EMPs can be produced by several actions, such as the detonation of nuclear weapons and other nonnuclear sources such as electromagnetic bombs (E-bombs).[12] When detonated on the ground, these weapons have a relatively small area of exposure; however, when detonated at high altitudes, the EMP result of these weapons can have wide-ranging devastating effects. It is estimated that a 1.4 megaton nuclear bomb detonated 250 miles above Kansas would destroy most of the nonprotected electronics in the continental United States.[12]

> **EPIC FAIL**
>
> In 1962, an atmospheric test of a 1.4 megaton nuclear bomb was detonated 250 miles above Johnston Island. The Hawaiian islands of Oahu and Kauai, which are located 800 miles east of Johnston Island, observed the effects of EMP when their street lights, fuses, and telephone service were disabled.[12] This was a test of a weapon though, so maybe it was an epic success.

NIST plans further research to study the potential affect of electromagnetic interference on smart grid communication technologies.[11] NIST states that "there is no intention to mandate the use of specific spectra (licensed or unlicensed) or the use of specific wireless technologies for Smart Grid equipment."[11] However, based on the results of their research and if a major electromagnetic incident occurs, the recommended communications technologies could become mandatory and massive updates may be recommended to smart grid implementations and devices. Overall, there may be several new standards to address electromagnetic threats to the security of the smart grid.

Smart Grid Cyber Security Strategy and Requirements

Section 6: Cyber Security Strategy and Section 7.3.3 of NIST SP 1108 focus on the Cyber Security Strategy and Privacy Issues in the Smart Grid, but only summarize the material in another document, NISTIR-7628: Smart Grid Cyber Security Strategy and Requirements. NISTIR-7628 is currently in its second draft status and can be obtained from http://csrc.nist.gov/publications/drafts/nistir-7628/draft-nistir-7628_2nd-public-draft.pdf. At the time this book was written, NISTIR-7628 was still in draft status, so there could be significant changes. However, the core information in this document will most likely remain.

Initially, the task of creating the Cyber Security Strategy and Requirements was undertaken by the Cyber Security Coordination Task Group (CSCTG), which has been renamed under the SGIP as the Cyber Security Working Group (SGIP-CSWG).[11] The SGIP-CSWG developed five high-level tasks to be performed in order to create the strategy, which are illustrated in Figure 4.2. Each utility company and smart grid technology vendor should perform a similar approach to develop their own cyber security strategy that is tailored to their own environment. NISTIR-7628 should be used as a baseline and to provide guidance to organization's developing their own cyber security strategy, as opposed to trying to force the NISTIR-7628 cyber security strategy on their organization.

Use Cases

As with the rest of NISTIR-7628, the use cases listed in Appendix A of NISTIR-7628 should be used as the starting point for your organization's use cases. Many of these use cases will apply directly to your organization; however, some will not, so it is important that each organization goes through their own analysis to

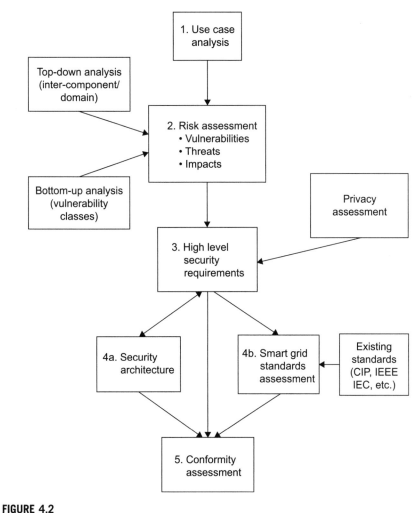

FIGURE 4.2

Smart grid cyber security strategy tasks.[13]

Reprinted courtesy of the National Institute of Standards and Technology, Technology Administration,
U.S. Department of Commerce. Not copyrightable in the United States

determine relevant use cases. As an example, a smart meter vendor will have a different set of use cases than a situational sensor device. For obvious reasons, a smart meter will be used for entirely different purposes than a sensor device.

Risk Assessment

The SGIP-CSWG used the documents listed in Table 4.3 to develop their risk assessment of the smart grid. Excluding the ISA documents, each of the documents listed in Table 4.3 are available to download for free. So, there should be

Table 4.3 Risk-assessment documents[13]

Document	URL
NIST SP 800-39: DRAFT Managing Risk from Information Systems: An Organizational Perspective	http://csrc.nist.gov/publications/drafts/800-39/SP800-39-spd-sz.pdf
NIST Federal Information Processing Standard (FIPS) 200: Minimum Security Requirements for Federal Information and Information Systems	http://csrc.nist.gov/publications/fips/fips200/FIPS-200-final-march.pdf
NIST FIPS 199: Standards for Security Categorization of Federal Information and Information Systems	http://csrc.nist.gov/publications/fips/fips199/FIPS-PUB-199-final.pdf
NERC: Security Guidelines for the Electricity Sector: Vulnerability and Risk Assessment	www.esisac.com/publicdocs/Guides/V1-VulnerabilityAssessment.pdf
DHS: The National Infrastructure Protection Plan (NIPP), Partnering to enhance protection and resiliency	www.dhs.gov/xlibrary/assets/NIPP_Plan.pdf
DHS: The IT, telecommunications, and energy sectors sector-specific plans (SSPs)	www.dhs.gov/files/programs/gc_1179866197607.shtm
ANSI/ISA-99.00.01-2007, Security for Industrial Automation and Control Systems: Concepts, Terminology and Models	www.isa.org/isa9900012007
ANSI/ISA-99.02.01-2009, Security for Industrial Automation and Control Systems: Establishing an Industrial Automation and Control Systems Security Program	www.isa.org/Template.cfm?Section=Standards2&template=/Ecommerce/ProductDisplay.cfm&ProductID=10243

no budgetary concerns for organization's to utilize these documents in performing risk assessments. In addition to risk assessments, these documents are also useful throughout the risk-management life cycle. As an example, consider DHS's NIPP Risk Management Framework, which is illustrated in Figure 4.3. Additionally, these are the document used by the SGIP-CSWG to develop their risk assessment, but that does not mean that every smart grid organization needs to use these documents. Other standards and guidelines that may be helpful are included in Table 4.4. The important issue is to be able to justify to auditors that the organization's risk assessment was based on proven, industry regarded standards.

High-Level Security Requirements

Despite having the label requirement, only one set of standards listed in the high-level security requirements of NISTIR-7628 is required or mandatory.[13] The high-level security requirement standards include the standards listed in Table 4.2, as well as the following additional standards listed in Table 4.5.

Reviewing and becoming an expert on every applicable standard, guideline, requirements documentation, and framework for the smart grid may seem like a daunting task. At this point in the chapter, we have listed more than

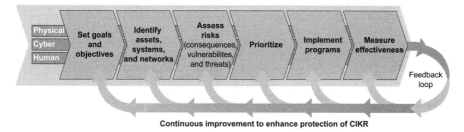

Continuous improvement to enhance protection of CIKR

FIGURE 4.3

DHS NIPP risk-management framework.[14]

Table 4.4 Additional risk-assessment documents

Document	URL
ISO/IEC Guide 73:2009: Risk Management – Vocabulary	www.iso.org/iso/iso_catalogue/catalogue_tc/catalogue_detail.htm?csnumber=44651
ISO/IEC 31000:2009: Risk Management – Principles and Guidelines	www.iso.org/iso/catalogue_detail?csnumber=43170
ISO/IEC 31010:2009: Risk management – Risk assessment techniques	www.iso.org/iso/catalogue_detail?csnumber=51073
Central Computing and Telecommunications Agency (CCTA) Risk Analysis and Management Method (CRAMM)	www.cramm.com/
COBIT	www.isaca.org/Template.cfm?Section=COBIT6&Template=/TaggedPage/TaggedPageDisplay.cfm&TPLID=55&ContentID=31519

Table 4.5 Additional cyber security documents[13]

Document	URL
UtilityAMI Home Area Network System Requirements Specification, 2008	www.utilityami.org/docs/UtilityAMI%20HAN%20SRS%20-%20v1.04%20-%20080819-1.pdf
ISA SP100 Wireless Standards	www.isa.org/isa100

25 documents for review. The good news is that organizations like SGIP-CSWG have done a lot of the baseline work for you and provide helpful tools such as the requirements tables in Chapter 3, "High Level Security Requirements," of NISTIR-7628. Additionally, not every document will be relevant to your organization or your individual role at the organization. However, a best effort must be performed to comply with as many of the requirements specified in the listed documents.

> **TIP**
>
> As opposed to regulatory requirements, industry standards are usually considered to be nice-to-haves but not absolutely necessary. However, regulatory requirements are usually based on standards such as those developed by NIST. Thus, smart grid–related organizations can save themselves time and money by complying with the standards developed by NIST now instead of waiting for the standards to be included in a regulatory requirement.

Standards and Requirements Assessment

When you compare your organization's use cases and the results of your organization's risk assessment against the requirements standards specified by NISTIR-7628, are all the use cases and risks addressed? The answer to this is probably not. In general, standards are written to apply to as many organizations and situations as possible, which means that highly specific conditions are usually not covered. The smart grid is intended to support as many different technologies as possible and as a result, there will always be unique situations that require additional security requirements.

If the smart grid becomes compliant with all the relevant security requirements specified by NISTIR-7628 and NIST SP 1108, will the smart grid be impervious to a cyber attack? Of course not! The goal of security professionals and security initiatives, such as the federal initiatives discussed in this chapter, is to manage the risk associated with the smart grid, not eliminate the risk. Eliminating risk is simply not possible. The cyber strategy detailed in NISTIR-7628 considers prevention to be the primary goal, but response and recovery to cyber attacks are considered critical requirements.[13] If your role in an organization is to develop the cyber security strategy, compliance with the security requirements and standards listed in the NIST documents should be a goal, but not the only goal.

DHS NIPP

As part of the Homeland Security Presidential Directive 7, DHS was instructed to create a National Infrastructure Protection Plan (NIPP) for the nation's critical infrastructure and key resources (CIKR).[14] Specifically, the stated goal for NIPP is to "build a safer, more secure, and more resilient America by preventing, deterring, neutralizing, or mitigating the effects of deliberate efforts by terrorists to destroy, incapacitate, or exploit elements of our Nation's CIKR and to strengthen national preparedness, timely response, and rapid recovery of CIKR in the event of an attack, natural disaster, or other emergency."[14] NIPP is a publicly accessible document that can be viewed at the URL specified in Table 4.3.

Although EISA of 2007 assigns NIST the responsibility of coordinating the cyber security efforts of the smart grid, the Homeland Security Act of 2002 assigns DHS the responsibility of securing the nation's critical infrastructure, which includes the smart grid. So, there are some gray areas for which responsibilities belong to the two organizations, but so far there has been cooperation in their efforts. For example, the NISTIR-7628 lists the DHS NIPP as one of the documents used to perform their risk assessment.

The original NIPP was created in 2006 and was later updated in 2009. One of the more interesting updates included in the 2009 version is in increasing the importance of resiliency.[14] Protection is still considered the main goal of the NIPP; however, the 2009 version of NIPP attempts to balance out the strategy with resiliency. The ability to respond and recover from attacks is now considered to be just as important, which is echoed in the NISTIR-7628 cyber security strategy.

Sector-Specific Plans

The electric grid is not the only entity classified as critical infrastructure, and in order to address the specific needs of each critical infrastructure, DHS created Sector-Specific Plans (SSP). Eighteen SSPs were created and can be reviewed at www.dhs.gov/files/programs/gc_1179866197607.shtm. The redacted Energy SSP can be downloaded at www.dhs.gov/xlibrary/assets/nipp-ssp-energy-redacted.pdf.

In the development of the Energy SSP, the illustration of the communication networks shown in Figure 4.4 was created. As shown, most of the communication goes across private (wired and wireless) networks and leased lines are used in public networks. Additionally, the illustration does not show any communication lines between the utility companies and residential, commercial, and industrial consumers. In the smart grid, there will be two-way communication lines between the consumers and the utility companies, and these communication lines will utilize multiple network types. Despite this, the document does include valuable insight and information that can help utility companies and smart grid technology vendors to secure their environments and products.

OTHER APPLICABLE LAWS

While there are and will be numerous initiatives and laws specifically directed at the smart grid, several security laws already exist that organizations should be aware of. This section will discuss the following laws:

- The Identity Theft Enforcement and Restitution Act of 2008
- Electronic Communications Privacy Act of 1986
- Breach Notification Laws
- Personal Information Protection and Electronic Documents Act (PIPEDA).

The Identity Theft Enforcement and Restitution Act of 2008

The Identity Theft Enforcement and Restitution Act of 2008 amends existing laws in order to make it easier to federally prosecute cyber criminals.[16] Specifically, the amendments to identity theft and cyber extortion that have implications with the

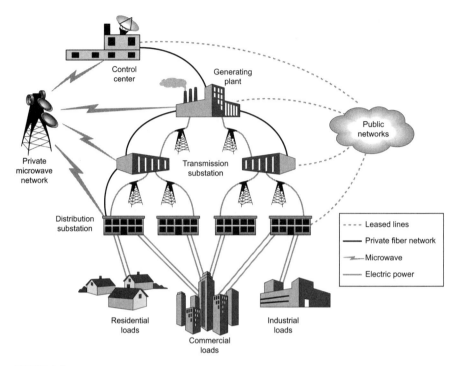

FIGURE 4.4

DHS SSP overview of the electric power system and control communications.[15]

smart grid. For example, consider an attacker who compromises a consumer's smart meter and shuts off their electricity. Then, the attacker demands the consumer pay the attacker to turn the electricity back on. The law should allow for federal prosecution of the attacker, which may require the utility company to provide network and device logs as evidence of the attack.

Electronic Communications Privacy Act of 1986

The Electronic Communications Privacy Act (ECPA) of 1986 prevents unauthorized access by the government to electronic communications that are stored or while in-transit. Utility companies need to be cautious when responding to requests by law enforcement for information regarding consumer's energy usage information. Although utility companies need to comply with valid requests that are backed by warrants, voluntarily providing consumer information to the government could lead to lawsuits filed by their customers. Chapter 5, "State and Local Security Initiatives," discusses these privacy issues in more detail.

Breach Notification Laws

Several attempts have been made to pass a national law requiring companies to immediately disclose a data breach to consumers. Most of these have not been passed into law yet, including the recent Data Accountability and Trust Act. However, 46 states, the District of Columbia, Puerto Rico, and the Virgin Islands have all enacted breach notification laws.[17] So, if a breach does occur, the utility company should be prepared to inform their affected customers.

Personal Information Protection and Electronic Documents Act

The United States is not the only country that is implementing a smart grid. Numerous other countries have their own initiatives and their own data privacy and security laws. As an example, let's consider Canada because the United States is part of the North American electric grid that includes the country of Canada. One particular Canadian law is the Personal Information Protection and Electronic Documents Act (PIPEDA), which relates to data privacy. The law requires organizations to comply with several mandates including the following:

- Obtain consent to use or disclose personal information
- Explain to individuals why they are collecting information
- Collect information by lawful means
- Maintain personal information policies that are clear and understandable
- Protect the personal information using appropriate security measures
- Provide individuals with easy access to their information.[18]

These mandates could materially impact the privacy policies and procedures of organizations that collect data from the smart grid. Additionally, any American smart grid–related company that wants to do business in another country needs to do its research to determine which laws will affect its products or services. Smart grid devices have the potential to collect massive amounts of data that may fall under the umbrella of federal laws.

Noncountry Specific Privacy Guidelines

If your organization plans to operate in more than one country, then using privacy guidelines that are not country specific will be a good approach to ensuring your organization complies with most, if not all, privacy laws. Specifically, the following guidelines provide recommendations for privacy that are not tied to specific countries:

- Organization for Economic Co-operation and Development (OECD) Guidelines on the Protection of Privacy and Transborder Flows of Personal Data – www.oecd.org/document/18/0,3343,en_2649_34255_1815186_1_1_1_1,00.html
- American Institute of Certified Public Accountants (AICPA) and the Canadian Institute of Chartered Accountants (CICA) Generally Accepted Privacy Principles – www.cica.ca/service-and-products/privacy/gen-accepted-privacy-principles/index.aspx.

SPONSORING SECURITY

The federal government should directly target organizations and consumers with information regarding security in the smart grid. Although security professionals recognize the need for proper security controls in the smart grid, some members of management at utility companies and smart grid technology vendors will still view cyber security threats as unrealistic. Future legislation is likely to mandate the adoption of the majority of the resulting security requirements from the federal security initiatives. As a result, organizations will eventually need to comply with these security best practices.

BUREAUCRACY AND POLITICS IN SMART GRID SECURITY

To state the obvious, the federal government is a large bureaucracy, which can affect the outcome of these security initiatives. As an example, consider the privacy impact assessment (PIA) performed and discussed as part of NIST SP 1108 and NISTIR-7628. Rebecca Herold, who leads the PIA effort, posted an entry on her blog (www.realtime-itcompliance.com/index.html) about the bureaucratic process involved with writing up the findings from the PIA in a NIST document. The initial draft PIA report to be included was 22 pages long; however, only seven pages were included.[19] In her words, "The portion of the PIA that was included within the first draft is 7 pages long. Much of the heart of the privacy details and related issues were removed, and I understand why. I blame myself for not understanding the amount of bureaucracy and need for discussion and explanation necessary, well in advance of report publication, to make sure that all of the folks not only within the NIST work group, but also the officials at NIST, including their lawyers, to make sure all information that (I firmly believe) is important is included."[19]

There may have been perfectly legitimate reasons to remove the other 15 pages from the PIA report. However, the point is that no process, initiative, standard, guideline, or best practice is perfect, and the federal initiatives should be interpreted accordingly. There will always be bureaucratic roadblocks and political influences that affect federal security initiatives, whether in a positive or a negative way.

SUMMARY

The federal government has made it clear that securing the electric grid is a matter of national security. As a result, the federal government has launched several security initiatives and has allocated billions of dollars to support the effort. Utilities and technology vendors have been sent a clear message that security is a top priority for the electric grid.

Staying up-to-date with all the federal standards, guidelines, requirements, and initiatives is a challenge to say the least. According to NIST SP 1108, "The Smart Grid will ultimately require hundreds of standards, specifications, and requirements."[11] The current security standards and initiatives by DOE, DHS, FERC, and NIST are only the beginning of what will need to be a close relationship between the federal government and the energy industry.

Endnotes

1. Cornell University Law School. Energy law: an overview [document on the Internet]. http://topics.law.cornell.edu/wex/energy; 2010 [accessed 30.04.10].
2. U.S. Energy Information Administration. Energy independence and security act of 2007: summary of provisions [document on the Internet]. www.eia.doe.gov/oiaf/aeo/otheranalysis/aeo_2008analysispapers/eisa.html; 2010 [accessed 30.04.10].
3. U.S. Government Printing Office. Public law 111 - 5 - American recovery and reinvestment act of 2009 [document on the Internet]. www.gpo.gov/fdsys/pkg/PLAW-111publ5/content-detail.html; 2010 [accessed 30.04.10].
4. U.S. Department of Energy. Breakdown of funding [document on the Internet]. www.energy.gov/recovery/breakdown.htm2010 [accessed 30.04.10].
5. U.S. Department of Energy. U.S. Department of energy national energy technology laboratory recovery act – Smart grid demonstrations funding opportunity number: DE-FOA-0000036 Announcement Type: AMENDMENT 000001 (FINAL) CFDA Number: 81.122 Electricity Delivery and Energy Reliability Research, Development and Analysis [document on the Internet]. www.energy.gov/media/xDE-FOA-00000.36.pdf; 2009 [accessed 07.05.10].
6. U.S. Department of Energy. Federal smart grid task force [document on the Internet]. www.oe.energy.gov/smartgrid_taskforce.htm; 2010 [accessed 30.04.10].
7. GovTrack. H.R. 5026: Grid act [document on the Internet]. www.govtrack.us/congress/bill.xpd?bill=h111-5026; 2010 [accessed .04.05.10].
8. U.S. Department of Energy Office of Electricity Delivery and Energy Reliability. Study of security attributes of smart grid systems – current cyber security issues [document on the Internet]. www.inl.gov/scada/publications/d/securing_the_smart_grid_current_issues.pdf; 2009 [accessed 01.05.10].
9. Federal Energy Regulatory Commission. FERC: about FERC [document on the Internet]. www.ferc.gov/about/about.asp; 2010 [accessed 04.05.10].
10. NIST. NIST announces three-phase plan for smart grid standards, paving way for more efficient, reliable electricity [document on the Internet]. www.nist.gov/public_affairs/releases/smartgrid_041309.cfm; 2009 [accessed 14.05.10].
11. National Institute of Standards and Technology. NIST Special publication 1108: NIST framework and roadmap for smart grid interoperability standards, Release 1.0 [document on the Internet]. www.nist.gov/public_affairs/releases/upload/smartgrid_interoperability_final.pdf; 2010 [accessed 14.05.10].
12. Washington State Department of Health, Division of Environmental Health, Office of Radiation Protection. Electromagnetic pulse [document on the Internet]. www.doh.wa.gov/ehp/rp/factsheets/factsheets-htm/fs41elecpuls.htm; 2009 [accessed 18.05.10].

13. National Institute of Standards and Technology. Draft NIST IR 7628: smart grid cyber security strategy and requirements [document on the Internet]. The Smart Grid Interoperability Panel – Cyber Security Working Group; http://csrc.nist.gov/publications/drafts/nistir-7628/draft-nistir-7628_2nd-public-draft.pdf; 2010 [accessed 18.05.10].

14. Department of Homeland Security. National infrastructure protection plan [document on the Internet]. www.dhs.gov/xlibrary/assets/NIPP_Plan.pdf; 2009 [accessed 18.05.10].

15. Department of Homeland Security. Energy critical infrastructure and key resources sector-specific plan as input to the National Infrastructure Protection Plan (Redacted) [document on the Internet]. www.dhs.gov/xlibrary/assets/nipp-ssp-energy-redacted.pdf; 2007 [accessed 18.05.10].

16. One Hundred Tenth Congress of the United States of America. Identity theft enforcement and restitution act of 2008 [document on the Internet]. www.govtrack.us/congress/billtext.xpd?bill=h110-5938; 2008 [accessed 18.05.10].

17. National Conference of State Legislatures. State security breach notification laws [document on the Internet]. www.ncsl.org/IssuesResearch/TelecommunicationsInformationTechnology/SecurityBreachNotificationLaws/tabid/13489/Default.aspx; 2010 [accessed 18.05.10].

18. Department of Justice Canada. Personal information protection and electronic documents act [document on the Internet]. http://laws.justice.gc.ca/eng/P-8.6/page-1.html; 2000 [accessed 18.05.10].

19. Herold R. 10 Smart grid consumer-to-utility privacy concerns; are there more? [document on the Internet]. www.realtime-itcompliance.com/privacy_and_compliance/2009/09/10_smart_grid_consumertoutilit.htm; 2009 [accessed 18.05.10].

State and Local Security Initiatives

INFORMATION IN THIS CHAPTER

- State Government
- State Regulatory Bodies
- State Courts
- Promoting Security Education
- Politics and the Smart Grid

Government agencies are becoming increasingly aware of cyber security threats. Federal agencies may take the lead on developing smart grid security regulations, requirements, standards, and best practices; however, utility companies will be required to adhere to state and local security initiatives as well. Additionally, companies that develop smart grid technologies will be required to support the requirements dictated by these government agencies if they want to sell their products to utility companies.

End users are often the weakest link in the security of a system. User awareness training is utilized by many organizations to mitigate this weakness within their employment ranks and even with their customers. Similarly, state and local governments will play critical roles in educating consumers on how to securely interact with smart grids.

STATE GOVERNMENT

Despite the fact that the North American electric grid regions span multiple states and international borders, state and local governments will seek to impose additional rules and regulations to the portions of the grid that operates within their jurisdiction. Several states, including California and Illinois, have already created their own smart grid development initiatives.

State Laws

Several states are in the process of creating laws, or launching other types of initiatives, to further regulate utility companies and promote the implementation of smart grids. The majority of these laws focus on setting deadlines for designing and implementing smart grids. Increased cyber security is usually mentioned as a goal; however, the majority of these laws do not state specific security requirements and rely solely on federal government and industry-based security initiatives. Additional states will most likely pass their own statewide laws and model their laws after the initial state laws. As such, utility and technology companies should monitor the state legislatures closely to ensure their products are compliant with new laws that are passed.

California

The state of California recently passed one of the first statewide smart grid laws in the United States, labeled Senate Bill (SB) 17.[1] The bill requires the California Public Utility Commission (PUC), in conjunction with several other state agencies, to create a smart grid deployment plan that is compliant with state and federal laws. Additionally, electrical corporations are required to develop and submit their smart grid deployment plan to the Californian PUC for approval. SB 17 imposed a deadline of July 1, 2010 for the PUC and July 1, 2011 for electric corporations, respectively.[1]

> **NOTE**
>
> California allows electric corporations who meet certain requirements to handle the requirements listed in SB 17 differently. Electric corporations with less than 100,000 service connections may have the requirements defined in the bill modified or adjusted.[1] However, the power to modify or adjust the requirements for these electric corporations is given to the PUC. Thus, the electric corporation would need to justify the modification.

According to section 8360 of the bill, California policy dictates that the state's smart grids meet 10 characterizations of smart grids, which apparently includes "cost-effective full cyber security."[1] Although there are good intentions in this statement, this characterization is neither practical nor realistic. "Full cyber security," or in other words eliminating the risk from cyber security threats, is simply not possible. As a result, the goal of cyber security, as well as most other types of security, is to manage risk, not eliminate risk. Additionally, cost-effective is a subjective term, which is why budgetary disputes are common. Implementing cyber security controls to defend against cyber security threats can be costly and will take a significant investment to achieve a best practice recommended level of cyber security, let alone full cyber security.

Commendably, the bill does require the California PUC adopt standards by NIST, the Gridwise Architecture Council (www.gridwiseac.org), the International Electrical and Electronics Engineers (IEEE – www.ieee.org), and NERC and FERC.[1] Mandating the adoption of standards from respected organizations such as these will assist California in achieving the listed characterizations of smart grids.

The California PUC and Californian electric corporations now have a deadline for developing a smart grid deployment plan. As a result, smart grid security will now become a priority for security and compliance departments within the California PUC and electric corporations. The deadline for electric corporations is one year later than the PUC deadline, which should allow the electric corporations sufficient time to ensure their plan is compliant with the PUC plan. Failure to comply with the regulatory bodies could cost the California electric corporations millions of dollars, which is what happened to a Texas-based utility company that is discussed later in the "PUC of Texas" section of this chapter.

Illinois

The Illinois Power Agency Act, SB 1592, requires utility companies to reduce peak demand by 0.1 percent each year for 10 years.[2] This requirement prompted smart grid initiatives by several of the state utility companies, including the deployment of hundreds of thousands smart meters. Additionally, Illinois has become a member of the Mid-Atlantic Distributed Resources Initiative (MADRI – http://sites. energetics.com/madri/). Although smart grid security requirements are not specifically mentioned in this act, these utility companies will still need to ensure their smart grid implementations meet the requirements of federal and industry regulations.

Maryland

The Maryland General Assembly passed the EmPOWER Maryland Energy Efficiency Act of 2008 (see Senate Bill 205) to reduce electricity consumption and peak demand by 15 percent by the end of 2015.[3] The law required the Maryland Public Service Commission (PSC) to determine the effectiveness of smart grids. Additionally, the law grants the PSC the ability to mandate the implementation of smart grids. Thus, utility companies in Maryland could be forced to implement smart grid technologies, although SB 205 does not mention compliance with or adoption of smart grid security standards.

State Mandates for Security

Currently, most state legislatures have not specifically mandated security in their smart grid initiative bills. The initiatives focus more on promoting or requiring utility companies to implement smart grid technologies and setting deadlines to ensure smart grid technology is deployed in a timely manner. Although the smart grids operating in their state will still be required to meet requirements defined by other organizations, such as the federal government and industry regulatory groups, the state legislatures are missing a critical opportunity to mandate cyber security controls that are appropriate for their state's specific implementation.

STATE REGULATORY BODIES

The state initiatives described in the previous section of this chapter, as well as most other state initiatives, have a common component. They empower or rely on the state energy regulatory body to produce requirements for smart grid deployments.

The name of the regulatory body varies between the states, but in general, the regulatory body will have one of the following labels:

- Board of Public Utilities
- Corporation Commission
- Commerce Commission
- PUC
- PSC
- Public Utility Control
- Public Service Board
- Utilities Board
- Utility Regulatory Commission (URC).

For a complete listing of the state regulatory bodies and their associated Web sites, see Table 5.1. Additionally, several countries have national regulatory bodies that perform similar functions on a national scale, such as the Belize PUC (www. puc.bz/). Some of these regulatory organizations do not appear to update their Web sites frequently; however, utility and smart grid technology companies should monitor these Web sites for information regarding new security requirements and other local smart grid news.

The purpose of these organizations is to regulate the utility companies that operate within their respective states. The most visible output of these organizations is the regulation of rates that utility companies can charge consumers. However, these organizations have much broader powers and responsibilities. As described previously in the "California" section of this chapter, the California PUC will be responsible for creating a deployment plan for smart grids that the utility companies will be required to comply with. Thus, these organizations have an incredible opportunity to lead utility companies and smart grid technology companies toward a more secure electrical grid. Even though smart grids are already actively being implemented as these organizations develop their own plans, these regulatory organizations and their regulated utility companies have sufficient time to ensure security plays an important role in smart grid implementations.

National Association of Regulatory Utility Commissioners

The National Association of Regulatory Utility Commissioners (NARUC – www. naruc.org/) is a nonprofit organization whose goal is to improve public utility regulation. NARUC was founded in 1889, and its membership includes the 50 states, Washington, D.C., and several U.S. territories. NARUC frequently testifies before Congress and federal government agencies to advance the interests of state utility regulatory bodies.

Normally, NARUC holds three annual meetings where new resolutions are proposed and voted on. The approved resolutions then serve as the basis for NARUC's political activities. Thus, NARUC's Web site should be monitored

Table 5.1 United States and District of Columbia utility regulatory bodies

State commission	Web site
Alabama Public Service Commission	www.psc.state.al.us/
Regulatory Commission of Alaska	http://rca.alaska.gov/
Arizona Corporation Commission	www.cc.state.az.us/
Arkansas Public Service Commission	www.arkansas.gov/psc/
California Public Utilities Commission	www.cpuc.ca.gov/puc/
Colorado Public Utilities Commission	www.dora.state.co.us/PUC/
Connecticut Department of Public Utility Control	www.ct.gov/dpuc/site/default.asp
Delaware Public Service Commission	http://depsc.delaware.gov/
District of Columbia Public Service Commission	www.dcpsc.org/
Florida Public Service Commission	www.floridapsc.com/
Georgia Public Service Commission	www.psc.state.ga.us/
Hawaii Public Utilities Commission	http://puc.hawaii.gov/
Idaho Public Utilities Commission	www.puc.state.id.us/
Illinois Commerce Commission	www.icc.illinois.gov/
Indiana Utility Regulatory Commission	www.in.gov/iurc/
Iowa Utilities Board	www.iowa.gov/iub/
Kansas Corporation Commission	www.kcc.state.ks.us/
Kentucky Public Service Commission	www.psc.ky.gov/
Louisiana Public Service Commission	www.lpsc.org/
Maine Public Utilities Commission	www.maine.gov/mpuc/
Maryland Public Service Commission	http://webapp.psc.state.md.us/
Massachusetts Department of Public Utilities	www.mass.gov/dpu
Michigan Public Service Commission	www.michigan.gov/mpsc
Minnesota Public Utilities Commission	www.puc.state.mn.us/
Mississippi Public Service Commission	www.psc.state.ms.us/
Missouri Public Service Commission	www.psc.mo.gov/
Montana Public Service Commission	www.psc.state.mt.us/
Nebraska Public Service Commission	www.psc.state.ne.us/
Nevada Public Utilities Commission	http://pucweb1.state.nv.us/PUCN/
New Hampshire Public Utilities Commission	www.puc.nh.gov/
New Jersey Board of Public Utilities	www.state.nj.us/bpu/
New Mexico Public Regulation Commission	www.nmprc.state.nm.us/
New York Public Service Commission	www.dps.state.ny.us/
North Carolina Utilities Commission	www.ncuc.commerce.state.nc.us/
North Dakota Public Service Commission	http://pc6.psc.state.nd.us/

(Continued)

Table 5.1 United States and District of Columbia utility regulatory bodies—*cont'd*

State commission	Web site
Public Utilities Commission of Ohio	www.puco.ohio.gov/
Oklahoma Corporation Commission	www.occ.state.ok.us/
Oregon Public Utility Commission	www.oregon.gov/PUC/
Pennsylvania Public Utility Commission	www.puc.state.pa.us/
Rhode Island Public Utilities Commission	www.ripuc.org/
South Carolina Public Service Commission	www.psc.sc.gov/
South Dakota Public Utilities Commission	http://puc.sd.gov/
Tennessee Regulatory Authority	www.tennessee.gov/tra/
Public Utility Commission of Texas	www.puc.state.tx.us/
Public Service Commission of Utah	www.psc.state.ut.us/
Vermont Public Service Board	http://psb.vermont.gov/
Virginia State Corporation Commission	www.scc.virginia.gov/pue/
Washington Utilities and Transportation Commission	www.wutc.wa.gov/
West Virginia Public Service Commission	www.psc.state.wv.us/
Wisconsin Public Service Commission	http://psc.wi.gov/
Wyoming Public Service Commission	http://psc.state.wy.us/

regularly for new initiatives that will most likely affect state regulations. Additionally, NARUC's Web site can be used as a valuable resource to observe how other states or regions are regulating smart grids. Specifically, NARUC's Web site has a Web page (www.naruc.org/SmartGrid/) dedicated to smart grid resources for state commissions.

Colorado PUC

The city of Boulder has become a test case for smart grid technology and will most likely influence how the rest of the state adopts smart grid technologies. In the meantime, the Colorado PUC has recently launched an investigation into the privacy concerns of smart metering.[4] Their major concern is the ability of other, nonutility industries to use consumer electric usage patterns and provide examples of marketing research firms and law enforcement agencies exploiting this data for their own uses. In Docket No. 09I-593EG, the commission states that information collected from the smart grid could have serious implications for consumer privacy.[4]

The results of the investigation could have a significant impact on smart grid security in the state of Colorado. The commission could be influenced to create new, stronger privacy policies to ensure that utility companies take adequate steps to protect the privacy of consumer usage data. In response to the investigation, the Colorado Office of Consumer Counsel (OCC – www.dora.state.co.us/occ/) has recommended the Colorado PUC implement new privacy protection policies and also recommended the implementation of an opt-in/opt-out service.[5] The opt-in/opt-out service would allow consumers to state whether the utility company would be allowed to disseminate their usage data to third parties.

The Colorado PUC could use the results of this investigation to create policies that mandate proper security controls around the transmission and storage of usage data. The implications could be broad for utility companies. Although this is not the first time that privacy concerns have been raised over the smart grid, the Colorado PUC has the authority to regulate how Colorado utility companies protect usage data. Because smart meters will create and transmit the usage data, smart meter vendors who hope to sell their products in Colorado will need to follow the results of this investigation to ensure their products are compliant with any resulting policy that dictates additional privacy and security controls.

PUC of Texas

Austin was one of the first cities in the United States to implement smart grid technology, and additional areas of Texas are implementing smart grid technology as well. Texas state law encourages utility companies to adopt smart grid technologies, which has accelerated the deployment.

Utility companies need to closely monitor all relevant regulatory bodies for new regulations, standards, and requirements that they will be required to comply with. Although future requirements may not be possible to predict, utility companies must be cautious when procuring new technologies to ensure that they meet all of the requirements. The purchase of insufficient technology could result in the loss of hundreds of millions of dollars, which is what could happen to a utility company in Texas.

EPIC FAIL

Several years ago, the state of Texas was facing a power supply deficit and the PUC of Texas urged utility companies to deploy smart meters to decrease demand. The Oncor utility company (http://oncor.com/) purchased about 900,000 smart meters for deployment. However, the PUC of Texas had not yet defined the functional requirements for smart meters. When the PUC of Texas later defined the operating standards for smart meters, the previously purchased smart meters were considered out of compliance.[6]

As a result, Oncor was required to replace the noncompliant smart meters with new smart meters. Additionally, Oncor requested a rate increase of $253 million to recover the cost of the smart meter replacement, which would have added about $5 a month to every customer.[7] However, the PUC of Texas only granted $130 million, or around $2.40 a month from customers.[7] The debate over this settlement has not ended and customers are angry about paying for the old meters, which they consider to be Oncor's mistake. Regardless of who is at fault, Oncor now has an angry customer base that could become potential security threats. As described in Chapter 3, "Threats and Impacts: Utility Companies and Beyond," an angry customer could seek revenge against Oncor to damage the utility company or

(Continued)

(Continued)
attempt to extract a monetary sum to compensate for the new monthly fees, mental anguish, or many other reasons.

Oncor has stated that the older meters can still be used for other purposes, such as streetlights.[7] Thus, Oncor will be using at least two different types of smart meters and will be responsible for securing at least two different models. Although smart grid technology is considered relatively new technology, Oncor will now have to deal with legacy smart grid systems, which will increase the complexity of securing their smart grid. Securing legacy systems is a known problem in the security world that many organizations have struggled to deal with.

Security departments often have to deal with issues such as nonexistent support for legacy systems and hiring personnel who are experienced with the legacy technology. For example, when a vulnerability is identified in a third-party system, the third-party vendor can be contacted to create a patch for the system. However, the vendor may not create the necessary patch because they no longer provide support for the legacy system. As a result, a mitigating security control may be required to reduce the risk of continuing to use the legacy system. The other alternatives would be to either accept the risk of using the legacy system or upgrade to a new version, which are usually not ideal options.

Planning for the Future

Although the situation in Texas was based on operational standards, a similar situation could occur because of new security standards pushed out by an authoritative organization. New security laws, regulations, and requirements are often instituted because of incidents, and with the electric grid being a big target, utility companies should expect and plan for changing rules. Utility companies need to be cautious when procuring new technology to avoid a repeat of the situation that occurred in Texas. When procuring new technology, a company should ensure that the device is compliant with all existing requirements, but the device should also meet or exceed the company's own set of requirements. Defining more stringent security requirements will help prevent the technology from becoming obsolete.

A common security problem has been so-called hard coded vulnerabilities, such as login credentials built into the code of a compiled application and insecure hardware settings that cannot be controlled with software. When procuring new smart grid technology, a company should investigate the ability to enhance a product's security controls and functionality and upgrade to new versions without requiring new hardware. Vendors should have development plans for future versions and should be able to provide some assurances for upgrade compatibility.

TIP
These security requirements, as well as functional requirements, should be defined during the beginning stages of a system development lifecycle (SDLC). When developing any type of system, including projects that result in the purchase of commercial-off-the-shelf (COTS) products, an SDLC should be used to ensure the system is developed accurately, efficiently, and securely. There are dozens of different SDLC models to choose from, but one model that puts an extra focus on security is the security SDLC (SecSDLC) model. This model

considers security before any other factor. Unfortunately, not all SDLC models will work within your organization, and you will need to determine which models will work within your particular organization. For more information on integrating security into your organization's system development processes, please review NIST SP800-64: "Security Considerations in the System Development Life Cycle," which can be found at http://csrc.nist.gov/publications/nistpubs/800-64-Rev2/SP800-64-Revision2.pdf.

STATE COURTS

Utility commissions have the authority to regulate utility companies that operate in their state; however, the state court systems will also play a critical role in deciding how the utility can operate smart grids. The state court systems will determine the legality of smart grid–related policies and may participate in data classification of smart grid produced information. Using history as a guide, one can expect the privacy policies of energy usage data to be weighed by state, as well as federal, courts.

Colorado Court of Appeals

In the case of *People v. Dunkin*, the Colorado Court of Appeals determined that a customer does not have a reasonable expectation of privacy in their energy consumption records because they do not reveal discrete information about the customer.[8] The Colorado Court of Appeals made this decision in 1994, when traditional, nondigital meters were utilized. However, the court would have most likely made the opposite decision if smart meters were in use.[8] The results of analyzing detailed power consumption from smart meters are well documented, and discussed in Chapter 2, "Threats and Impacts: Consumers," of this book.

Implications

The *People v. Dunkin* court case has privacy implications for utility companies that work with law enforcement agencies. Although the utility company is obviously expected to provide law enforcement with usage data when presented with a warrant, should a utility company voluntarily provide law enforcement with usage data? Additionally, would the utility company compromise their customer's right to privacy in doing so? The courts will most likely determine the legality of providing law enforcement with usage data from smart grids.

Utility companies will need to pay close attention to the federal and state laws, as well as any decisions made by the courts to ensure they both protect their customer's privacy and comply with the law. As described in Chapter 3, "Threats and Impacts: Utility Companies and Beyond," the over disclosure of customer data to law enforcement could create a backlash against the utility company and smart grid technologies.

PROMOTING SECURITY EDUCATION

Even with properly implemented security controls, end-users will help attackers circumvent security controls through insecure activity. For example, password complexity controls can force users to choose passwords that meet minimum requirements such as length, and alphanumeric and special characters. However, users will find ways to choose easy-to-remember passwords such as using their dog's name and their dog's birth year (pickles@2002), which could be found on the user's social networking profile.

> **WARNING**
>
> Security controls that are too restrictive can frustrate users and may cause users to revolt against the security controls that hinder the usability of a system. Although the users may complain about the difficulty of using an application, the complaints will be much louder when they receive an electric bill that is erroneously three times their average bill.

In Chapter 2, "Threats and Impacts: Consumers," we discussed how the smart grid will put consumers at risk. Through the smart grid, utility companies will allow consumers to interact with the electrical grid in many new ways. Electrical usage information will be made available from anywhere and delivered to consumers through e-mail, SMS, social networking Web sites, and many other new ways. More concerning, consumers will be able to control their energy usage, such as controlling thermostats or even HVAC settings, through Web-based gateways that can be accessed by anyone. However, consumers will likely not recognize the critical role they play in securing the smart grid, which is why state and local government agencies and local regulatory bodies should play an active role in educating consumers on smart grid security. Programs targeted directly to consumers and indirectly through utility companies will help reduce the security risk posed by uninformed consumers.

State and local governments should directly target consumers with information regarding secure practices, such as choosing strong passwords and not publicly sharing certain information. Although user awareness training for every consumer is not practical, television, Web, and other types of advertising campaigns can be used to disseminate this information. These mediums have been utilized in the past to disseminate information regarding energy efficiency that can reduce consumer electric bills, such as buying energy-efficient devices and turning down your air conditioner by a few degrees. Because consumers are familiar with these mediums, utility companies should utilize them to promote strong security practices by their customers.

Utility companies could also use their new mediums for disseminating usage data to promote security. For example, wall-based units that normally display the current usage data and control smart devices, could cycle through different security best practices. Similar to the smart grid vision of consumption data being plentiful and omnipresent, utility companies can use the same methods to make security best practice reminders ubiquitous.

POLITICS AND THE SMART GRID

The initiatives at all levels, including state and local, may provide guidance for implementing smart grids properly, or more appropriately how that particular organization perceives the proper way to implement smart grids. Political and economical interest groups will most likely have some influence on government smart grid initiatives, which could have significant security implications.

As an example, consider a venture capitalist group that has invested in smart grid technology companies. The venture capitalist group lobbies state senators to rush the implementation of a smart grid in their state. As a result, the deadlines for implementing a smart grid become too aggressive and do not allow enough time for proper planning and design. Thus, the smart grid deployment is rushed, and the recommended security controls are not properly implemented.

As another example, consider a smart meter vendor whose product does not meet the proposed stringent security requirements of an upcoming state bill. The vendor makes large campaign contributions to several senators, who amend the bill to remove several critical security requirements. As a result, the smart meter vendor is now allowed to compete for the state utility companies' smart meter contracts with their less secure products.

SUMMARY

Hundreds of regulations, standards, and guidelines have already been created to define requirements for a recommended level of security and provide instruction on the best practices in smart grid security. These documents will continually be reviewed, scrutinized, revised, and improved. Additionally, new documents will be created to address new smart grid technologies when they are developed. The majority of these documents provide a tremendous wealth of knowledge in integrating security controls into smart grid components. Thus, smart grid security professionals must regularly monitor for new requirements and best practices.

Several states already have initiatives to promote, or even require, the deployment of smart grids. With the amount of federal money available, the remaining states will most likely create their own initiatives. California state law specifically states that smart grids should follow the best practices defined in several standards. By including similar verbiage in their own initiatives, state legislatures around the country will help create a more secure electrical infrastructure. Companies take different approaches in handling compliance. Larger companies may have separate compliance departments, whereas smaller companies may place that responsibility on the security departments. Whichever department is ultimately responsible, they will need to closely monitor their state legislature and utility regulatory body to ensure compliance. Being compliant with the state and local security regulations, as well as with other levels of regulation, may not guarantee the security of smart grids. The state and local security requirements will not be perfect, and companies should only view these requirements as setting a minimum level. Doing the bare minimum may be the most cost-effective approach upfront; however, a breach of security or privacy will likely cost significantly more than implementing appropriate controls.

Most consumers will not be privacy or information security experts and will need assistance to understand their role, what strong security practices are critical to the security of the smart grid and their information and electricity, and why.

Endnotes

1. California State Senate. Senate bill no. 17 [document on the Internet]. Alex Padilla, Patricia Wiggins; http://info.sen.ca.gov/pub/09-10/bill/sen/sb_0001-0050/sb_17_bill_20091011_chaptered.pdf; 2009 [accessed 09.01.10].
2. Illinois General Assembly. SB 1592 [document on the Internet]. http://ilga.gov/legislation/95/SB/PDF/09500SB1592lv.pdf; 2007 [accessed 09.01.10].
3. Maryland General Assembly. EmPOWER Maryland Energy Efficiency Act of 2008 [document on the Internet]. http://mlis.state.md.us/2008rs/chapters_noln/Ch_131_hb0374E.pdf; 2008 [accessed 09.01.10].
4. Public Utilities Commission of the State of Colorado. Docket no. 09I-593EG decision no. C09-0878 [document on the Internet]. www.dora.state.co.us/puc/DocketsDecisions/decisions/2009/C09-0878_09I-593EG.doc; 2009 [accessed 11.01.10].
5. Colorado Office of Consumer Counsel. Initial comments of the Colorado office of consumer counsel pursuant to decision no. C09-0878 [document on the Internet]. https://www.dora.state.co.us/pls/efi/efi_p2_v2_demo.show_document?p_dms_document_id=15389; 2009 [accessed 10.01.10].
6. NBC DFW. Oncor customers to pay for "Smart Meter" mistake [document on the Internet]. Stacy Morrow; www.nbcdfw.com/news/local-beat/Oncor-Customers-To-Pay-for-Smart-Meter-Mistake-53177347.html; 2009 [accessed 10.01.10].
7. The Dallas Morning News. Electricity customers may pay for Oncor meters. Elizabeth Souder; www.dallasnews.com/sharedcontent/dws/bus/stories/DN-oncor_03bus.ART.State.Edition1.3cf2fb0.html; 2009 [accessed 10.01.10].
8. Colorado Office of Consumer Counsel. Initial comments of the Colorado office of consumer counsel pursuant to decision no. C09-0878 [document on the Internet]. www.dora.state.co.us/pls/efi/efi_p2_v2_demo.show_document?p_dms_document_id=15389; 2009 [accessed 10.01.10].

Public and Private Companies

INFORMATION IN THIS CHAPTER

* Industry Plans for Self-Policing
* Compliance Versus Security
* How Technology Vendors Can Fill the Gaps
* How Utility Companies Can Fill the Gaps

In this chapter, we will discuss how public and private entities plan to secure the smart grid. Ranging from industry standards to private certifications, there are many tools at the disposal of utility companies. We will explore how compliance with industry standards, while required for many smart grid entities, does not always equate to security. Finally, we will discuss how both technology vendors and the utility companies themselves can fill the gaps between compliance and security.

INDUSTRY PLANS FOR SELF-POLICING

The five hundred pound gorilla in industry self-regulation is the NERC Critical Infrastructure Protection (CIP) standards. As a refresher, NERC is the U.S. Electric Reliability Organization (ERO), as ordered by FERC on July 20, 2006.[1] Prior to becoming an ERO, NERC collaborated within the industry and developed policies that power companies voluntarily followed. Once NERC was designated as an ERO, NERCs policies became required standards for power companies operating in the United States and parts of Canada. As an ERO, NERC is also charged with the enforcement of compliance with the CIP standards. Noncompliance with the CIP standards can result in significant financial penalties for the power companies ranging from $1,000 to $1,000,000, per day.[2]

WARNING

If you think that the fines that FERC can impose for violations of NERC standards are empty threats, think again. In October 2009, FERC and Florida Power and Light Company (FPL) reached a settlement where FPL paid $25 million as a result of a power loss that affected millions of consumers in South Florida on February 26, 2008.[3] FERCs Director of the Commission's Office of Enforcement stated that, "The message to the industry is clear: Compliance with the standards is critical."[3]

NERC Critical Infrastructure Protection Standards

The NERC CIP standards are comprised of eight primary standards that, for the purposes of this book, can be classified into two categories as follows:

1. Electronic security
2. Physical and personnel security

To understand the strengths and weaknesses of the CIP standards, the following sections will highlight the requirements, how compliance will be assessed, and the applicable noncompliance levels.[4] The terms that you should be familiar with are as follows:

- Responsible entity – NERC standard CIP-002 lists the following as "responsible entities"[5];
- Reliability coordinator
- Balancing authority
- Interchange authority
- Transmission service provider
- Transmission owner
- Transmission operator
- Generator owner
- Generator operator
- Load serving entity
- NERC
- Regional reliability organizations.

The same standard also excludes the following from being considered "responsible entities"[5];

- Facilities regulated by the U.S. Nuclear Regulatory Commission or the Canadian Nuclear Safety Commission
- Cyber assets associated with communication networks and data communication links between discrete electronic security perimeters
- **Electronic security perimeter** – A logical boundary that separates a network housing critical cyber assets.

Electronic Security

The following NERC CIP standards can be grouped in the electronic security category as follows:

- **CIP-002** – Critical cyber asset identification
- **CIP-003** – Security management controls
- **CIP-005** – Electronic security protection
- **CIP-007** – System security management
- **CIP-008** – Incident reporting and response planning
- **CIP-009** – Disaster recovery.

We will now go over each of these standards in order to better understand how they will help protect the smart grid.

CIP-002 – Critical Cyber Asset Identification

NERC standard CIP-002 requires that applicable entities identify and document their critical cyber assets that are associated with the critical assets that enable the reliable operation of their bulk electric system. These entities must identify their critical assets through the use of a risk-based assessment. Documentation of this assessment is required and must include the methodology used, evaluation criteria, and associated processes and procedures. Risk-based assessments must be performed on at least an annual basis.

The risk-based assessment performed by the applicable entities must consider numerous asset categories, including the following:

- Primary and backup control centers that can perform critical functions
- Transmission substations that support the reliable operation of the bulk electric system[5]
- Other general resources that support the reliable operation of the bulk electric system[5]
- Systems and facilities that are critical to system restoration and automatic load shedding
- Special protection systems that support the reliable operation of the bulk electric system[5]
- Any other assets that support the reliable operation of the bulk electric system deemed appropriate by the entities themselves.

The process for identifying critical cyber assets is somewhat easier. Critical cyber assets are defined by standard CIP-002 as possessing at least one of the following characteristics:

- Using a routable protocol to communicate outside the electronic security perimeter
- Using a routable protocol within a control center
- Allows access via dial-up capabilities.

WARNING

Interestingly enough, the NERC CIP-002 standard does not apply to cyber assets that are associated with the data and communication networks between discrete electronic security perimeters. Under this exemption, communication lines between business partners over a wide area network (WAN) would be out of scope.

To demonstrate compliance with standard CIP-002, entities must present the following:

- Risk-based assessment methodology documentation
- Their list of critical assets

Table 6.1 Levels of noncompliance with NERC CIP-002	
Level	**Criteria**
1	The risk assessment has not been performed annually.
2	The list of critical assets or critical cyber assets exists, but it has not been approved or reviewed in the last calendar year.
3	The list of critical assets or critical cyber assets does not exist.
4	The lists of critical assets and critical cyber assets do not exist.

- Their list of critical cyber assets
- Documentation of the annual approval of the above lists by a senior manager or their delegate(s).

If an entity is found to be out of compliance, it is classified into one of four levels for noncompliance. These levels and their criteria are listed in Table 6.1.[5]

CIP-003 – Security Management Controls

NERC standard CIP-003 requires entities to implement minimum-security management controls to protect their critical cyber assets (as identified per standard CIP-002). At the core of the requirements outlined in standard CIP-003 is the entities' cyber security policy. This policy must address the requirements of standards CIP-002 through CIP-009, as well as include provisions for emergency situations.

> **NOTE**
>
> Entities that have met the requirements of standard CIP-002, but have not identified any critical cyber assets, are exempt from the requirements included within standard CIP-003. This is the case for a majority of the CIP standards and is noted in each standard's section.

Expanding on the requirements of entities' cyber security policy, they must also ensure it is available to all personnel responsible for, or who have access to, critical cyber assets. Much like the requirements of standard CIP-002, entities' cyber security policy must be reviewed and approved by the senior manager on an annual basis.

Beyond a cyber security policy, standard CIP-003 covers the roles and responsibilities of those involved with critical assets and cyber critical assets. Specifically, standard CIP-003 requires that a senior manager responsible for the entity's implementation of, and adherence to, standards CIP-002 through CIP-009, be identified by the following:

- Name
- Title
- Business phone

- Business address
- Date of designation.

Changes to the designated senior manager must be documented within 30 calendar days of the effective change. This designated senior manager is responsible for the authorization and documentation of any exceptions from the requirements of the cyber security policy mentioned above.

Standard CIP-003 also covers exceptions to the cyber security policy that it requires. Where entities cannot confirm their cyber security policy, documentation for these exceptions, as well as documented authorization by the senior manager or delegate(s), must be in place. The following specific requirements are in place for exceptions to cyber security policy:

- Documentation for exceptions must be in place within 30 days of senior manager or delegate(s) approval.
- Approved exceptions must include an explanation that includes its necessity as well as any compensating controls or acceptance of risk.
- An annual review and acceptance of each exception is required by the senior manager or delegate(s). This process is also required to be documented.

TIP

Standard CIP-003 allows for the acceptance of risk when dealing with exceptions from entities' cyber security policy. As risk acceptance should be the option of last resort, providing the senior manager or delegate(s) with complete information is essential. When presenting exceptions, ensure that current and future risks are covered and probe decision makers to confirm their understanding of what they are accepting.

Moving from policy to implementation, standard CIP-003 requires entities to establish, document, and maintain program(s) to protect information related to critical cyber assets. Specifically, standard CIP-003 requires the following for the protection of related information:

- At a minimum, protect operation procedures, the lists required by standard CIP-002, network diagrams, data center floor plans (for those data centers housing critical cyber assets), equipment layouts of critical cyber assets, disaster recovery plans, and security configurations.
- Information that will be protected by the aforementioned program(s) will be based on the sensitivity of the critical cyber asset information.
- Entities must perform, at least annually, an assessment to determine if their established program(s) are being followed. The results of this assessment must be documented and an action plan must be implemented to remediate any identified deficiencies.

Standard CIP-003 also requires entities to establish, document, and implement program(s) to control the access to protected critical cyber asset information.

Specifically, the following requirements related to access control must be in place:

- A list of personnel who are responsible for the authorization of logical or physical access to protected information must exist. These personnel should be identified by name, title, business phone, and the list should indicate the information for which they are responsible for authorizing. Like the aforementioned lists, this list must be reviewed and verified on an annual basis.
- Granted access must be reviewed for appropriateness at least annually. Appropriateness should be determined by the roles and responsibilities of the authorized personnel.
- Entities must annually assess and document the process for controlling access to protected information.

Finally, standard CIP-003 identifies specific requirements for change control and configuration management related to critical cyber assets. These requirements include establishing and documenting a change control process and the implementation of controls for adding, modifying, replacing, or removing critical cyber asset hardware or software (change management). A process must also exist to identify, control, and document all entity or vendor-related changes to critical cyber asset hardware and software components pursuant to the change control process.

To demonstrate compliance with standard CIP-003, entities must possess the following:

- Cyber security policy documentation that references its availability
- Documentation of leadership assignment, including any changes
- Exception documentation
- Information protection program documentation
- Access control documentation
- Change control and configuration management documentation.

If an entity is found to be out of compliance, it is classified into one of four levels for noncompliance. These levels and their criteria are listed in Table 6.2.[6]

CIP-005 – Electronic Security Protection

Standard CIP-005 requires entities to identify and protect the electronic security perimeter(s) that house critical cyber assets. This includes protecting all access points on these perimeters. Like standard CIP-003, entities that do not identify any critical cyber assets are exempt from the requirements of standard CIP-005.

Specifically, standard CIP-005 requires entities to ensure that all critical cyber assets are housed within an electronic security perimeter. These perimeters, and their associated access points, must be identified and documented. Included within the access points to the electronic security perimeters are any external communication end points, such as dial-up modems, which terminate within the electronic security perimeter. Noncritical cyber assets that exist within electronic security perimeters are considered in scope for the requirements of standard CIP-005. Additionally, standard

Table 6.2 Levels of noncompliance with NERC CIP-003

Level	Criteria
1	Changes to the designation of senior manager were not documented within 30 calendar days of the effective date; or,
1	Exceptions from the cyber security policy have not been documented within 30 calendar days of the approval of the exception; or,
1	An information protection program to identify and classify information and the processes to protect information associated with critical cyber assets has not been assessed in the previous full calendar year.
2	A cyber security policy exists, but has not been reviewed within the full calendar year; or,
2	Exceptions to policy are not documented or authorized by the senior manager or delegate(s); or,
2	Access privileges to information related to critical cyber assets have not been reviewed within the previous full calendar year; or,
2	The list of designated personnel responsible to authorize access to the information related to critical cyber assets has not been reviewed within the previous full calendar year.
3	A senior manager has not been properly identified; or,
3	The list of designated personnel responsible to authorize logical or physical access to protected information associated with critical cyber assets does not exist; or,
3	No changes to hardware or software components of critical assets have been properly documented.
4	No cyber security policy exists; or,
4	No identification and classification program for protecting information associated with critical cyber assets exists; or,
4	No documented change control and configuration management process exists.

CIP-005 notes that cyber assets involved in the access control, such as active directory domain controllers, and monitoring, such as intrusion detection systems (IDS), are bound to the applicable controls of the following CIP standards:

- CIP-003
- CIP-004
- CIP-005
- CIP-006
- CIP-008
- CIP-009

Standard CIP-005 requires the implementation and documentation of organizational processes and technical procedures to control the access to electronic security perimeters. It requires that these technical procedures follow a default deny model, to require explicit access to cyber assets, both critical and noncritical, housed in the electronic security perimeter. Expanding on the default deny model,

Standard CIP-005 requires that only the ports and services required for the operation and monitoring of cyber assets within the electronic security perimeter be enabled. These required ports and services must be documented, either individually or by specified groups.

Other requirements covered by standard CIP-005 pertaining to the access controls protecting the electronic security perimeter include securing dial-up access, requiring an Appropriate Use Banner, and ensuring the authenticity of those with external inter-active access to cyber assets within the electronic security perimeter. The technical controls implemented to ensure this authenticity must be documented and include the following specific information:

- The process for requesting access and authorization
- The authentication methods used
- The process used to review authorization rights, in accordance with the requirements of standard CIP-004
- The controls for securing dial-up access.

Standard CIP-005 also covers the monitoring of electronic access to cyber assets within the electronic security perimeter. The listed requirements for entities include the implementation and documentation of electronic or manual processes for monitoring and logging access on a constant basis for access points to the electronic security perimeter. Monitoring processes for nonroutable dial-up access to critical cyber assets is also required; however, the standard notes only where "technically feasible."[7] Along these lines, standard CIP-005 requires the detection and alerting of unauthorized access attempts, where technically feasible, to cyber assets housed within the electronic security perimeter.

> **NOTE**
>
> For cyber assets within the electronic security perimeter where the detection and alerting of unauthorized access attempts is not technically feasible,[7] standard CIP-005 requires that access logs be reviewed at least every 90 calendar days. The goal of these reviews is to identify unauthorized attempts, whether successful or not.

Standard CIP-005 also requires that entities perform vulnerability assessments of their electronic security perimeter(s) at least annually. Beyond simply perform-ing the vulnerability assessment, entities must document their vulnerability assess-ment process, include a process for ensuring only the ports and services required for operations are enabled, discover all points of entry into the electronic security perimeter(s), and identify default accounts, passwords, and Simple Network Man-agement Protocol (SNMP) community strings. The results of vulnerability assess-ments must be documented and an action plan to remediate or mitigate identified vulnerabilities must be established.

Finally, standard CIP-005 requires that entities review and update the documentation required by the standard at least annually. This review should support compliance with the standard and ensure that documentation reflects the actual configurations, processes, and procedures in place. It also requires that any changes to the entities' network or implemented controls must be documented within 90 days of the change. A requirement to retain access logs for at least 90 calendar days is included to support incident investigation, which is covered in standard CIP-008.

To demonstrate compliance with standard CIP-005, entities must possess the previously discussed documentation for the following:

- Electronic security perimeter(s)
- Access controls
- Logging and monitoring controls
- Vulnerability assessments
- Access log reviews
- Documentation reviews and changes.

If an entity is found to be out of compliance, it is classified into one of four levels for noncompliance. These levels and their criteria are listed in Table 6.3.[7]

Table 6.3 Levels of noncompliance with NERC CIP-005

Level	Criteria
1	All document(s) identified in CIP-005 exist, but have not been updated within 90 calendar days of any changes as required; or,
1	Access to less than 15% of electronic security perimeters is not controlled, monitored, and logged; or,
1	Document(s) exist confirming that only necessary network ports and services have been enabled, but no record documenting annual reviews exists; or,
1	At least on, but not all, of the electronic security perimeter vulnerability assessment items has been performed in the last full calendar year.
2	All document(s) identified in CIP-005 exist, but have not been updated or reviewed in the previous full calendar year as required; or,
2	Access to between 15% and 25% of electronic security perimeters is not controlled, monitored, and logged; or,
2	Documentation and records of vulnerability assessments of the electronic security perimeter(s) exist, but a vulnerability assessment has not been performed in the previous full calendar year.
3	A document defining the electronic security perimeter(s) exists, but there are one or more critical cyber assets within the defined electronic security perimeter(s); or,
3	One or more identified noncritical cyber assets is within the electronic security perimeter(s) but not documented; or,
3	Electronic access controls document(s) exist, but one or more access points have not been identified; or,
3	Electronic access controls document(s) do not identify or describe access controls for one or more access points; or,

(Continued)

Table 6.3 Levels of noncompliance with NERC CIP-005—*cont'd*

Level	Criteria
3	Access to between 26% and 50% of electronic security perimeters is not controlled, monitored, or logged; or,
3	Access logs exist, but have not been reviewed within the past 90 calendar days, or,
3	Documentation and records of vulnerability assessments of electronic security perimeter(s) exist, but a vulnerability assessment has not been performed for more than two full calendar years.
4	No documented electronic security perimeter exists; or,
4	No records of access exist; or,
4	51% or more electronic security perimeters are not controlled, monitored, and logged; or,
4	Documentation and records of vulnerability assessments of the electronic security perimeter(s) exist, but a vulnerability assessment has not been performed for more than three full calendar years; or,
4	No documented vulnerability assessment of the electronic security perimeter(s) process exists.

CIP-007 – Systems Security Management

Standard CIP-007 requires entities to define processes, methods, and procedures in order to secure critical cyber assets, as well as cyber assets that reside within electronic security perimeter(s). Entities that do not posses critical cyber assets are exempt from the requirements included within standard CIP-007.

The first category of requirements published in standard CIP-007 relates to the testing procedures in place to prevent adverse affects from significant changes to cyber assets within the electronic security perimeter. A significant change includes at a minimum: security patches, service packs, updates, and upgrades to operating systems, applications, database platforms, or other software or firmware.

Specifically, standard CIP-007 requires entities to develop, implement, and maintain procedures to test the security of significant changes. Entities must document testing activities and ensure that they are conducted in a manner that reflects their own production environments. Finally, the results of such tests must be documented.

As required by standard CIP-005, standard CIP-007 goes one step further and requires entities to develop and document a process to ensure only required ports and services, for normal and emergency operations, are enabled. Specifically, it requires that only the required ports and services be enabled on systems during normal and emergency operating situations, as well as ensuring that all other ports and services are disabled on systems prior to their introduction into the electronic security perimeter. If ports and services not required for normal or emergency operating situations cannot be disabled, entities are required to document such cases and indicate any compensating controls implemented to reduce their risk. As a last resort, unnecessary ports and services that cannot be disabled can be deemed an acceptable risk.

Patch management is also covered in standard CIP-007. It requires entities to develop and document a security patch management program for the tracking, evaluation, testing, and installation of security patches for all cyber assets within the electronic security perimeter. This program can be an independent program or can be included in the configuration management program required by standard CIP-003.

Entities are required to document the evaluation of security patches for their applicability within 30 calendar days of their release. If applicable, security patch implementation must be documented, and in cases where that patch is not installed, compensating controls or risk acceptance documentation is required.

Standard CIP-007 includes a category for the prevention of malicious software. Required controls, where technically feasible, include antivirus software and other antimalware tools. Specifically, entities are required to document and implement antivirus and malware prevention tools. If such tools are not installed, entities are required to document compensating controls or risk acceptance. Updates to antivirus and malware prevention signatures must follow a documented process that also includes the testing and installation of said signatures.

The fifth requirement category contained within standard CIP-007 covers account management. Entities are required to develop, implement, and document controls to enforce access authentication of and ensure accountability for all user activity. The goal of account management controls is to reduce the risk of unauthorized access to cyber assets.

Account management requirements outlined by standard CIP-007 include implementing the principle of "least privilege" for individual and shared accounts when granting access permissions. Entities must also develop methods, processes, and procedures to produce logs that provide historical audit trails of individual user account access. These logs must be retained for at least 90 days. Entities must also review user account access at least annually to ensure their access is still required.

Entities must also implement policy that governs administrator, shared, and generic account privileges (including vendor default accounts). This governance requires that these types of accounts be modified when possible. Available modification methods include removal, disabling, or renaming. If such accounts must be enabled, entities must change default passwords prior to introducing the systems into production. Users of shared accounts must be identified, and entities must include policy verbiage that limits access to only authorized users and provides for the securing of shared accounts in the case of personnel changes. Finally, entities must establish and audit trail for the usage of shared accounts.

Requirement 5.3 of standard CIP-007 provides entities with password complexity requirements, but adds a condition of "technical feasibility."[7] These requirements are as follows:

- Six character minimum
- A combination of alpha, numeric, and special characters
- Expiration of no longer than annual, but shorter when warranted by risk.

The sixth requirement covered by standard CIP-007 deals with the monitoring of devices within the electronic security perimeter. Specifically, entities must develop and implement procedures and technical mechanisms for monitoring all cyber assets within electronic security perimeters. This monitoring must alert on, via automated or manual processes, and log system events related to cyber security incidents. Entities are required to review these logs as well as retain them for at least 90 days. Although no mention of the frequency of review is mentioned, entities must document their reviewing of system event logs related to cyber security.

Continuing down the requirements of standard CIP-007, requirement seven covers the disposal and redeployment of cyber assets within the electronic security perimeter. Entities are required to securely destroy or erase data storage media prior to disposal. Similarly, entities must erase data storage media prior to redeployment. Both of these requirements aims to prevent unauthorized retrieval of the data housed on the storage media. In either case, entities are required to maintain records of cyber asset disposal or redeployment.

Standard CIP-007 includes a requirement for Cyber Vulnerability Assessment. The requirements under this section mirror those covered in standard CIP-005, except that standard CIP-007 does not require the identification of all access points into the electronic security perimeter.

The last requirement of standard CIP-007 simply states that the previously required documentation must be reviewed and updated at least annually. Any changes that are a result of modifications to systems or controls must be documented within 90 days of the change.

To demonstrate compliance with standard CIP-007, entities must possess the previously discussed documentation for the following:

- Security test procedures
- Ports and services documentation
- Security patch management program
- Malicious software prevention program
- Account management program
- Security status monitoring program
- Disposal or redeployment of cyber assets program
- Vulnerability assessments
- Documentation reviews and changes.

If an entity is found to be out of compliance, it is classified into one of four levels for noncompliance. These levels and their criteria are listed in Table 6.4.[8]

CIP-008 – Incident Reporting and Response Planning

Standard CIP-008 requires entities to identify, classify, respond to, and report on cyber security incidents related to critical cyber assets. The standard only includes

Table 6.4 Levels of noncompliance with NERC CIP-007

Level	Criteria
1	System security controls are in place, but fail to document one of the measures (M1 to M9) of standard CIP-007; or
1	One of the documents required in standard CIP-007 has not been reviewed in the previous full calendar year as specified by requirement R9; or,
1	One of the documented system security controls has not been updated within 90 calendar days of a change as specified by requirement R9; or,
1	Any one of:
	Authorization rights and access privileges have not been reviewed during the previous full calendar year; or,
	A gap exists in any one log of system events related to cyber security of greater than seven calendar days; or,
	Security patches and upgrades have not been assessed for applicability within 30 calendar days of availability.
2	System security controls are in place, but fail to document up to two of the measures (M1 to M9) of standard CIP-007; or,
2	Two occurrences in any combination of those violations enumerated in noncompliance level 1, 2.1.4 within the same compliance period.
3	System security controls are in place, but fail to document up to three of the measures (M1 to M9) of standard CIP-007; or,
3	Three occurrences in any combination of those violations enumerated in noncompliance level 1, 2.1.4 within the same compliance period.
4	System security controls are in place, but fail to document four or more of the measures (M1 to M9) of standard CIP-007; or,
4	Four occurrences in any combination of those violations enumerated in noncompliance level 1, 2.1.4 within the same compliance period.
4	No logs exist.

two requirements and as with most CIP standards, entities without critical cyber assets are not bound by those requirements.

The first requirement of standard CIP-008 requires entities to develop and maintain a cyber security incident response plan. This plan is required to include, at a minimum, the following:

- Classification procedures to determine which event are reportable cyber security incidents
- Actions to properly respond to cyber security incidents. These actions must include the roles and responsibilities of incident response teams, the procedures for handling incidents, and plans for communication of incidents.
- A process for escalating and reporting cyber security incidents to the Electricity Sector Information Sharing and Analysis Center (ES ISAC)
- A process to ensure response plans are updated within 90 calendar days of any changes

Table 6.5 Levels of noncompliance with NERC CIP-008

Level	Criteria
1	A cyber security incident response plan exists, but has not been updated within 90 calendar days of changes.
2	A cyber security incident response plan exists, but has not been reviewed in the previous full calendar year; or,
2	A cyber security incident response plan has not been tested in the previous full calendar year; or,
2	Records related to reportable cyber security incidents were not retained for three calendar years.
3	A cyber security incident response plan exists, but does not include required elements requirements R1.1, R1.2, and R1.3 of standard CIP-008; or,
3	A reportable cyber security incident has occurred but was not reported to the ES ISAC.
4	A cyber security incident response plan does not exist.

- A process to ensure response plans are reviewed at least annually
- A process to ensure response plans are exercised at least annually.

The second and last requirement of standard CIP-008 simply requires entities to make available all documentation related to cyber security incidents for at least three calendar years.

To demonstrate compliance with standard CIP-008, entities must possess the previously discussed documentation for the following:

- Incident response plan
- Cyber security incident documentation for the last three calendar years.

If an entity is found to be out of compliance, it is classified into one of four levels for noncompliance. These levels and their criteria are listed in Table 6.5.[9]

CIP-009 – Disaster Recovery

NERC standard CIP-009 requires entities to establish recovery plan(s) for critical cyber assets, as well as ensure that these plans follow established business continuity and disaster recovery techniques and practices. Like many of the previous standards, entities that do not posses critical cyber assets are exempt from the requirements included within standard CIP-009.

In total, standard CIP-009 includes five requirements, the first of which covers recovery plans. Specifically, entities must establish and annually review recovery plans for cyber critical assets that specify the actions required to respond to events or conditions. These recovery plans must include actions to respond to events or conditions of varying length and severity. Finally, these plans must include definitions for the roles and responsibilities associated with recovery.

Standard CIP-009's second requirement simply states that entities must test their recovery plans at least annually. Mentioned tests include paper-based exercises, as well as full operational exercises, and the recovery from an actual incident.

Change control of recovery plans are covered in the third requirement of standard CIP-009. Specifically, entities should incorporate lessons learned from the aforementioned exercises into their recovery plans. Any changes must be communicated to the responsible parties within ninety calendar days.

The fourth requirement of standard CIP-009 discusses the backup and restoration processes and procedures required for entities. Simply stated, this requirement states that entities must include documentation for the successful backup, storage, and recovery of information on critical cyber assets.

Finally, standard CIP-009 requires entities to test their backup media at least annually for information deemed "essential"[10] to recovery. These tests can be performed off site by the entity at an alternative operations center.

To demonstrate compliance with standard CIP-009, entities must possess the previously discussed documentation for the following:

- Recovery plans documentation
- Required exercise documentation
- Documentation reviews, changes, and communications
- Backup and storage documentation
- Backup media testing documentation.

If an entity is found to be out of compliance, it is classified into one of four levels for noncompliance. These levels and their criteria are listed in Table 6.6.[10]

Table 6.6 Levels of noncompliance with NERC CIP-009	
Level	**Criteria**
1	Recovery plan(s) exist and are exercised, but do not contain all elements as specified in requirement R1; or,
1	Recovery plan(s) are not updated and personnel are not notified within 90 calendar days of the change.
2	Recovery plan(s) exist, but have not been reviewed during the previous full calendar year; or,
2	Documented processes and procedures for the backup and storage of information required to successfully restore critical cyber assets do not exist.
3	Testing of information stored on backup media to ensure that the information is available has not been performed at least annually; or,
3	Recovery plan(s) exist, but have not been exercised during the previous full calendar year.
4	No recovery plan(s) exist; or,
4	Backup of information required to successfully restore critical cyber assets does not exist.

Physical and Personnel Security

The following NERC CIP standards can be grouped in the Physical and Personnel Security category:

- **CIP-004** – Personnel and training
- **CIP-006** – Physical security of critical cyber assets.

Although the Physical and Personnel Security category contains only two standards, its implications on the security of the smart grid are significant. Let us review them both in detail to better understand how they will help protect the smart grid.

CIP-004 – Personnel & Training

NERC standard CIP-004 requires entities ensure that those with physical access to critical cyber assets possess the appropriate level of personnel risk assessment, training, and security awareness. Entities without critical cyber assets are not bound by the requirements of standard CIP-004. Standard CIP-004 includes the following four specific requirements:

- Awareness
  Entities are required to develop, maintain, and document a security awareness program for those personnel with access to cyber critical assets. This awareness program should be ongoing, with at least quarterly updates via direct or indirect means of communications. Other acceptable updates include management presentations and meetings.
- Training
  Entities are required to develop, maintain, and document a cyber security training program for personnel with access to cyber critical assets. Standard CIP-004 requires this training to occur at least annually and those granted physical access to cyber critical assets must be trained within 90 calendar days of being granted said access. Specifically, this training must cover the policies, access controls, and procedures related to critical cyber assets. Finally, entities are required to document that training is conducted at least annually.
- Personnel risk assessment
  Requirement three requires entities to implement and document a personnel risk assessment program. This program must be in accordance with federal, state, provincial, and local laws, as well as collective bargaining unit agreements. Personnel risk assessments must be performed for personnel with physical access to cyber critical assets within 30 days of said access being granted. Personnel risk assessments must include, at a minimum, the following:
  - Verification of social security number and a seven-year criminal background check
  - Reassessment at least every seven years or if for cause
  - Documentation of assessment results.

- Access

The final requirement of standard CIP-004 covers physical access. Specifically, entities must maintain lists of personnel authorized to physically access critical cyber assets. These lists must be reviewed at least quarterly and be updated within seven calendar days of any personnel change or change of access rights for specific personnel. Additionally, physical access must be revoked within 24 hours for terminated personnel and within seven calendar days for personnel who no longer need physical access.

To demonstrate compliance with standard CIP-004, entities must possess the previously discussed documentation for the following:

- Security awareness program
- Cyber security program
- Personnel risk assessment program
- Lists, list reviews and updates, and revocation records.

If an entity is found to be out of compliance, it is classified into one of four levels for noncompliance. These levels and their criteria are listed in Table 6.7.[11]

Table 6.7 Levels of noncompliance with NERC CIP-004	
Level	**Criteria**
1	Awareness program exists, but is not conducted within the minimum required period of quarterly reinforcement; or,
1	Training program exists, but records of training either do not exist or reveal that personnel who have access to critical cyber assets were not trained as required; or,
1	Personnel risk assessment program exists, but documentation of that program does not exist; or,
1	List(s) of personnel with their access rights is available, but has not been reviewed and updated as required.
1	One personnel risk assessment is not updated at least every 7 years, or for cause; or,
1	One instance of personnel (employee, contractor, or service provider) change other than for cause in which access to critical cyber assets was no longer needed was not revoked within seven calendar days.
2	Awareness program does not exist or is not implemented; or,
2	Training program exists, but does not address the requirements identified in standard CIP-004; or,
2	Personnel risk assessment program exists, but assessments are not conducted as required; or,
2	One instance of personnel termination for cause (employee, contractor, or service provider) in which access to critical cyber assets was not revoked within 24 hours.

(Continued)

Table 6.7 Levels of noncompliance with NERC CIP-004—*cont'd*

Level	Criteria
3	Training program exists, but has not been reviewed and updated at least annually; or,
3	A personnel risk assessment program exists, but records reveal program does not meet the requirements of standard CIP-004; or,
3	List(s) of personnel with their access control rights exists, but does not include service vendors and contractors.
4	No documented training program exists; or,
4	No documented personnel risk assessment program exists; or,
4	No required documentation created pursuant to the training or personnel risk assessment programs exists.

CIP-006 – Personnel & Training

The final NERC standard within the Physical and Personnel Security category is standard CIP-006. Specifically, standard CIP-006 requires entities to develop and implement a physical security program to protect critical cyber assets. The standard includes six unique requirements, which are detailed below.

The first requirement of standard CIP-006 covers physical security plans. Entities are required to develop and maintain a physical security plan that addresses the following:

- A process and documentation of all cyber assets within the Electronic Cyber Perimeter are housed within a physical security perimeter. If they are not, compensating controls must be in place and documented.
- A process for identifying and controlling access to all access points to physical security perimeters
- The ability to monitor physical access to physical security perimeters
- A procedure for appropriately applying access controls to the physical security perimeters. Such controls covered include visitor passes and how to respond to unauthorized access.
- A process for ensuring access authorization requests and revocations are reviewed
- A procedure for escorting unauthorized personnel within the physical security perimeter
- Ensuring that updates to the physical security plan are made within 90 calendar days of any changes. Changes include access, monitoring, and logging control changes.
- Cyber assets used in controlling access to physical security perimeters provided the same protections of Cyber Assets specified in other CIP standards
- A process for reviewing the physical security plan at least annually.

The second requirement in standard CIP-006 covers physical access controls. This requirement specifies that entities must implement controls to manage access to physical security perimeters on a 24/7 basis. Within this requirement are specifics for Card Keys, Special Locks, Security Personnel, and Other Authentication Devices.

Standard CIP-006 requires that entities monitor and log physical access to physical security perimeters in the next two requirements. Alarm systems or human observation are both acceptable methods of monitoring physical access. As for logging, computerized, video, or manual logging are acceptable methods for logging physical access.

The final two requirements of standard CIP-006 cover access log retention and maintenance and testing. Specifically, entities are required to keep physical access logs for at least 90 calendar days. For maintenance and testing, entities must test and maintain all components of their physical security at least every three years and maintain records of said testing. Finally, outages of access controls, logging, and monitoring must be retained for at least one calendar year.

To demonstrate compliance with standard CIP-006, entities must possess the previously discussed documentation for the following:

- Physical security plan
- Physical access control documentation
- Monitoring physical access documentation
- Logging physical access documentation
- Access logs
- Testing and maintenance logs, as well as outage logs.

If an entity is found to be out of compliance, it is classified into one of four levels for noncompliance. These levels and their criteria are listed in Table 6.8.[12]

Table 6.8 Levels of noncompliance with NERC CIP-006	
Level	**Criteria**
1	The physical security plan exists, but has not been updated within 90 calendar days of a modification to the plan or any of its components; or,
1	Access to less than 15% of a responsible entity's total number of physical security perimeters is not controlled, monitored, and logged; or,
1	Required documentation exists but has not been updated within 90 calendar days of a modification; or,
1	Physical access logs are retained for a period shorter than 90 calender days; or,
1	A maintenance and testing program for the required physical security systems exists, but not all have been tested within the required cycle; or,
1	One required document does not exist.
2	The physical security plan exists, but has not been updated within six calendar months of a modification to the plan or any of its components; or,

(Continued)

Level	Criteria
	Table 6.8 Levels of noncompliance with NERC CIP-006—*cont'd*
2	Access to between 15% and 25% of a responsible entity's total number of physical security perimeters is not controlled, monitored, and logged; or,
2	Required documentation exists but has not been updated within six calendar months of a modification; or
2	More than one required document does not exist.
3	The physical security plan exists, but has not been updated or reviewed in the last 12 calendar months of a modification to the physical security plan; or,
3	Access to between 26% and 50% of a responsible entity's total number of physical security perimeters is not controlled, monitored, and logged; or,
3	No logs of monitored physical access are retained.
4	No physical security plan exists; or,
4	Access to more than 51% of a responsible entity's total number of physical security perimeters is not controlled, monitored, and logged; or,
4	No maintenance or testing program exists.

COMPLIANCE VERSUS SECURITY

Although entities are required to comply with NERCs CIP standards, compliance does not equate to security. Compliance demonstrates an organization's adherence to documented requirements within an arbitrary time frame, such as an annual audit. However, compliance requirements are generally vague and are not updated frequently enough to keep up with the constantly changing information security threat landscape. Moreover, many organizations treat compliance as an afterthought until the months leading up to an audit.

Additionally, compliant organizations' management often possess a false sense of security. The Payment Card Industry's (PCI) data security standard (DSS) is one of the most prevalent industry standards that influence information security. Although the PCI DSS does provide some of the most specific implementation requirements to date amongst regulatory mandates, several organizations that were deemed "PCI compliant" suffered breaches since PCI DSS' inception. One of the highest profile breaches came in 2008 when Heartland Payment Systems, a credit card processor, was breached.[13] During the period that the breach occurred, Heartland was considered "compliant" with PCI DSS requirements.

Heartland's Chief Executive Officer, Robert Carr, echoed the belief that compliance does not equate to security in an interview he gave to *Computerworld* in June of 2009.[14]

> "Just because you have a certificate of compliance doesn't mean that you can't get breached … I think everyone would agree the PCI standard is necessary, but it is also the lowest common denominator and the bad guys have figured out how to get around some of the weaknesses."

> **NOTE**
>
> Heartland Payment Systems is a Princeton (New Jersey)-based bank card payment processor for merchants in the United States.[15] Since being breached in 2008, Heartland has been developing its own end-to-end encryption solution known as E3. To learn more about E3, visit www.e3secure.com.

For merchants who do a certain amount of credit card transactions, PCI requires them to fill out a self-assessment questionnaire (SAQ), as opposed to an on-site assessment by an approved third party, to determine whether the merchant adheres to certain security controls. This approach relies on the "honor system" to ensure that companies are compliant with the PCI DSS. As a result, a company could potentially report inaccurate security controls in their SAQ. Similarly, a recent analysis by NERC reported, "many utilities are underreporting their critical cyber assets, potentially to avoid compliance requirements."[16] These results show that the utilities should not be trusted to ensure that proper security is implemented.

Simply stated, "security" is not an achievable goal. However, managing risk to an acceptable level is. Entities involved with the smart grid must distinguish between compliance and security, understanding that compliance can be a result of implementing a comprehensive information security program. Building and implementing a comprehensive information security program is covered in Chapter 8, "Securing the Utility Companies."

HOW TECHNOLOGY VENDORS CAN FILL THE GAPS

The gap between compliance and security presents significant opportunities for technology vendors. Existing organizations will position their products to aid in securing the smart grid using traditional techniques such as intrusion detection systems (IDS), network encryption, and application firewalls. Cisco has jumped on the smart grid security wagon by launching smart grid security professional services offerings that include utility compliance assessments, physical site security vulnerability assessments, and networking security design and deployment.[17]

New organizations will also be created, identifying new techniques and technologies aimed at filling these gaps. These organizations will undoubtedly position themselves to provide unique solutions that add value to smart grid initiatives in order distinguish themselves from established firms like Cisco. The market conditions are ripe for these new organizations and new technologies, as an estimated $21 billion[18] will be spent on smart grid security over the next five years.

As more and more smart grid deployments and products are introduced, it is a safe assumption that the number of vendor security solutions will also continue to evolve. What remains to be determined is if these vendor solutions will actually increase the security of smart grid technologies and deployments, or will they simply serve as the proverbial security "check box."

HOW UTILITY COMPANIES CAN FILL THE GAPS

When properly implemented and utilized, vendor technologies can significantly improve entities' information security posture. However, in the current economical climate, it remains to be seen if utility companies will receive the funding to appropriately secure their smart grid deployments. When technologies cannot be purchased and implemented, the responsibility for implementing secure smart grid deployments will fall solely on the abilities of the utility companies.

Although the challenge is daunting, utility companies can secure their smart grid deployments through strong and comprehensive policies, procedures, and standards. Utility companies will have to go beyond regulatory mandates and build their information security programs on industry best practices, such as the ISO 27000 series. Building such a program is covered in Chapter 8, "Securing the Utility Companies."

SUMMARY

Adequately securing the smart grid cannot be accomplished solely by utility companies; they will need the technologies, knowledge, and tools of the private sector. Likewise, the private sector cannot solely secure the smart grid as they will need utility companies to appropriately leverage the private sector's technologies, knowledge, and tools as well as implement strong policies, procedures, and standards.

The current approach toward securing the smart grid relies on the broken model of self-regulation and misconception that compliance and security are synonymous. NERC's own President and Chief Executive Officer, Rick Sergel, stated in their 2008 Annual Report that, "[NERC is] in a unique position to make the self-regulatory model work,"[19] suggesting that the self-regulation model has historically failed.

To better secure smart grid deployments and technologies, both the regulatory bodies and utility companies must recognize their current gaps and appropriately address them. Unfortunately, as often is the case with information security, it will most likely take a significant event to change the current approach. Let us hope this is not the case.

Endnotes

1. Federal Energy Regulatory Commission. NERC certified as Electric Reliability Organization; Western Region Reliability Advisory Body Accepted [document on the Internet]. www.ferc.gov/news/news-releases/2006/2006-3/07-20-06-E-5.asp; 2006 [accessed 14.01.10].

2. Control Global. Becoming NERC CIP-Compliant [document on the Internet]. PutnamMedia; www.controlglobal.com/articles/2007/284.html; 2007 [accessed 14.01.10].

3. Federal Energy Regulatory Commission. FERC approves settlement, $25 million fine for FPL's 2008 Blackout [document on the Internet]. www.ferc.gov/news/news-releases/2009/2009-4/10-08-09.asp; 2009 [accessed 14.01.10].

4. North American Electric Reliability Corporation. Standards: Reliability Standards [document on the Internet]. www.nerc.com/page.php?cid=2|20; 2006 [accessed 18.01.10].

5. North American Electric Reliability Corporation. Standard CIP–002–1 — Cyber Security — Critical Cyber Asset Identification [document on the Internet]. www.nerc.com/files/CIP-002-1.pdf; 2006 [accessed 04.03.10].

6. North American Electric Reliability Corporation. Standard CIP–003–1 — Cyber Security — Security Management Controls [document on the Internet]. www.nerc.com/files/CIP-003-1.pdf; 2006 [accessed 04.03.10].

7. North American Electric Reliability Corporation. Standard CIP–005–1 — Cyber Security — Electronic Security Perimeter(s) [document on the Internet]. www.nerc.com/files/CIP-005-1.pdf; 2006 [accessed 04.03.10].

8. North American Electric Reliability Corporation. Standard CIP–007–1 — Cyber Security — Systems Security Management [document on the Internet]. www.nerc.com/files/CIP-007-1.pdf; 2006 [accessed 04.03.10].

9. North American Electric Reliability Corporation. Standard CIP–008–1 — Cyber Security — Incident Reporting and Response Planning [document on the Internet]. www.nerc.com/files/CIP-008-1.pdf; 2006 [accessed 04.03.10].

10. North American Electric Reliability Corporation. Cyber Security — Recovery Plans for Critical Cyber Assets [document on the Internet]. www.nerc.com/files/CIP-009-1.pdf; 2006 [accessed 04.03.10].

11. North American Electric Reliability Corporation. Standard CIP–004–1 — Cyber Security — Personnel and Training [document on the Internet]. 2006. [cited 2010 Mar 4]. Available from: www.nerc.com/files/CIP-004-1.pdf.

12. North American Electric Reliability Corporation. Standard CIP-006-1 — Cyber Security — Physical Security [document on the Internet]. www.nerc.com/files/CIP-006-1.pdf; 2006 [accessed 04.03.10].

13. USA TODAY. Hackers breach Heartland Payment credit card system [document on the Internet]. Gannett Co. Inc; www.usatoday.com/money/perfi/credit/2009-01-20-heartland-credit-card-security-breach_N.htm; 2009 [accessed 20.01.09].

14. Computerworld. Heartland CEO says data breach was 'devastating' [document on the Internet]. International Data Group Inc; www.computerworld.com/s/article/9134516/Heartland_CEO_says_data_breach_was_devastating_?taxonomyId=17&pageNumber=1; 2009 [accessed 04.03.10].

15. NYSE. Heartland Payment Systems, Inc [document on the Internet]. www.nyse.com/about/listed/hpy.html; 2010 [accessed 20.01.10].

16. United States House of Representatives Committee on Homeland Security Press Center. Homeland Security Committee Introduces HR 2195, a Bill to Secure the Nation's Electric Grid [document on the Internet]. http://homeland.house.gov/press/index.asp?ID=450; 2009 [accessed 21.01.10].

17. Cisco. Cisco Continues Global Smart Grid Momentum [document on the Internet]. http://newsroom.cisco.com/dlls/2009/prod_091709.html; 2009 [accessed 21.01.10].

18. Government Technology. Feds Will Spur Smart Grid Cyber-Security Investment Growth to $21 Billion by 2015, Report Claims [document on the Internet]. eRepublic, Inc; www.govtech.com/gt/744630; 2010 [accessed 04.03.10].

19. North American Electric Reliability Corporation. Annual Report 2008 [document on the Internet]. www.nerc.com/files/2008-Annual-Report.pdf; 2009 [accessed 21.01.10].

Attacking the Utility Companies

INFORMATION IN THIS CHAPTER

- Motivation
- Network Attacks
- System Attacks
- Application Attacks
- Wireless Attacks
- Social Engineering Attacks
- Physical Attacks
- Putting It All Together

A well-coordinated attack against a smart grid will most likely utilize multiple attack vectors. A combination of application, network, social engineering, and many other types of attacks may be used to achieve the attacker's goals. Utility companies will also have to deal with attacks from attackers with less incentive or resources, including curious customers and random script kiddies that will attempt individual attack vectors.

Understanding the attacks that you will face can help you understand how to prevent a successful attack. Moreover, running a staged attack against your environment will help you identify the security gaps in your environment. Thus, performing a comprehensive vulnerability assessment or penetration test is critical. This chapter will discuss how attacks may be carried out against current and future smart grids and, from a similar perspective, discuss how to perform a comprehensive security assessment against a utility company's smart grid environment.

MOTIVATION

In Chapter 3, "Threats and Impacts: Utility Companies and Beyond," we discussed several motives for malicious attacks against the utility companies. However, not all motives are of the malicious kind. Internal vulnerability management programs, which involve vulnerability assessments and/or penetration testing, are critical in evaluating an organization's security posture and identifying areas for improvement in security controls. Additionally, NERC CIP-005 requires that entities perform vulnerability assessments of their Electronic Security Perimeter(s) at least annually. So in order to be compliant with NERC CIP, utility companies will need to perform at least a perimeter vulnerability assessment annually.

Vulnerability Assessment versus Penetration Test

The generic term "security assessment" will be used throughout this chapter; however, a security assessment can have many different meanings. For the purposes of this chapter, security assessment will refer to vulnerability assessment or penetration test. The goal of a vulnerability assessment is to identify hosts and associated vulnerabilities. A penetration test will take a vulnerability assessment one step further where the identified vulnerabilities, or a few selected vulnerabilities, are exploited to gain more access networks, systems, and data.

I Want a Pen Test! Are You Sure?

Organizations will often decide they need to perform a penetration test or a vulnerability assessment without considering the business drivers for the assessment. If the goal of performing a security assessment is to discover vulnerabilities for remediation purposes, is exploitation of the vulnerabilities really necessary? Depending on various political factors within your organization, the answer very well may be yes. However, a vulnerability assessment would satisfy the goal of discovering vulnerabilities, albeit with a higher potential for false positives. Alternatively, if the goal of the security assessment is to prove to upper management that the threat of electricity theft is real, then a penetration test may be the more appropriate choice.

In general, the advantages of performing a vulnerability assessment over a penetration test are as follows:

- It takes less time since vulnerabilities will not be exploited.
- It is cheaper because a vulnerability assessment should take less time.
- It is less likely to interrupt normal business operations.

Alternatively, the general advantages of performing a penetration test over a vulnerability assessment are as follows:

- There are fewer false positives due to the verification of vulnerabilities through exploitation.
- The risk assigned to a particular vulnerability or group of vulnerabilities can be more accurately evaluated.
- It provides concrete evidence of the impact to skeptics.

NOTE

A false positive refers to a vulnerability identified during a security assessment that does not actually exist. For example, a vulnerability scanner may have determined that your Web server is susceptible to a buffer overflow based on the version listed in the Web server's banner. However, the banner lists an incorrect version because the applied security patch fixed the buffer overflow condition, but did not change the version number in the banner. Conversely, a false negative refers to a vulnerability that does exist but was not identified during the assessment.

Other Aspects of a Security Assessment

In addition to deciding whether to perform a vulnerability assessment or a penetration test, an organization will need to determine other factors of the security assessment as well. Security assessment conditions include the following:

- External (perimeter) or internal perspective
- Level of covertness
- Authentication.

The internal perspective would more closely resemble an insider attack scenario, such as an attack by an employee or contractor or by an external attacker with physical access to internal resources. The internal security assessment would evaluate only the internal security controls. Alternatively, an external security assessment would require the test team to breach the perimeter security controls in order to access internal resources. The focus of an external security assessment is to evaluate the external security controls. In a perfect world, the comprehensive security assessment would involve both the external and internal security assessments; however, budgetary and resource limitations may prevent this.

Security assessments can be performed at different levels of covertness to determine how well the organization's personnel and monitoring devices can detect an attack. Specifically, a security assessment can be performed as covert, hybrid-covert, and overt. When a new security device, such as an intrusion prevention system (IPS) or intrusion detection system (IDS), has been installed, a covert security assessment can be used to evaluate its effectiveness and to tune its rule set and policies. The drawback in performing a covert test is cost and efficiency. In the IPS/IDS assessment scenario, two of the main methods used to perform a covert test are (1) to slow down the network testing and (2) periodically change your source IP address through an anonymous network, such as Tor (www.torproject.org/). Both of these methods will significantly slow down the speed of testing though, thus increasing the cost and time it takes to perform the assessment. As a compromise, in a hybrid-covert security assessment, the assessment team could perform the test covertly until detected. Then, perform the remainder of the assessment in an overt manner.

Additionally, a security assessment can be performed in a full-disclosure, hybrid-disclosure, or nondisclosure manner. This determines the amount of information provided to the assessment team and levels of communication between the utility company's personnel and the assessment team during the assessment. In a nondisclosure security assessment, the assessment team is provided with your organization's name and not much else. This type of assessment is designed to simulate an attack perpetrated by an attacker with no inside knowledge of your organization. In a hybrid-disclosure assessment, the assessment team may be provided IP address ranges or some other small amount of information. In a full-disclosure assessment, there is open communication between the assessment team and the utility company's personnel, who may provide network diagrams and other useful information to the assessment team.

Some would consider it cheating to provide administrative credentials to the assessment team; however, it shouldn't be considered cheating if your internal security assessment team (as opposed to a vendor assessment team) is provided the credentials. The benefits of an authenticated assessment will reduce both false positives and false negatives. For example, when you run a vulnerability scanning tool without credentials against a system, the scan will identify vulnerabilities in networked services, such as Web servers and FTP servers. However, the tool will be unable to identify vulnerabilities in client applications, such as Web browsers and office productivity suites. When you provide the tool with administrative credentials, the tool should be able to discover vulnerabilities in client tools and perform checks on operating system configuration settings.

NETWORK ATTACKS

At its core, a smart grid contains an information network that transmits data to improve the efficiency and availability of the electric grid. Back in Chapter 1, "Smart Grid: What Is It?," Figure 1.7 presented a very basic diagram of a smart grid as an introduction to the reader. However, smart grid implementations will not be so simple and will contain multiple networks. Figure 7.1 illustrates some of the information networks in a smart grid implementation.[1] As shown in the diagram, information networks will be connecting each of the different components to each other. There will also be multiple information networks within each of the components. As you can see from Figure 7.1, data will flow between many different systems, networks, and subnetworks. Thus, attacks could come from many different locations.

There have been dozens of books dedicated solely to attacking networks and performing network security assessments, including *Hacking Exposed™ 6: Network Security Secrets & Solutions* and *Professional Penetration Testing: Creating and Operating a Formal Hacking Lab* (ISBN: 978-1-59749-425-0, Syngress). The majority, if not all, of smart grid networks will be IP-based networks and, as a result, the same techniques discussed in these books will apply to networks in smart grid implementations. If this is your first time hearing the phrases vulnerability assessment or penetration test, then reading a book that is dedicated solely to that topic would be recommended ... in addition to this chapter of course. This section of the chapter will focus on applying the general principles and standards in these books to smart grid networks.

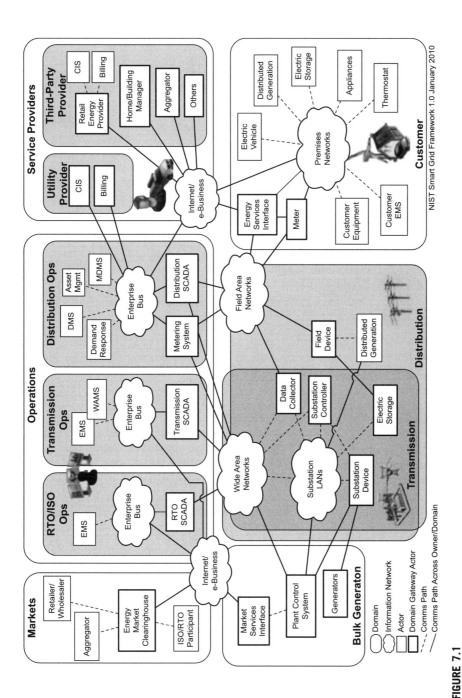

FIGURE 7.1

Smart grid information networks.[1]

Reprinted courtesy of the National Institute of Standards and Technology, Technology Administration, U.S. Department of Commerce. Not copyrightable in the United States

Methodologies

Whether you are trying to set up an internally managed vulnerability assessment or evaluating third-party vendors, the methodology is the best place to start. Several industry regarded methodology standards exist including the following:

- NIST SP800-53A – Guide for Assessing the Security Controls in Federal Information Systems
- Information Design Assurance Red Team (IDART – www.idart.sandia.gov/methodology/index.html)
- DOE Electric Power Infrastructure Vulnerability Assessment Methodology (www.esisac.com/publicdocs/assessment_methods/VA.pdf)
- Information Systems Security Assessment Framework (ISSAF – www.oissg.org/issaf)
- *Open Source Security Testing Methodology* (OSSTMM – www.isecom.org/osstmm/).

Although every methodology will be slightly different, they will all follow the same relative approach and should be modeled after the standards. Additionally, well-coordinated attackers will utilize these methodologies to perform their attacks. For this section of the chapter, we will use the following phases for the network security assessment.

- Reconnaissance
- Discovery
- Vulnerability identification
- Penetration.

Reconnaissance

Passive testing, which involves no direct interaction with the targets, is usually performed during this stage of the assessment to identify the utility company's infrastructure. Many Web sites will provide detailed information regarding any organization's perimeter network. While you can visit these online tools manually, several other tools will automate this process. See Table 7.1 for a listing of just a few of these tools. During this phase, the following information will be obtained:

- Perimeter IP address ranges assigned to the target utility company
- IP addresses and/or host names for at least the following:
  - Web servers
  - DNS servers
  - E-mail servers
  - Routers
  - Gateways
  - Remote access (VPN Concentrators)
  - Service provider Web applications (Example: thermostat controlling Web application)
- Incidental information disclosures (Example: organizational charts, network diagrams, ...)

Table 7.1 Network security testing tools – free tools are denoted with a "*"

Category	Name	Link
Reconnaissance	Fierce*	http://ha.ckers.org/fierce/
	Maltego	www.paterva.com/web4/index.php/maltego
	PassiveRecon*	https://addons.mozilla.org/en-US/firefox/addon/6196
	tcpdump*	www.tcpdump.org/
	Wireshark*	www.wireshark.org/
Discovery	Nmap*	http://nmap.org/
	UnicornScan*	www.unicornscan.org/
Vulnerability Identification	Nessus	www.tenablesecurity.com/nessus/
	NeXpose	www.rapid7.com/
	Nipper	www.titania.co.uk/
	OpenVAS*	www.openvas.org/
	Qualys	www.qualys.com/
	SAINT	www.saintcorporation.com/
Exploitation	Core Impact	www.coresecurity.com/
	Metasploit*	www.metasploit.com/
Live Linux Distros	BackTrack*	www.backtrack-linux.org/

Undertaking a smart grid implementation is big news and involves big money. Marketing departments from utility companies, technology vendors, and service providers want to promote their projects and as a result will disclose details regarding implementation details. For example, consider the city of Miami's smart grid initiative. Perform a Google search for "Miami smart grid" and you will discover the utility company and its partners. Just knowing the partners is not going to give you instant, unfettered access, but without sending one network packet to your target utility company, you already know the smart meter and network vendors, as well as their entire Internet presence, which gives you plenty to start with.

Internally Passive

Performing the aforementioned reconnaissance will work when you are starting off with an external security assessment. However, if the security assessment is internal, the best approach will be to run a packet sniffer, such as Wireshark. Running a packet sniffer will allow you to identify the IP address scheme, as well as identify active hosts.

TIP

Although uncommon, if you are performing an evasive internal security assessment, remember to disable your DHCP client while you are capturing network packets. You do not need an IP address to capture traffic, and a DHCP-assigned address could be used by alert personnel to find you.

Discovery

In this phase, we will determine what is available to target and is normally done using ping sweeps and port scans. Examples of popular discovery tools are listed in Table 7.1. One of the many benefits to security assessments is identifying rogue systems on the network. In many cases, these rogue systems were placed on the network for testing purposes and never removed. However, rogue smart meters, that really are not smart meters at all, may be identified with this method.

Although identifying hosts is an important part of this phase, discovering available network routes is just as important. Going back to Figure 7.1, there will be dozens of networks and domains involved in a smart grid. The utility company will need to determine how each of these networks and domains can connect with each other, as well as how to protect itself from an attack that originates from each of these networks. In a secure implementation, each of these networks will be properly segmented with strict access control lists (ACL), as well as other security controls and devices, that restrict the systems and network services that are allowed to interact with each other. For example, smart devices in the Customer domain should not be able to communicate with plant control systems in the Bulk Generation domain.

WARNING

The diagram in Figure 7.1 is an example smart grid diagram and may not reflect your particular implementation. Outdated network diagrams can lead to confusion and mistakes in implementing access controls. Maintaining updated network diagrams is critical in ensuring that the proper security controls are in place to protect your network.

To ensure proper network segmentation, port scanning should be performed to and from each domain and network. Although this will take a considerable amount of time, complete port scans (all 65,536 ports TCP and UDP ports) should be performed to ensure only necessary communication is allowed. In particular, business partner networks should not be given unrestricted access to the utility company's internal networks. Attackers will use these networks as a way to bypass the perimeter security controls. Read the "Epic Fail" sidebar for examples of why network segmentation is so critical. Also, Chapter 9, "Third-Party Services," will cover how to properly address the security of third-party services.

EPIC FAIL

Back in 2002, the Slammer worm infiltrated the Davis-Besse nuclear power plant in Ohio, which crashed a safety monitoring system. The firewall protecting the plant was configured to block the port Slammer used to spread; however, a T1 line that bridged the

---

Davis-Besse corporate network with a Davis-Besse contractor's network was left open. The Slammer worm first infected the contractor's network, and then it used the T1 line to spread to the Davis-Besse corporate network, bypassing the plant's firewall. The worm then spread from the corporate network to the plant network, where it crashed the system that monitored the coolant systems, core temperature sensors, and external radiation sensors.[2] Thankfully, the power plant had backup analog systems that were used until the problem was remediated.

But that was six years ago. We have, of course, learned our lesson since then, right?

Near Epic Fail, Redux: In 2009, numerous workstations at an Australian utility company were infected with the W32.Virut.CF virus. Although details are still scarce, the utility company stated that the virus was contained within their information technology network. The control systems for the electric power system were not running Windows, so they were not at risk to this particular virus. However, the control room operator displays were running a vulnerable version of Windows and were not segregated from the infected network. Thankfully, these systems were replaced in time to prevent any major impact.[3] The obvious response is to blame outdated antivirus signatures and patch management. However, the more concerning problem is the lack of separation between the business systems and the control systems.

Vulnerability Identification

The goal of the vulnerability identification phase is to create an inventory of vulnerabilities for the systems and services discovered in the previous phase. See Table 7.1 for example tools to use during this phase. Although the smart grid will utilize new technologies, the traditional vulnerability scanners will still work because these new technologies will rely mostly on traditional networking technologies and services. However, there will be exceptions to this rule and proprietary protocols and services will be used. More information on how to assess these services can be found in the "Application Attacks" section later in this chapter.

In general, network vulnerability scanners identify vulnerabilities by first identifying the service running on the open port and then interrogating that service. Specifically, the vulnerability scanner will inspect the service's banner, which will typically include the name and version of the service. Based on the version information, the vulnerability scanner will determine what security patch-based vulnerabilities the service is susceptible to. Vulnerability scanners may also manipulate normal requests by, for example, increasing the length of the value in a data parameter and then determine susceptibility based on the service's response. Additional testing, such as checking for default passwords, will also be performed, but the majority of vulnerabilities are identified by checking the version number in the banner.

Penetration

In a vulnerability assessment, the risk assigned to a vulnerability is sometimes hypothetical. We can say that by exploiting vulnerability, we will be able to obtain complete control of the vulnerable host. However, we may not know what exactly can be obtained from that host. Is there sensitive information stored on that host? Does that host provide a critical service, such as monitoring the temperatures of the nuclear reactor? Alternatively, a penetration test will answer those questions because we will exploit the vulnerability and obtain complete control of the vulnerable hosts to determine its purpose, which may include storing sensitive data or providing critical services.

Exploiting a vulnerability can have numerous outcomes including denial of service, information disclosure, and remote code execution. Remote code execution is usually accomplished by spawning a remote command shell that allows the attacker to execute operating system commands on the target system. The list below is just one common technique, albeit at a high level, used to gain remote control of a vulnerable host:

1. Exploit the vulnerability to spawn a remote shell.
2. Use the default utilities in the target operating system to steal the password file.
   a. On a Windows system, use a file transfer program (Example: TFTP) to upload a script, such as fgdump (www.foofus.net/fizzgig/fgdump/), that will grab the password file and the locally cached network domain credentials.
   b. Run fgdump to grab the password file.
   c. Use the same file transfer program to transfer the output of fgdump to the attackers system.
   d. Remove the evidence, including deleting the scripts, output files, and any relevant audit logs.
3. Use Rainbow tables to crack the local Administrator password hash.
4. Use your new administrator password to log in to systems that were configured with the same local Administrator password, using Remote Desktop or Server Message Block (SMB).
5. If the victim system was accessed by a domain user, say for example, a domain administrator for troubleshooting purposes, the victim system most likely cached that administrator's password, and the attacker will be able to crack that password, given enough time to do so.
6. Use your new domain administrator password to log into any system in that domain.

Some of you may be thinking that cracking the administrator password will take too long, especially that 15-character password that contains uppercase and lowercase letters, numbers, and special characters. The latest techniques, such as Graphics Processing Unit (GPU) password cracking, botnets,[4] and cloud computing will be able to crack your password efficiently. However, if you are still not convinced, does the attacker really need to crack your password? PSEXEC, which was originally released by Sysinternals (http://technet.microsoft.com/en-us/sysinternals/bb897553.aspx), allows you to remotely execute commands on a Windows system by providing a valid user name and password. The popular exploit framework Metasploit contains a PSEXEC module that allows you to either enter the password or the password hash to remotely execute commands; thus, saving the attacker time to crack that supposedly strong password of yours. For more information on this method, review the description at www.metasploit.com/modules/exploit/windows/smb/psexec.

SYSTEM ATTACKS

Network attacks are not the only way to attack the utility company. Perimeter security controls such as firewalls and IPS/IDS made it harder to remotely attack organizations, so attackers shifted their attacks to other approaches, such as malicious e-mail attachments and Web sites. Vulnerabilities are frequently identified in local applications such as Web browsers and office productivity suites. Attackers can and have easily exploited these vulnerabilities to gain control of systems, which is why performing authenticated vulnerability scans to identify these vulnerabilities is critical.

SCADA

Supervisory control and data acquisition (SCADA) systems are commonly used in electric grids. SCADA systems were originally thought to be too obscure to have legitimate threats because they were mostly proprietary systems that used proprietary protocols. However, SCADA systems have evolved and can now run on common hardware and software platforms. Now, the same tools discussed earlier and listed in Table 7.2 can be used to assess SCADA systems.

If you are new to the utility industry, you are likely to encounter new terms that you are unfamiliar with. With SCADA in particular, you are likely to be presented with numerous acronyms including PLC, RTU, and HMI, which stand for programmable logic unit, remote terminal unit, and human machine interface, respectively. Although you may not be familiar with these SCADA components, you will be familiar with most of the results of profiling and scanning these

Table 7.2 System security testing tools – free tools are denoted with a "*"

Category	Name	Link
Vulnerability identification	MBSA*	http://technet.microsoft.com/en-us/security/cc184924.aspx
	Nessus	www.tenablesecurity.com/nessus/
	NetChk	www.shavlik.com/
	NeXpose	www.rapid7.com/
	Nipper	www.titania.co.uk/
	OpenVAS*	www.openvas.org/
	Qualys	www.qualys.com/
	SAINT	www.saintcorporation.com/

components. Most SCADA devices will support Web servers, telnet, and FTP servers for remote access, among other common network services. If you have a vulnerability scanner at your disposal, take a second to look at the SCADA vulnerability checks. The majority of the vulnerability checks will be for default passwords to common network services and missing patches for specific SCADA vendor models. If you do not have a vulnerability scanner at your disposal or your vulnerability scanner does not include SCADA security checks, take a look at OpenVAS (www.openvas.org/) for a free open-source vulnerability scanner.

Numerous books that focus solely on SCADA security have been written, including *Techno Security's Guide to Securing SCADA: A Comprehensive Handbook On Protecting The Critical Infrastructure* (ISBN: 978-1-59749-282-9, Syngress) and *Securing SCADA Systems*. Additionally, white papers and standards for assessing SCADA systems have been written, including *Cyber Assessment Methods for SCADA Security* (www.oe.energy.gov/DocumentsandMedia/ Cyber_Assessment_Methods_for_SCADA_Security_Mays_ISA_Paper.pdf).

Legacy Systems

Smart grids will not be implemented in one day and older legacy systems will persist in the electric grid for many years to come. The problem for utility companies is that support for these systems will end and as a result, security patches will no longer be created when new vulnerabilities are discovered. However, vulnerability scanners will still be able to identify these vulnerabilities and exploits will still be available.

War Dialing

Many organizations, including utility companies, have phased out the use of dial-up modems. However, viable alternatives are not always available in rural areas. Even in high-bandwidth locations, organizations often install dial-up modems as part of a backup plan in cases of network outages. Dial-up modems provide an affordable and easy-to-use alternative for remote access to critical systems. War dialers should be utilized to identify and scan these dial-up modems for vulnerabilities, such as default passwords. See Table 7.3 for examples of war dialers.

Table 7.3 War dialing testing tools – free tools are denoted with a "*"		
Category	**Name**	**Link**
Vulnerability identification	PhoneSweep	www.sandstorm.net/products/ phonesweep/
	Telesweep*	www.securelogix.com/
	THC-SCAN*	http://freeworld.thc.org/thc-tsng/
	WarVOX*	www.warvox.org/

APPLICATION ATTACKS

As in almost every other type of organization, utilities companies are rolling out Web applications in order to automate traditionally inefficient, manual business processes and to provide better functionality and accessibility to their customers. Organizations are also replacing traditional client-server applications – also referred to as "thick client" or "compiled code" applications – with Web application alternatives. The ongoing explosion of Web browser–based application development is continuing to push innovation, functionality, and interoperability at a staggering rate that application security has failed to match … or even come close to matching.

Life-Imitating Art

Watching recent Hollywood movies could make you believe that hacking into traffic command centers, intelligence agency networks, nuclear missile facilities, and the current electrical grid can be easily accomplished by randomly pounding away at the keyboard. Although not impossible, there are some technical roadblocks such as segregated networks for the business and the command and control systems, applications, and users that may impede even a determined attacker. Pretty graphical user interfaces with large "Shut down power" buttons may or may not exist either, though determined attackers are not typically stopped by a lack of pretty interfaces.

The scary (or exciting, depending on your point of view) aspect of smart grid implementations is the integration of Web servers and custom Web applications. The entry level to the world of Web application security is much lower than that of non-Web applications. Although security analysis of compiled code applications requires deep knowledge of computer architecture and low-level programming languages and concepts, a simple Web search and a few clicks of the mouse can enable a novice Web application security person to carry out some of the most complex and powerful attacks. And not only are there powerful attacks, but there are many more types of attacks against Web applications, some of which cannot be detected by traditional security devices, such as intrusion detection systems and firewalls, or Web application security devices such as Web application firewalls.

WARNING

Don't believe it is that easy? Visit your favorite Web search provider and submit searches for the attack terms in this chapter. Adding the phrase "cheat sheet" (with quotes) to any of these searches will only help to increase the novice's attack range and firepower. It's like having a "how to" guide to have a major impact on daily life in the networked world. For starters, try the following Web sites:

- http://search.yahoo.com/search?p="sql+injection"+"cheat+sheet"
- www.google.com/#q=cross+site+scripting+"cheat+sheet"

One more related comment: The reader will have to look elsewhere for the "how to" on hiding one's identity as the source of said major impact.

Attacking Utility Company Web Applications

As explained throughout this book, Web servers – and the Web applications and Web services they support – are going to be a tremendous player in smart grid implementations. Because Web browsers are part of any laptop, desktop, cell phone, and probably many other future user computing devices, in addition to the so-called smart devices for the home (see Chapter 13, "Home Area Network: Smart Devices and Interfaces"), the Web server will be the bridge that connects the dots and enables the simple-to-use control that everyone has been dreaming about. Before drifting off to sleep to dream of remotely changing the thermostat, consider this: The control and functionality being included in smart grid implementations is made possible by the same software applications (Web browsers) that utility company employees and consumers use to tell the world where they went to eat last night and watch the latest YouTube video. The same software applications that are used to pay bills online, check e-mail, read and watch the news, download music and movies and other software, and just happened to be the first whipping boy of the "Month of Bugs" phenomenon.[5] There is more of this tirade to come, but first let's delve further into the Web applications.

The security issues related to utility company Web applications can be broken down into two categories: Web applications that support business operations and those that support smart grid functionality and accessibility (in other words, smart grid operations). The purpose for this distinction lies in risk management. Regardless of title, roles, and responsibilities, most utility company employees (and contractors) must perform certain tasks, such as submitting timesheets, that are common among all personnel. The use of such business operations applications are now commonly implemented as Web applications and present information security risks directly to the utility company and indirectly to the consumer. Web applications used to support smart grid operations present different information security risks directly to both the utility company and its consumers.

Web Applications for Corporate Operations

The threat to a utility company's corporate operations should not be underestimated. Not only could a successful attack against these applications enable an attacker to compromise the confidentiality of personnel information and customer billing data, but also such an attack may be leveraged as a jumping point to the power control and smart grid operations systems. Because many IT systems require a deep knowledge of the specific technology, many organizations' IT administrators are organized based on the technology used. For example, separate groups for Windows and UNIX server administrators, another group for application administrators, and similarly separate groups of administrators for databases from different vendors. This type of dedicated staffing organization has, in the past, led to the security weakness of common passwords.

In other words, the administrator account password for the personnel time-keeping application's database is the same as that for a smart meter interface application database. And, unfortunately, because we have not yet learned from history, this type of security weakness continues to plague IT network environments.

Even if due diligence has been followed such that the corporate network is segregated from the control operations network, a successful attack against these applications could allow for widespread control of personally identifiable and financial information that could be utilized in a litany of social engineering attacks or blackmail. With access to a customers' account information – account number, current balance, home address – one could likely convince unsuspecting customers to give up more sensitive data. A more sophisticated attacker could possibly convince other utility company personnel to, for example, shut off power to an existing customer by impersonating a customer billing representative and flagging the account(s) for lack of payment.

Alternatively, imagine an attack that enables remote access to the utility company's payroll application, which is leveraged to manipulate all paycheck amounts on a given pay period. The ensuing mild (or possibly severe) chaos could bog down personnel and allow for service disruptions, poor public relations for the utility company, and many other undesirable outcomes. It is easy to imagine a similar outcome if the attack targeted a customer payment application and forced over- or under-charging of customers en masse.

Regardless of a utility company's selection of Web applications for business operations – developed internally, outsourced, or commercial-off-the-shelf purchase – and regardless of the company's internal network architecture, the implementation of and reliance on Web applications for business operations introduce a host of new attack vectors that present increased risk as opposed to manual processes and/or traditional client-server applications.

Web Applications for Smart Grid Operations

A successful attack against a utility company's corporate Web applications is a serious threat, but it has been done before. Not necessarily a successful attack against every utility company, but organizations are hit by attacks against their corporate Web applications every day – they just may not know it or admit to it publicly. Attackers (and talented information security professionals) thrive on challenges and breaking new ground; smart grid Web applications can at least fulfill the latter. With respect to the former, I present to you one utility company's "Advanced Web Services Secure Login" Web form in Figure 7.2 that does not accept the HTTPS protocol; only HTTP is allowed here. One example is not enough? Okay, here's another Web application providing access to "the Energy Conservation Program" (with packet capture goodness and HTML source in Figures 7.3 and 7.4).

Identifying information has been removed from the screenshots to protect the identities of the organizations. The main point of including these two

FIGURE 7.2

Advanced web services secure login.

examples is to illustrate that the smart grid industry seems to be starting at security square one. It is a widely accepted practice to protect Web applications that handle sensitive data and/or provide access to powerful functionality against network eavesdropping by implementing transport layer security. This means anyone with a network sniffer and some free time can travel throughout a utility company's service area, connect to open home networks, and capture their authentication credentials for use in a future widespread attack against those consumers.

The first generation of smart grid applications simply provide near real-time access to energy rate and consumption information in the hope of helping consumers reduce their overall energy consumption and to use their energy more efficiently. Some applications are being developed to provide users with the ability to remotely operate smart devices, such as the thermostat. This functionality is, of course, being provided by Web applications.

By implementing these Web applications, utility companies may also be implementing a single point of failure. Attacks that would require exploits of multiple vulnerabilities to bypass multiple layers of control and a lack of interoperability among systems in the old dumb power grid may now be simplified to a single attack vector in a smart grid. What used to be difficult or nearly impossible – turning off lights, cranking up the heat, or shutting off power entirely to a large area – may now become a competition between

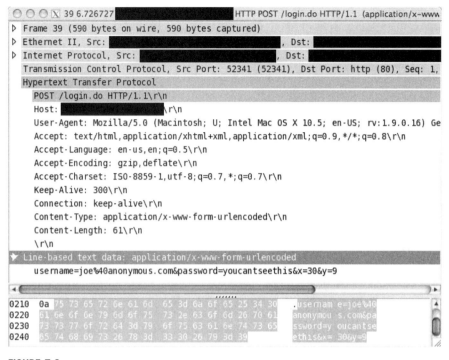

FIGURE 7.3

Energy conservation program packet capture.

FIGURE 7.4

Energy conservation program HTTP source.

attackers around the world. Who can blackout the most homes? Who can make the coolest light show? Who can play chopsticks with a row of street houses.

So how exactly could an attacker carry out such attacks? For this part of the discussion, we divide Web applications into its two externally accessible components: (1) the Web server application and (2) the application user interface.

Attacking Custom Web Application Code

Attacks against Web applications began long before we called them "Web applications." As Web server applications and Web application languages and frameworks became more powerful and flexible, attacks against them also grew in power and flexibility. So how could an attacker use a relatively simple exploit against a Web application in order to carry out the attacks described throughout this book? The answer is, unfortunately, in using one or more of many, many methods.

Attacks against custom Web applications can be split into two categories based on the immediate or direct target of the attack: the client (Web browser) or the application. The same attack objectives may be accomplished by utilizing either category of attack, which is yet another reason that Web applications are such fun targets for attackers. Specifically, an attack against certain application users could result in privileged access to the application itself, thereby gaining access to the functionality and data necessary to accomplish the attack objectives. One could easily write an entire book devoted to application vulnerabilities, attacks, and threats, so we will cover the most relevant parts beginning with an attack methodology.

NOTE

At the writing of this book, the Web application security industry is changing from what has traditionally been based on attacks to a more threat-based viewpoint. This transition is a good sign that the industry is maturing and becoming more in-line with the rest of the information security industry. From organizations' perspective, Web application security goals and objectives can be better aligned to the prevailing, industry-accepted guidelines such as those purported by the Open Web Application Security Project (OWASP – www. owasp.org/)[6] and the Web Application Security Consortium (WASC – www.webappsec.org/).[7] The transition to a threat-based approach can be seen by reviewing the OWASP Top Ten and WASC Threat Classification projects, and then comparing their current state to previous versions and other information resources that were generally accepted just a few years ago.

Even though the end result may be the same, Web application attacks that directly target the application are still commonly considered more severe than those against the client. This observation is evidence that the transition from attacks to threats is not complete. If history is any lesson, this transition can be expected to continue for several years before something better comes along.

Attack Methodology

A general attack methodology involves three phases: reconnaissance, vulnerability identification, and exploit creation. An attacker must first know what he is attacking before determining the subsequent correct steps. Reconnaissance will include analysis of an application's functionality; data in the form of information stored in and used by the application as well as input data fields presented to the client; and design and architectural aspects. The task of identifying vulnerabilities and weaknesses and then creating a successful exploit becomes easier as more useful information is obtained.

Identifying vulnerabilities in an application is somewhat systematic as most exploits involve manipulation of data available to the client. The difficult part is identifying which data fields can and should be manipulated and how they are used by the application. The easy part is basically a checklist of configuration settings and algorithms. Applications that have a particular vulnerability will most likely be vulnerable to a corresponding exploit. For example, applications that fail to set the "Secure" flag for a cookie that stores the user's session token may be vulnerable to session hijacking. Once a set of potential vulnerabilities and weaknesses are identified in an application, the attacker can proceed to identify and validate exploitable vulnerabilities – possibly in tandem – and map out an attack.

A successful attack will often involve repetition of the aforementioned phases. Rarely will an attacker have access to all of the functionality and data built into the application; if he did, then the attack pretty much boils down to the unmentioned "How do I get away with it?" phase. Instead, an attacker must first identify the available functionality and data, then successively gain access to more and more components of the application by exploiting various vulnerabilities. Because this is a book on the security of smart grids and not on breaking applications, certain details are left as an exercise for interested readers. Instead, we will now discuss some of the most critical Web application attacks that could be used to accomplish the attack objectives described earlier in the "Motivation" section of this chapter.

Attacking the Web Application

Probably the most severe type of attack against a Web application is the injection of executable malicious content. Depending on the platform that receives the injected input (SQL database, operating system, other application, or service), this could be an injection of application code, script, commands, or queries. Regardless of the platform, the end result of a successful exploit is unauthorized application execution. The platform will determine the type of injection possible, which in turn will help determine the immediate risk associated with a successful injection. For example, an injection targeting a SQL database (SQL Injection) could be used to extract sensitive data stored in database tables, insert new values into the database, or drop some tables for fun. Imagine your shiny new billing Web application has suddenly stopped working; all functionality in the application simply generates more and more error log file content. Then imagine sifting through those application log files – assuming there are log files to sift through – and coming across "userid = Owned'; DROP TABLE customers; – " in the HTTP request. Hopefully your backup and recovery procedures were more effective than the application's input data validation and database querying code.

Injection attacks exploit a lack of proper input data validation and insecure interaction between the application and the receiving platform. Improper input data validation allows a client to submit requests with invalid or unexpected data, which could include more characters than the expected maximum length or may – in the case of an injection – include a partial command or set of commands to be executed as part of a predefined command built into the application code. The injected command submitting by the attacker is executed just as any normal command as long as the resulting command (intended + injected command) is in a valid form for the target platform. If it is invalid, an error is generated and said error message is often mistakenly sent to the client.

The reason that injection attacks are considered so severe is that the attacker's injected command will be executed with the privileges of the executing entity. For example, a SQL Injection query will be executed with the privileges of the application querying the database. Because many applications are configured with administrator level access to one or more databases, the SQL Injection query will be associated with administrator level access and thus allow the attacker to perform any desired query against any desired database table. Hopefully, this helps explain the reason Information Security professionals respond with a horrifying stare when you mention that the application is running with domain administrator privileges. Depending on the application configuration and other factors, a successful injection exploit could result in information disclosure, unauthorized access (by extracting user credentials), or full system compromise.

Although injection attacks may present the most risk to an application's security, there are many more types of attacks that could be used to achieve similar goals. The authentication component is often the first target in the search for vulnerabilities because most useful functionality (to an attacker) is inaccessible unless one provides valid authentication credentials. With most Web applications, pretty much any authentication attack could be used with almost certain success.

Brute force attacks can be easily automated, especially because most Web applications still only require user identification and password fields and almost never implement an account lockout control. If a brute force attack against user credentials doesn't work well enough, some Web applications may allow you to simply reset the accounts' passwords. CAPTCHAs or other Turing tests[8,9] are implemented to stop automated attacks, but they have been defeated with some percentage of success. Another common technique is to require users to provide answers to challenge questions when attempting to reset their password or perform other account management actions. Presumably, this technique is implemented because it is believed impossible that an attacker could automate a brute force attack with 2 or 3 answers to a set of 6 to 12 known questions. Please read that last sentence again with a very sarcastic tone in mind.

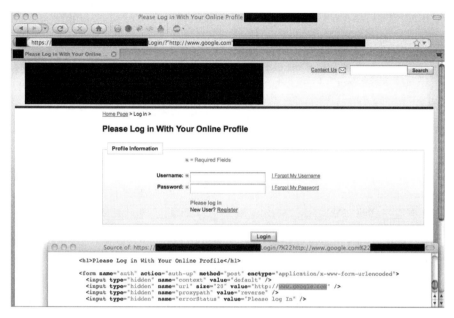

FIGURE 7.5

URL redirection.

Additional types of attacks against the Web application include manipulation of data fields exposed to the client, analysis of encryption algorithms, and many others. The result of manipulating data fields exposed to the client will vary based on how the application uses the manipulated data fields. For example, one utility company's Web application authentication form includes a hidden parameter that is used as the target when a user submits the form with valid credentials as shown in Figure 7.5. This design aspect could be exploited with URL redirection, which could trick the user into requesting any URL following successful authentication. This type of attack could exploit browser bugs, install malicious software, or implement additional attacks against the utility company's Web application with the access privileges of the authenticated user.

These attacks exploit a variety of possible vulnerabilities and weaknesses that can be implemented in a Web application and, as described earlier, can have disastrous results. The point is that there are many types of vulnerabilities and exploits that attackers could use to carry out the attacks described throughout this book. And those vulnerabilities are already being implemented in smart grid Web applications.

Attacking the Web Application User

Attacks against Web application users can cause just as much damage as attacks against the application directly, depending on the data and functionality available to users. The most common types of user attacks are cross-site scripting (XSS) and cross-site request forgery (CSRF). Although the details may vary, attacks against Web application users will typically force the user's client (Web browser) to perform some action(s) on the user's behalf, with the user's access privileges, and without the user's knowledge. To this end, a XSS or CSRF attack could produce the same result as an injection attack.

Cross-site scripting attacks involve the injection of malicious HTML into a Web page that is sent from the Web application to a user's client. The client happily interprets the malicious (attacker generated) HTML along with the intended (application generated) HTML because they both appear as simply HTML to the client. As indicated earlier, a XSS payload can force the user's client to perform an unwanted action. This may be accomplished by inserting HTML that instructs the client to make one or more requests to the application. As long as the attacker can determine the correct request(s) to make, the proper request order, and appropriate input data values to use in the request(s), then the attacker can deliver the XSS payload as desired.

The simplest and most common method to determine whether a cross-site scripting attack is possible against a particular Web application is to cause the receiving Web browser to open an alert popup box. This can often be accomplished by setting a data field to "<script>alert(1)</script>" (without quotes) in a request. Alternatively, it may require much more effort on the part of the attacker to defeat input filters or other defenses put in place to protect an application.

FIGURE 7.6

Cross-site scripting.

When it comes to utility company Web applications, it may not be so difficult, as illustrated in Figure 7.6.

As illustrated in Figure 7.6, the Web form requesting "Customer Billing Information" during the user registration process is vulnerable to cross-site scripting attacks. This test was performed without access to valid user credentials, meaning that anyone with access to an Internet-accessible computer can use this Web form to attack unsuspecting victims' Web browsers without first obtaining authenticated access to the Web application.

Cross-site request forgery is very similar to the first XSS payload described earlier and is given away by the name. Essentially, a CSRF payload will include one or more *requests* that *forge* the user's account signature because the client will automatically attach the user's session identification token to the requests. CSRF exploits are relatively easy to create; the more difficult part is in delivering the exploit to the users' clients. From a utility company's perspective, this could have disastrous results as users are unwittingly forced to make excessive payments on bills, reset their passwords, or start their dishwashers at 04:00 P.M. every day.

Because we're on the subject, there are many payloads available for use in XSS attacks. An attacker could harvest cookies to obtain session tokens (assuming they are stored in a cookie) or harvest user credentials by inserting a fake authentication form into the Web page. An attacker could even gain complete control of the user's operating system by using XSS to deliver a browser exploit in the payload. Much like an injection, an attacker could then execute arbitrary code on the user's system with the privileges of the client. Although the owner of the vulnerable Web application, that was used to deliver the XSS payload, may not consider this as significant a risk as a successful injection attack, the user's security and privacy could be seriously affected. Of course, the public relations situation that could result from such an attack may work to change the owner's assessment of risk.

As previously mentioned, it would be impossible to do justice to Web application attacks in one section of one chapter. Basically, it comes down to two things: applying a set of standard tests for security vulnerabilities, and exploiting the application's custom (and possibly unique) functionality. The standard tests would include injection testing, attempting authentication attacks, analyzing the implementation of encryption algorithms and session management, and many others. Exploiting custom functionality requires detailed analysis of how the use cases are intended to function, the types of input data used in those functions, and then manipulation of the input data in a manner that can produce a desired (malicious or unintended) result. Whether directly targeting the application or its users, attackers have many tools and techniques at their disposal and can usually take more than one route in order to reach their ultimate goal.

Tools of the Trade

One of the ironic aspects of Web application security is that attackers may not need any special and expensive tools to perform the most powerful attacks. Injections, brute force authentication attacks, and cross-site scripting attacks can sometimes be conducted with just the intended client tier of the application. These exploits are possible using only the client (Web browser) because the code and data values used by the Web browser can be analyzed and modified by attackers, which is possible because HTML (and JavaScript) must be interpreted by the Web browser and is therefore in a human readable state.

Aside from the client itself, the most common type of attack tool is a Web proxy. Essentially, the proxy can capture all requests and responses sent by the client and server, respectively, and allow the proxy owner to inspect and manipulate the content as desired. Additional tools can integrate with a proxy in order to automate common tasks, such as scanning for unknown Web pages, repeating previous requests, comparing and contrasting multiple requests or responses, and systematically changing input data values in subsequent requests. The last example is commonly known as "fuzzing," a technique that can effectively assist analysis of an application but can be very resource intensive.

Probably the most common type of Web application security tool used by information security departments and professionals is the automated vulnerability scanner. Much like their patch and configuration scanning predecessors, the Web application scanners submit requests to the application and analyze the response(s). Although largely based on signatures, these tools can help a user map out an application and help to identify simple vulnerabilities. When conducting authorized security testing of a Web application, at least one automated scanner is typically used to build a map of the application and as an initial search for vulnerabilities. Luckily for those of us in the application security industry, a significant majority of the work must be completed by intelligent human minds.

Many Web application security analysis tools offer these and other small tools into a single suite, thereby allowing the user to transfer data seamlessly (in theory) from one tool to another. Table 7.4 includes some of these tool suites

Table 7.4 Security testing tools for Web applications

Category	Name	Link
Freeware	Burp Suite	http://portswigger.net/suite/
	Paros Proxy	www.parosproxy.org/index.shtml
	w3af	http://w3af.sourceforge.net/
	Wapiti	http://wapiti.sourceforge.net/
	WebScarab	www.owasp.org/index.php/Category:OWASP_WebScarab_Project
Commercial	AppScan	www.ibm.com/software/awdtools/appscan/
	Hailstorm	www.cenzic.com/products/software/overview/
	Netsparker	www.mavitunasecurity.com/netsparker/
	NTO Spider	www.ntobjectives.com/ntospider/
	WebInspect	https://download.spidynamics.com/webinspect/default.htm

currently available. There are also many Web browser plug-ins (also referred to as "add-ons") and other single purpose tools that can be extremely helpful in identifying vulnerabilities, but are far too numerous to include here. The usefulness of the tools listed in Table 7.4 is the subject of continued debate within the industry, but the tools themselves can be considered a good baseline tool set.

Attacking Web Server Software

With all the recent industry hype surrounding Web application security, specifically some of the things described earlier, it may be easy to overlook the all-too-common Web server vulnerabilities. Just as the operating system supports Web servers and other applications, Web servers support the custom Web applications that will bring the smart grid to consumers' fingertips. Despite the mature software development life cycles in use and many talented developers working on these applications, there are bugs (just as there are with any software applications). What this means is that all the attention paid to the Web application code may overshadow another attack vector that is just as important: exploiting Web server vulnerabilities.

Apache and Microsoft IIS currently dominate the Web server software market. A quick scan through the latest security patch releases[10,11] is one indication of the type and number of vulnerabilities that have been *publicly* reported for these applications. Of course the word *publicly* is key here: It is possible that only a few vulnerabilities have been identified but not disclosed. However, given the size and complexity of these applications, it is more likely that there are many more unknown – or at least undisclosed – vulnerabilities waiting to be found and exploited.

There are two significant differences between attacks against Web server software and those against custom Web application code. The first is related to how vulnerabilities are identified. Whether open source or closed, Web server software is almost guaranteed to have a much larger code base than even the most complex and feature-rich Web application. This translates into a lot more tedious work on the part of the attacker in order to identify a vulnerability and then to craft a working exploit. Closed source applications, for which the source code is not made available to the public, must be analyzed using binary analysis techniques, which may involve disassembly, decompilation, debugging, and fuzzing.

The second difference between attacks against Web server software and Web application code involves the pool of targets for any given vulnerability exploit. Whereas a Web application vulnerability may only be applicable to a small number or group of custom Web applications (dependent on specific code or script techniques or common frameworks); an exploitable vulnerability in any supported version of the Apache Web server could affect tens of millions of systems and the Web applications they support. Put in the scope of smart grid security, a vulnerability in one utility company's Web application may be used to disrupt service to that company's consumers, but an Apache vulnerability may be used to disrupt service to half of all utility companies' consumers. The latter may just require a bit more time and resources to pull off.

Attacking Compiled Code Applications

Even though Web applications will likely account for a majority of smart grid applications, we should not overlook the importance of the compiled code application attack vector. Actually, we already started this discussion with the Web server software earlier, specifically regarding the Apache and IIS Web servers. As mentioned earlier, identifying vulnerabilities in compiled code applications can be a much more difficult process that requires more time, perseverance, and skill set ... not to mention a more expensive tool set. However, it is possible that some organizations will continue using (or possibly even transition back to) compiled code applications for some functions as Web applications continue to present such an easy attack vector.

The most sought after type of exploit against compiled code is typically the overflow, as in the buffer, heap, and stack overflows. This type of exploit can often allow for the execution of arbitrary code on the system with the privileges of the vulnerable application that failed to properly validate the size and other aspects of some input data. Basically, overflow exploits can inject new code to be executed and change the execution flow by the system to allow for this type of unauthorized and unexpected code execution. The basics of this type of exploit have been available for a long time.[12] More recent advancements in overflow protections and associated workarounds and new exploit methods are well beyond the scope of this book. Your favorite Web search engine and other Internet resources can provide plenty of details for the interested and technically advanced reader.

Similar to Web applications, compiled code applications may suffer from many types of security vulnerabilities and weaknesses. Other common problems include the use of hard-coded passwords, which are simply passwords that are included in the application during development and placed into production and allow one component of the application to gain access to some other component of the application. Typically, such passwords are included with the client (commonly referred to as a "thick client" compared with a "thin client" Web browser) with the goal of enabling the server to require an access password without requiring the user to submit a password. Hard-coded passwords can be located in the code, in a registry entry (for Windows applications), or in data files used by the application. Depending on the location of such a password and the type of storage, gaining unauthorized access through a hard-coded password may be as simple as reading a flat text file or as difficult as gaining access to the appropriate registry entry or analyzing a binary file.

Speaking of binary analysis, the ability to identify these types of security issues (and others) will be greatly aided by the use of some powerful tools mentioned earlier. First, there are the disassemblers and decompilers that can convert incomprehensible-to-humans executable files into a semicomprehensible code form. Although this conversion cannot produce the exact code files that were created during application development and used to build the executable files, it does produce output that can be much more easily interpreted and analyzed by humans given enough time, energy, and skill set (and some luck). This conversion produces static files for analysis; another type of analysis tool is the debugger, which allows the user to analyze an

Table 7.5 Security testing tools for compiled code applications

Category	Name	Link
Disassembler	IDA Pro	www.hex-rays.com/idapro/
	objdump/binutils	www.gnu.org/software/binutils/
	OllyDbg	www.ollydbg.de/
	Proview/PVDasm	http://pvdasm.reverse-engineering.net/
Debugger	GDB	www.gnu.org/software/gdb/
	IDA Pro	www.hex-rays.com/idapro/
	Immunity Debugger	www.immunitysec.com/products-immdbg.shtml
	OllyDbg	www.ollydbg.de/
	Microsoft Windows Debugging Tools	www.microsoft.com/whdc/devtools/debugging/default.mspx
Other Tools	ospy	http://code.google.com/p/ospy/
	ProcHeapViewer	http://securityxploded.com/ProcHeapViewer.php

application as it is being executed. Through debugging, an attacker can pause execution at any desired execution point in order to analyze the current state of the application, including storage locations such as hard drives, memory, and even registers. Debuggers also allow the attacker to manipulate the data values in these storage locations in order to alter the current state, which can be extremely useful when trying to determine, for example, how the application handles input data – to identify potential overflow attack vectors – and where critical data fields are stored – to identify potential hard-coded passwords.

Tools of the Trade, Round 2

If attacking non-Web applications sounds appealing, and you are in need of help building a tool set (and don't have a friend that can "Google that for you"), Table 7.5 contains some of the tools available to the public. Similar to the previous statement regarding endorsements, none of the tools mentioned in this book are recommended over others. Specific tools can only be preferred when specific information on the target application, goal(s) of the analysis, and large quantities of our favorite drinks are provided. Please also reconsider the prior warning, but taken to a new extreme: These tools should only be used by skilled minds. In other words, mind your studies and research before diving into the deep end of the pool. Alternatively, stick to analyzing Web applications, which will now be referred to as the "kiddie pool."

WIRELESS ATTACKS

Back in Chapter 1, "Smart Grid: What Is It?," we discussed several wireless technologies that may be used in a smart grid. Although new wireless technologies will be developed and utilized in the future, the current most widely used wireless technologies include the following:

- RF with Narrow Band, Direct-sequence spread spectrum (DSSS), and Frequency-hopping spread spectrum (FHSS)
- Wi-Fi
- Bluetooth
- Cellular.

For detailed information about how to carry out specific wireless attacks, several books have been written on wireless security assessments and attacks including *WarDriving and Wireless Penetration Testing* (ISBN: 978-1-59749-111-2, Syngress), *Hacking Exposed™ Wireless: Wireless Security Secrets & Solutions*, and *Seven Deadliest Wireless Technologies Attacks* (ISBN: 978-1-59749-541-7, Syngress). Additionally, the following NIST guidelines discuss wireless security and wireless testing:

- SP800-48 – Guide to Securing Legacy IEEE 802.11 Wireless Networks
- SP800-97 – Establishing Wireless Robust Security Networks: A Guide to IEEE 802.11i
- SP800-115 – Technical Guide to Information Security Testing and Assessment
- SP800-120 – Recommendation for EAP Methods Used in Wireless Network Access Authentication
- SP800-121 – Guide to Bluetooth Security
- SP800-127 – Guide to Security for Worldwide Interoperability for Microwave Access (WiMAX) Technologies.

In this section, we will describe the components of a wireless security assessment at a high-level and provide example attacks tailored to a smart grid. In general, a wireless attack will have the following flow:

- Discovery
- Device profiling
- Exploitation.

The initial goal of the attacker or assessment team will be to identify the wireless technology in use. A wireless scanning tool, such as Kismet (www.kismet-wireless.net/), and an RF spectrum analyzer can be used to determine the types of wireless technologies in use. In addition to the technology used, the different wireless networks, wireless clients, and access points should be catalogued in order to identify rogue (unauthorized) wireless networks and clients. In most cases, the attacker will attempt to attack the utility company's wireless networks in order to:

- Cause a denial of service
- Obtain sensitive information
- Bypass perimeter security controls and gain access to the internal networks.

Table 7.6 Wireless security testing tools

Category	Name	Link
Scanning	Kismet	www.kismetwireless.net/
	Netstumbler	www.netstumbler.com/
Packet Sniffer	Tcpdump	www.tcpdump.org/
	Wireshark	www.wireshark.org/
Exploit	Aircrack	www.aircrack-ng.org/
	Asleap	http://asleap.sourceforge.net/
	Metasploit (Karmetasploit)	www.metasploit.com/redmine/ projects/framework/wiki/ Karmetasploit
Live Linux Distros	BackTrack	www.backtrack-linux.org/

Table 7.6 lists a few of the many available wireless tools at an attacker's disposal. The smart grid components that will most likely use wireless technology are the smart meters and associated AMI/AMR networks. Smart meters will use wireless technology to transport the usage data back to the utility company. The data from smart meters will be used by the utility company to bill their customers, adjust electrical demand estimates, inform the customer of their usage through third-party applications, and much more. In other words, wireless networks may be used to transport data from a customer's home to the utility company's internal networks, as well as their partner networks. However, these wireless networks will most likely not have direct access into the utility company's internal networks. From the meter, the data will go through field networks and up to management stations before it touches the utility company network. Still, these wireless networks will be a good starting point for an attacker to gain access into a utility company network.

One of the goals of AMI is to allow remote administration of meters. If the attacker's goal is to turn off a victim's electricity, he or she could break into the wireless network used by the utility company for remote administration. Once on the wireless network or once the wireless encryption has been cracked, the attacker could use a packet sniffer to steal the remote administration credentials and use them to disable the victim's electricity.

Wireless Clients

Even if the utility company does not have any wireless networks, attackers can still perform client-based attacks against employee laptops, handheld devices, and smart devices. Most laptops, and the majority of any type of computing device sold today, have some internal wireless radio and unless these radios are disabled, attackers could target them. One such tool that an attacker can use to target wireless clients is Karma (http://trailofbits.com/karma/), which is now part of Metasploit as Karmetasploit.

Karmetasploit turns the attacker's laptop into a wireless access point in an attempt to convince wireless clients to associate with it. The tool takes advantage of the fact that most systems are configured to probe for wireless networks that they were previously connected to. So when a victim probes for their "preferred" wireless network, the Karma attacker will respond to the probe as that "preferred" wireless network. When a victim has associated with the Karma box, any type of request the victim makes will take them to a malicious service.

Wi-Fi

Due to the widespread availability of Wi-Fi products that follow the 802.11a/b/g/n standards, these wireless networks may crop up on any of the smart grid domains depicted in Figure 7.1. Due to the pervasive security problems with Wi-Fi networks, most organizations have either banned Wi-Fi networks or have strict policies that require wireless networks to have no access to internal corporate networks. Regardless, some organizations do permit Wi-Fi networks to access their internal networks and attackers will target these wireless networks to bypass perimeter security controls.

Bluetooth

Bluetooth has notoriously been an insecure technology and many attacks have been developed to exploit weaknesses in the technology. Bluetooth scanning tools can be used to discover Bluetooth devices, their operating mode, and the strength of the device's PIN. Additionally, the Bluetooth 3.0 specification uses Wi-Fi radios for transferring large amounts of data, so the strengths and weaknesses of Wi-Fi may apply to these devices as well.

Cellular

Cellular networks were once thought to be relatively secure wireless networks; however, the encryption scheme for Global System for Communications (GSM) has recently come under scrutiny. Theoretical weaknesses in GSM have been known for many years, but practical public exploits did not exist. However, Karsten Nohl and Sascha Kribler, recently, gave presentations at security conferences on practical attacks on the encryption scheme used in GSM networks.[13] The point to take away is that every type of wireless network will have some security-related drawback, which is why additional security controls should be implemented.

SOCIAL ENGINEERING ATTACKS

Social engineering attacks will test the security awareness of utility company employees. The attack may attempt to trick an employee into revealing information, such as their user name and password, or providing the attacker with additional access. Common examples of social engineering attacks include the following:

- Impersonating an employee to the IT Help Desk to change his or her password
- Impersonating service vendors (Examples: document shredder service, backup tape pickup, maintenance workers) to obtain potentially sensitive information or sabotage equipment
- Leaving USB key drives at strategic locations, such as the parking lot outside the headquarters, that contain malicious software that will provide a backdoor into the IT infrastructure
- Sending "phishing" e-mails to solicit sensitive information and/or IT infrastructure information from the clients' employees.

Selecting Targets

Although incidental disclosure was more common in the 1990s, it still exists today. With the explosion in popularity of social networking sites, it has never been easier to identify targets. Most social networking sites will have a space for the person's employer and some social networking sites are dedicated to the person's career. Performing a search for the name of the utility company in these social networking sites will most likely provide you with numerous employee names, and their positions. Additionally, automated tools such as Maltego and Passive Recon, discussed earlier in the "Network Attacks" section of this chapter will also identify targets for you.

PHYSICAL ATTACKS

Most types of organizations have their physical assets located within the walls of their offices. Alternatively, utility companies can have thousands of miles of transmission lines and smart meters installed in customers' homes and businesses. Realistically, there will be little a utility company can do to prevent a motivated person from cutting down a transmission line or physically tampering with a smart meter. However, there are physical access attacks that utility companies can try to prevent including the following:

- Gaining physical access to location(s) without an access badge
- Photocopy or take picture of any sensitive information that is in plain sight
- Shoulder-surfing and eavesdropping
- Stealing an unattended and unlocked mobile device (Blackberry)
- Using an unattended, unlocked computer.

Attacking with a Friend

Breaking into physical locations will usually involve social engineering techniques. Granted, sometimes you can just find an unlocked and unmonitored door and walk in. However, most doors are usually locked and an attacker will need to convince an employee to let them in. When performing these types of security assessments, a more bold goal is to walk through the front door and obtain a badge from the security guard or receptionist. To achieve this, a favorite attack is using a cell phone trick and a friend, let's call him John. The following steps are usually taken in this attack:

1. Identify an employee of the utility company, let's call him Bob.
2. In your cell phone address book, change the name of your friend John to the employee's name, Bob.
3. Before walking into the lobby, call John whose name should now appear as Bob on your cell phone's screen.
4. Tell the receptionist/security guard (Charlie) that you are here to see Bob.
5. When Charlie attempts to call Bob, tell them you already have Bob on the phone and hand your cell phone to Charlie to verify.
6. Your friend John now convinces Charlie that he can't escort the visitor because he is at home with the flu or with some other sad story, but convinces Charlie to give you a badge and thanks Charlie for helping him.

Now even if you fail to get past the main lobby, there may be plenty of time when you are just waiting in the lobby. If available, try to choose the seat right next to the lobby phone, which is hopefully a Voice over Internet Protocol (VoIP) phone. A lot of VoIP phones have a network switch built into the phone, which is perfect for connecting a small, travel size wireless access point. Because most organizations do not separate their voice networks from their data networks, the wireless access point will allow access to the internal network. So even if Charlie refuses to let the tester past the main lobby, they can just go back out to the parking lot and connect to the wireless access point.

PUTTING IT ALL TOGETHER

It makes logical sense to break up the chapter into the different types of attacks/assessments. However, in a real attack, the attacker(s) will not stick to one category or attack. For example, an attacker sets up a malicious Web site whose URL looks very similar to the remote operations access Web application. The attacker sends an e-mail that convinces a utility company employee to visit the site, which exploits a vulnerability in the employee's browser. Then, the attacker uses the new employee workstation (the one that was just exploited) to map out the internal networks, and is successful because the network is flat. Think flat networks do not exist any more? Turn back to the "Epic Fail" sidebar in this chapter. Because every system was configured with the same administrator password, the attacker is able to log into the customer-billing database and decrease their monthly bill, resulting in a revenue loss for the utility company. In this example, the attacker utilized social engineering, application, network, and system attacks to carry out his or her goal.

This example had many clauses to it, such as an employee visiting a malicious Web site and proper network segmentation not existing, but this is exactly how an attack or penetration test may turn out. The attacker/tester finds a vulnerability and exploits it to escalate his or her access, which leads to finding another vulnerability to further increase his or her unauthorized access. This continues until the attacker has met or exceeded his or her goal.

SUMMARY

Utility companies cannot rely on the obscurity of smart grid technologies to protect themselves from smart grid attacks. Although some technology components will be new, smart grids will utilize technology that has existed for decades and have well-known and well-documented vulnerabilities. With the more connected nature of smart grids, attackers and security testers will more easily be able to identify and exploit vulnerabilities in electric grids. Attacks can be initiated from many different locations, thus utility companies should perform comprehensive security assessments of their implementation to determine if they are protected from the many different attack vectors.

Security is a lopsided battle in that defenders must protect against any potential attack vector; however, an attacker may only need to find one vulnerability to exploit. Performing regular security assessments will help identify these vulnerabilities in your smart grid implementation.

Endnotes

1. National Institute of Standards and Technology. NIST Special Publication 1108: NIST framework and roadmap for smart grid interoperability standards, release 1.0 [document on the Internet]. www.nist.gov/public_affairs/releases/upload/smartgrid_interoperability_final. pdf; 2010 [accessed 8.02.10].
2. Poulsen K. Security Focus. Slammer worm crashed Ohio nuke plant network [document on the Internet]. www.securityfocus.com/news/6767; 2003 [accessed 8.02.10].
3. Zheng AY. SmartGridNews.com. Australian grid threatened by computer virus. www. smartgridnews.com/artman/publish/News_Blogs_News/Australian-Grid-Threatened-by-Computer-Virus-1296.html; 2009 [accessed 8.02.10].
4. Stokes J. ars technica. Russian crackers throw GPU power at passwords [document on the Internet]. http://arstechnica.com/business/news/2007/10/russian-crackers-throw-gpu-power-at-passwords.ars; 2007 [accessed 15.02.10].
5. Moore HD. Browser bugs, tricks, and hacks. Browser fun [homepage on the Internet]. [updated 2006 August 17]. http://browserfun.blogspot.com; 2006 [accessed 31.01.10].
6. The Open Web Application Security Project. Category:OWASP Top Ten Project [document on the Internet]. [updated 2009 December 2]. www.owasp.org/index.php/Category: OWASP_Top_Ten_Project; 2009 [accessed 31.01.10].
7. The Web Application Security Consortium. The WASC threat classification v2.0. threat classification [homepage on the Internet]. [updated 2010 January 3]. http://projects. webappsec.org/Threat-Classification; 2010 [accessed 31.01.10].

8. Association for the Advancement of Artificial Intelligence. Turing Test [document on the Internet]. [updated 2008 December 14]. www.aaai.org/AITopics/pmwiki/pmwiki. php/AITopics/TuringTest; 2008 [accessed 31.01.10].

9. World Wide Web Consortium. Inaccessibility of CAPTCHA. Alternatives to visual turing tests on the web [document on the Internet]. [updated 2005 November 23]. www.w3.org/TR/turingtest; 2005 [accessed 31.01.10].

10. The Apache Software Foundation. Apache HTTP server project. Apache httpd 2.2 vulnerabilities [document on the Internet]. [updated 2009 October 5]. http://httpd. apache.org/security/vulnerabilities_22.html; 2009 [accessed 31.01.10].

11. Microsoft TechNet. Security bulletin search products technologies KB articles service packs. Microsoft security bulletin search [homepage on the Internet]. [updated 2010 January 21]. www.microsoft.com/technet/security/current.aspx; 2010 [accessed 31.01.10].

12. Phrack. Smashing the stack for fun and profit. phrack issue 49 [document on the Internet]. Phrack 49 - Volume Seven, Issue Forty-Nine; www.phrack.com/issues.html?issue=49& id=14#article; 1996 [accessed 31.01.10].

13. Nohl K, Kribler S. Subverting the security base of GSM. https://har2009.org/program/ attachments/119_GSM.A51.Cracking.Nohl.pdf; 2009 [accessed 16.02.10].

Securing the Utility Companies

INFORMATION IN THIS CHAPTER

- Smart Grid Security Program
- Top 12 Technical Practices to Secure the Smart Grid

We previously discussed the threats to utility companies in Chapter 3, "Threats and Impacts: Utility Companies & Beyond." We also reviewed how to attack utility companies in Chapter 7, "Attacking the Utility Companies." In this chapter, we will take a look at how to secure the utility companies. First, we will examine the softer side of security; how to develop and mature an effective information security program through the use of standards. Then, we will dive into the technical side of security; reviewing the technologies that can protect the utility companies' smart grid deployments.

SMART GRID SECURITY PROGRAM

Depending upon the maturity of the utility company's current information security program, one of two approaches can be taken to further develop it. First, if the organization has a partially functioning information security program, a gap analysis should be performed. The second approach, for organizations that do not currently operate a functioning information security program, the complete adaptation of chosen frameworks should be performed. Regardless of which approach is taken, a framework for building an information security program must be chosen. Let us review the more mature options.

> **TIP**
>
> Before choosing a standard on which to build or mature your information security program, consult upper management to determine if certification of your information security program is desired. Of the two standards reviewed in this chapter, only the ISO/IEC 27000 series standards can be certified. To learn more about ISO/IEC 27000 certification, visit the ISO 27001 and ISO 27002 frequently asked question (FAQ) located at www.17799.com.

ISO/IEC 27000

The International Organization for Standardization (ISO – www.iso.org/iso/home.html) along with the International Electrotechnical Commission (IEC – www.iec.ch) have developed and published the ISO/IEC 27000 series standards. These standards are specific to "Information Technology – Security Techniques – Information Security Management Systems (ISMS)."[1] These standards provide organizations with a set of international best practices for information security that focuses on risk assessment and control implementation. The standards apply to most every organization, large or small, for profit or nonprofit.

Currently, the ISO/IEC 2700 series is comprised of six standards, with several additional standards planned.[2] The currently published standards are as follows:

- ISO/IEC 27000 – Information technology – Security techniques – Information security management systems – Overview and vocabulary
- ISO/IEC 27001 – Information technology – Security techniques – Information security management systems – Requirements
- ISO/IEC 27002 – Information technology – Security techniques – Code of practice for information security management
- ISO/IEC 27003 – Information technology – Security techniques – Information security management system implementation guidance
- ISO/IEC 27004 – Information technology – Security techniques – Information security management – Measurement
- ISO/IEC 27005 – Information technology – Security techniques – Information security risk management
- ISO/IEC 27006 – Information technology – Security techniques – Requirements for bodies providing audit and certification of information security management systems
- ISO/IEC 27011 – Information technology – Security techniques – Information security management guidelines for telecommunications organizations based on ISO/IEC 27002.

Despite the breadth of the existing ISO/IEC 27000 series standards, the following standards are currently being prepared:

- ISO/IEC 27007 – Information technology – Security techniques – Guidelines for information security management systems auditing
- ISO/IEC 27008 – Information technology – Security techniques – A Guideline for information systems management auditing
- ISO/IEC 27013 – Information technology – Security techniques – A Guideline on the integrated implementation of ISO/IEC 20000-1 and ISO/IEC 27001
- ISO/IEC 27014 – Information technology – Security techniques – An information security governance framework
- ISO/IEC 27015 – Information technology – Security techniques – Information security management guidelines for the finance and insurance sectors

- ISO/IEC 27031 – Information technology – Security techniques – A guideline for information and communications technology readiness for business continuity
- ISO/IEC 27032 – Information technology – Security techniques – A guideline for cyber security
- ISO/IEC 27033 – Information technology – Security techniques – Information technology security
- ISO/IEC 27034 – Information technology – Security techniques – A guideline for application security.

While a majority of the aforementioned published and future ISO/IEC 27000 series standards would benefit utility companies build or mature their information security programs, we will focus on ISO/IEC 27002.

ISO/IEC 27002 – Code of Practice for Information Security Management

The second standard in the ISO/IEC 27000 series focuses on providing guidance on the information security management. This guidance is aimed at those tasked with developing, implementing, or managing information security management systems. This guidance is broken down into the following 12 sections[3]:

1. Risk assessment
2. Security policy
3. Organization of information security
4. Asset management
5. Human resources security
6. Physical and environment security
7. Communications and operations management
8. Access control
9. Information systems acquisition, development, and maintenance
10. Information security incident management
11. Business continuity management
12. Compliance.

Each of the ISO/IEC 27002's 12 sections contains what are referred to as information security controls and objectives.[3] Each documented Information security objective has at least one corresponding information security control. For each information security control contained within ISO/IEC 27002, implementation guidance is provided. This guidance provides organizations with insights as to how best apply the associated information security control to support the associated information security objective.

Organizations utilizing ISO/IEC 27002 to mature or build their information security programs are not required to implement every identified information security control. Every information security control is not required to be implemented because of the following two reasons:

1. Organizations utilizing ISO/IEC 27002 should perform an information security risk assessment, which is discussed in the first section of ISO/IEC 27002. This

information security risk assessment provides organizations with a prioritized list of information security objectives, which results in a prioritized list of information security controls to implement.

2. The implementation of every information security control to achieve every information security objective is impractical for organizations of all sizes. The ISO/IEC recognizes this by issuing industry-specific implementation guidance in the form of additional ISO/IEC 27000 series standards. The ISO/IEC 27015 standard on information security management guidelines for the finance and insurance sectors is an example of such industry-specific implementation guidance.

In order to best understand how ISO/IEC 27002 can help utility companies mature or build effective information security programs, we will discuss, at a high level, each of the 12 sections mentioned above.

Risk Assessment

Utility companies should perform risk assessments, at least annually, to identify, quantify, and prioritize the risks of their information systems. Once utility companies have identified, quantified, and prioritized their risks, they can identify the actions necessary to minimize the identified risks to a level acceptable to their respective organization. Here, the utility companies must choose one of the four risk control strategies available:

1. Risk avoidance – The goal of the risk avoidance strategy is to prevent a vulnerability from being exploited.
2. Risk transference – The goal of the risk transference strategy is to move the risk to other assets, processes, or organizations.
3. Risk mitigation – The goal of the risk mitigation strategy is to minimize the impact of a successful exploitation of a vulnerability.
4. Risk acceptance – The risk acceptance strategy is utilized when the utility companies chose to accept the risk of a vulnerability and the impact of a successful exploitation.

In the context of using ISO/IEC 27002 to build or mature an information security program to protect the smart grid, utility companies should first choose to avoid risks or mitigate them. Most of the time, risk avoidance involves the implementation of information security controls, many of which are covered in depth in the 12 sections of ISO/IEC 27002.

Security Policy

Information Security Policies serve as the backbone of any mature information security program. Utility companies must implement information security policies that support their organizations' business objectives while also adhering to industry standards and regulations. Simplified, information security policies must exist in order to direct and evaluate the information security programs of the utility companies. Without information security policies, violations or deviations from documented information security policies cannot be identified and remediated. As with most information security initiatives, management must fully support and participate in the development, distribution, and enforcement of information security policies in order for them to be successful.

Organization of Information Security

Much like information security policies, the organization of information security within the utility companies can be a significant factor in their successful implementation of a functional information security program. As also mentioned for information security policies, management must support the information security functions within the utility companies for them to be effective. This support should be manifested in the approval of information security policies, the assignment of information security roles, including clearly defined roles and responsibilities, as well as periodic reviews of the information security program.

Asset Management

In order to build an effective information security program, utility companies must take asset management seriously. Specifically, in order to effectively protect the organizations' assets, they must all be associated with a particular owner. These owners will ultimately be responsible for the system, including any of its required controls. Utility companies may or may not allow their asset owners to delegate certain aspects of their duties as asset owners; however, the owners must ultimately be responsible for their systems. This clear definition of asset owners allows the utility companies to easily identify who is responsible for particular assets, as well as hold specific asset owners accountable. Without accountability, utility companies will find it hard to implement any of their information security controls.

Human Resources Security

Perhaps one of the most important sections of ISO/IEC 27002 highlights the human aspect in implementing an effective information security program. Utility companies must disseminate information to their employees, contractors, and third parties that clearly articulate their roles and responsibilities in regards to information security. Vehicles that utility companies could use to disseminate this information include detailed job roles and responsibilities, terms of employment, and in the case of contractors or third parties, legal verbiage in contracts. Without ensuring that those operating within the utility companies, or on their behalf, have a strong understanding of their roles and responsibilities for the security of the utility companies, their information security program's success will be materially impacted.

Physical and Environmental Security

This section of ISO/IEC 27002 covers topics that utility companies should be familiar to both. However, topics such as preventing unauthorized access, protecting critical systems, and ensuring provided protections are commensurate with the associated risks should serve as baseline for utility companies to measure their current physical and environmental security against. One area that will most likely require a significant evaluation of current controls is the smart grid devices that will be deployed to customers of the utility companies. Here, the topics discussed by the Physical and Environment Security section of ISO/IEC 27002 should serve as a starting point. Additional controls should be implemented for smart grid devices deployed to customers who are commensurate with the identified risks; such as those covered previously in Chapter 2, "Threats and Impacts: Consumers." Without ensuring the physical and environmental security of the smart grid, utility companies will leave themselves exposed to increased threats from attack vectors that may have otherwise been protected.

Communications and Operations Management

The previous Asset Management section of ISO/IEC 27002 ensures that utility companies hold someone responsible and accountable for the organizations' information systems. The Communications and Operations Management section of ISO/IEC 27002 ensures that utility companies develop processes and procedures for the development, operation, and ongoing management of the identified information systems. Additionally, it calls for these processes and procedures to ensure that segregation of duties is implemented. Implementing clear processes and procedures will allow the utility companies to ensure consistent operation and management of their information systems while also helping to ensure that information security controls are being properly implemented and followed. Without implementing clear processes and procedures, utility companies will be subject to the shortcomings of operational chaos. Without implementing proper segregation of duties, information security controls may easily be circumvented or minimized.

Access Control

Principles such as least privilege are contained within the next section of ISO/IEC 27002, Access Control. Utility companies should utilize the information security controls within this section to ensure that access to information systems is both required and authorized. Required access should be evaluated from both a business and security aspect, while authorization may follow the proper channels to ensure that only those who need access to information systems have it. Utility companies can utilize access controls as a significant contributor to their defense in depth approach to information security. Without effective access controls properly implemented, the utility companies will have a significant disadvantage in combating the inappropriate and unauthorized access to information systems, including those that support the smart grid.

Information Systems Acquisition, Development, and Maintenance

The Information Systems Acquisition, Development, and Maintenance section of ISO/IEC 27002 covers what is often referred to as Systems Development Life Cycle, or SDLC. Utility companies should utilize the controls within the Information Systems Acquisition, Development, and Maintenance section to ensure that during the requirements phase of any project that all information security requirements are included. A common phrase within the information security world is that "Security costs less when it is integrated from the start, and more expensive when it is bolted on." Utility companies can use the controls within this section of ISO/IEC 27002 to enforce that security is built-in from the start and recognize cost savings while also increasing their information systems security posture. The controls within this section of ISO/IEC 27002 highlight that security needs to exist on all aspects of information systems, including the operating systems, network infrastructure, applications, and more. Without integrating information security requirements into the development phase of utility companies' SDLC, they will be forced to take a reactive approach to securing their information systems. A reactive approach to security will result in additional costs to the utility companies and leaves them vulnerable to threats that might otherwise have been avoided.

Information Security Incident Management

A reality for the utility companies is that it is only a matter of when, not if their smart grid deployments will come under attack. In order to deal with these attacks, from both an impact minimization and future prevention aspect, the utility companies must implement mechanisms that allow for the timely identification and containment of information security incidents. The Information Security Incident Management section of ISO/IEC 27002 covers information security controls that will allow the utility companies to respond to attacks in a timely manner, minimize their impact, and implement corrective actions to prevent their reoccurrence. Without implementing such information security controls, the utility companies will be "asleep behind the wheel" and may not be able to recover from successful attacks.

Business Continuity Management

The Business Continuity Management section of ISO/IEC 27002 should position utility companies to withstand incidents that threaten the continuity of their operations, whether these incidents are natural disasters, attacks, or accidents. The utility companies should utilize the information resulting from the Risk Assessment activities covered in the first section of ISO/IEC 27002. Critical infrastructure must be identified, along with their associated risks, and information security controls should be implemented to minimize the impact of disasters, security breaches, and denials of service. Without thorough Business Continuity Management, the utility companies will be hard pressed to withstand a coordinated and targeted cyber attack.

Compliance

The final section of ISO/IEC 27002 covers compliance with applicable standards and legal requirements. Utility companies can implement the information security controls contained within the Compliance section of ISO/IEC 27002 to help maintain their adherence to applicable laws, regulations, contractual obligations, or security requirements, such as NERCs Critical Infrastructure Protection standards. In implementing these information security controls, the utility companies should utilize their legal counsel to verify their compliance and provide advice on integrating all applicable regulations and standards. Compliance audits should provide the utility companies with an outside perspective on the implementation of their information security controls as well as a validation of their effectiveness. Without implementing the information security controls contained within the compliance section of ISO/IEC 27002, the utility companies may leave themselves open to legal actions or find themselves operating in a vacuum.

The Information Security Forum's Standard of Good Practice (SoGP)

The Information Security Forum, or ISF, is an international association that is comprised of organizations from numerous industries, including the financial services, consumer products, manufacturing, and telecommunications.[5] In 2007, the Information Security Forum published the most recent version of their Standard of Good Practice (www.isfsecuritystandard.com/SOGP07/index.htm). The Information Security Forum's Standard of Good Practice provides organizations with a documented set of best practices that should be implemented to develop and maintain an effective information security program.

> **NOTE**
>
> The Information Security Forum was founded in 1989 as a nonprofit organization aimed to provide opinion and guidance on information security.[4] With over 300 members, the Information Security Forum strives to address a diverse range of information security challenges and deliver solutions that are practical. More information about the Information Security Forum is available on their Web site located at www.securityforum.org.

Unlike the ISO/IEC 27000 series standards, the Information Security Forum's Standard of Good Practice is available to all free of charge.[4] The Standard of Good Practice is organized into the following six aspects[5]:

1. Security management
2. Critical business applications
3. Computer installations
4. Networks
5. Systems development
6. End user environment.

Each of the aspects contained within the Information Security Forum's Standard of Good Practice contains areas and sections.[5] An area covers a specific topic within an aspect, while a section is a subset of an area that contains a set of statements.[5] Each area contains a principle and an objective.[5] The principles guide organizations toward complying with the Standard of Good Practice, while the objective explains why the statements provided within the section are required. In terms of comparing the Information Security Forum's Standard of Good Practice to the ISO/IEC 27002 standard, you can equate the Standard of Good Practice's statements to the 27002's information security controls. There are a total of 36 areas and 166 sections within the aforementioned six aspects of the Standard of Good Practice.[5]

In order to best understand how the Information Security Forum's Standard of Good Practice can help utility companies mature or build effective information security programs, we will discuss, at a high level, each of the six aspects mentioned above.

Security Management

The Security Management aspect of the Information Security Forum's Standard of Good Practice consists of 7 areas and 36 sections.[5] These 7 areas and 36 sections aim to establish an effective information security management function within the organization. In order for the utility companies to implement an effective information security management function, they must secure upper management's support, via both managerial and resource support. Without an effective information security management function within the utility companies, they will be left fighting to implement the necessary processes, procedures, and technologies required to secure the smart grid.

Critical Business Applications

The next aspect of the Information Security Forum's Standard of Good Practice, Critical Business Applications, consists of 6 areas and 25 sections.[5] The goal of this aspect of the Standard of Good Practice is to identify applications that are critical to the organization and subsequently identify and mange their risks. Utility companies must implement a risk identification and management process in order to effectively and efficiently manage their critical infrastructure. Without an effective and efficient risk identification and management process, the utility companies will potentially overlook the potential risks to critical business applications or misappropriate their limited resources to the wrong critical business applications.

Computer Installations

The Computer Installations aspect of the Information Security Forum's Standard of Good Practice contains 6 areas and 31 sections.[5] The Computer Installations aspect aims to ensure that organizations understand that information systems on which their critical business applications run must also properly secured. Utility companies must meet the objectives of the Computer Installations aspect of the Standard of Good Practice in order to accurately identify the requirements of the information systems that support their critical business applications and subsequently implement the appropriate controls to protect them. Without identifying the information systems requirements of their critical business applications or properly implementing controls to protect them, utility companies may expose the smart grid to additional risk via unnecessary services or misconfigurations.

Networks

The Standard of Good Practice's fourth aspect pertains to networks and contains 5 areas and 25 sections.[5] The Network aspect is very similar to the previously mentioned Computer Installations aspect of the Standard of Good Practice. Specifically, the Network aspect aims to ensure that organizations understand the network infrastructure that supports their critical business applications. This network infrastructure must be adequately protected against attacks and disruptions. Utility companies must meet the objectives of the Networks aspect of the Standard of Good Practice to address the network design, management, operations, and maintenance of the networks that support their critical business applications. Without meeting the objectives of the Networks aspect, the utility companies will leave the smart grid vulnerable to preventable disruption and abuse.

Systems Development

The Systems Development aspect of the Information Security Forum's Standard of Good Practice consists of 6 areas and 23 sections.[5] The Systems Development aspect aims to integrate information security requirements and controls into the SDLC. Utility companies must meet the objectives of the Systems Development aspect of the Standard of Good Practice in order to both develop more secure systems and recognize significant cost savings when compared with implementing information security controls once the systems have been deployed into production. If the utility companies do not integrate the identification of information security requirements or control into their SDLC, they will leave themselves vulnerable to preventable attacks and increase the cost of securing the smart grid.

End User Environment

The last aspect of the Information Security Forum's Standard of Good Practice covers the end user environment. This aspect contains 6 areas and 26 sections aimed at ensuring that organizations arrange for the education and awareness of their end users on the acceptable and secure ways to utilize the organization's information systems.[5] Utility companies must meet the objectives of the end user environment aspect of the Standard of Good Practice to ensure that the utility companies' employees protect their sensitive information regardless of the application they use or the medium in which they access the information. Without implementing the objectives contained within the end user environment aspect, utility companies will condone the inappropriate access and dissemination of sensitive information. While ensuring that end users will always act appropriately in respects to information systems and data access is nearly impossible, the objectives of the end user environment aspect provide utility companies with a strong approach to minimizing the frequency of abuse.

TOP 12 TECHNICAL PRACTICES TO SECURE THE SMART GRID

Now that we have reviewed the softer side of information security and how it can help the utility companies develop and build an effective information security program, let us get a little more technical and discuss the best ways that the utility companies can secure the smart grid. These technologies apply to both the utility companies' corporate environments and smart grid deployments.

The following top 12 technical practices are not listed in the order of their importance. Rather, the utility companies should review this list and determine which practices are aligned with their risk management controls for the assets that the practice would protect. This list is not intended to be all-encompassing nor will all of the practices discussed apply to all utility companies and smart grid deployments.

The top 12 technical practices are as follows:

1. Threat modeling
2. Segmentation
3. Default deny firewall rules
4. Code and command signing
5. Honeypots
6. Encryption
7. Vulnerability management
8. Penetration testing
9. Source code review
10. Configuration hardening
11. Strong authentication
12. Logging and monitoring.

Threat Modeling

Threat modeling attempts to have the architects or developers of any solution or software identify the potential attack vectors against their deployment. Architects and developers are usually the most knowledgeable of the functionality of the solution or software, which is why they are usually considered the best to perform the threat modeling. However, information security professionals must be engaged to provide the necessary training for the architects and developers. Architects and developers are usually more focused on the functionality and go through a common exercise known as developing use cases or user stories. Use cases and user stories generally define how a valid user would properly use the solution of software and are sometimes called *functional requirements*. However, in threat modeling, the focus is on developing how the solution or software can be misused for malicious intentions. Information security professionals can assist the architects and developers by training them to think like an attacker and consider the malicious use of their solution or software. In order to make the transition to an evil mind, using similar terminology that the architect and developers are familiar with will help the process. While developing their use cases or user stories, architects and developers should be trained to develop abuse cases or evil user stories in parallel.

Once the attack vectors have been identified, information security controls can be implemented to mitigate the attacks. The attack vectors can be broken down into attacks against the confidentiality, integrity, and availability of the deployment. An example of threat modeling against the smart meter software could be the following:

- **Use case** – Utility company maintenance worker remotely authenticates to the smart meter to update the firmware across the wireless network.
- **Abuse case** – Attackers could intercept the credentials being sent from the smart meter to the utility companies via wireless communications.

Thus, the software developers could utilize encryption to obfuscate the credentials, rendering them useless to the attackers.

WARNING

Use case to abuse case, or user story to evil user story, is not always a one-to-one function. There can be many abuse cases for a single-use case, and the proper time should be spent to consider every abuse case for each use case.

Threat modeling has become an integral part of many organizations' development life cycle. Microsoft has integrated threat modeling into their Security Development Life Cycle.[6] More information on threat modeling and Microsoft's specific approach is available at http://blogs.msdn.com/sdl.

Segmentation

The Payment Card Industry's Data Security Standards (PCI DSS) strongly encourage those bound by the standards to segment their cardholder data environment from the rest of their network in order to limit the scope of the standard's requirements.[7] This concept should also be applied to the utility companies and the smart grid. However, the goal of segmentation for the utility companies and the smart grid should not be to limit the scope of standards requirements. Rather, it should be to minimize the impact of a successful attack. For example, if the utility companies were to segment their smart meter deployments by geographic locations and forbid traffic between the locations, a worm would be contained to only the geographic location in which it was introduced. Segmentation should be implemented through the use of stateful firewalls, and not through the use of switch or router access control lists (ACLs).

EPIC FAIL

In October 2009, Integral Energy, an Australian power supplier, was hit with a worm that affected all of the organization's corporate desktops and propagated to their control room machines.[8] While the worm did not affect the system control and data acquisition (SCADA) systems that run Integral's power grid because it targeted machines running Microsoft's Windows operating system, it did affect the control room machines that were running the Windows operating system. The media's reaction to this incident focused on the fact that Integral had not updated their antivirus software since February 2009; however, several Web sites caught on to the fact that the organization had not implemented even basic segmentation between their corporate and control room systems. Had the organization implemented segmentation, they would not have had to rely on the Solaris operating system to prevent a catastrophe. You can read more about Integral's woes at www.theinquirer.net/inquirer/news/1556944/linux-saves-aussie-electricity.

Default Deny Firewall Rules

While the practice of implementing default deny firewalls rules is commonplace in many organizations from an outside in perspective, it continues to elude many organizations from an inside out perspective. The utility companies should implement default deny rules on their firewalls for all inbound and outbound access. Outbound connections should only be allowed from systems that must have direct access to the Internet. All other systems should be forced through a proxy that provides protections such as content filtering, SSL termination, and malware detection. Implementing a proxy server and default deny outbound firewall rules will materially decrease the probability that a successful compromise of a utility company's internal asset is able to communicate with remote command and control servers.

Code and Command Signing

Software developers for smart grid devices such as smart meters must implement signing of their code as well as critical commands issues to and from the smart meters. Code signing uses cryptographic hashes to validate software's authors as well as the integrity of the code to be executed. Command signing provides the same validation of authorship and the integrity of the command. Without implementing code and command signing, attackers will be able to run their own arbitrary code on smart meters and issues commands that will be trusted by the smart grid infrastructure. Code and command signing could have prevented the successful worm developed by IOActive's Mike Davis during his security research of smart meters.[9] Davis noted that "many of the security vulnerabilities we found are pretty frightening and most smart meters don't even use encryption or ask for authentication before carrying out sensitive functions like running software updates and severing customers from the power grid." More information on Mike Davis's research is available at www.ioactive.com/news-events/DavisSmartGridBlackHatPR.html.

Honeypots

Honeypots are used to identify and trap attackers by presenting vulnerable systems that appear to be a production system, but in fact they are a dummy system that is isolated from the production environment. Honeypots can be used to identify attackers because they can be configured to alert when they are being attacked or have been successfully compromised. They can also be used to trap attackers by presenting them with false information that is also set to trigger alerts when accessed. Utility companies should set up honeypots throughout their organization and particularly in their perimeter and smart grid environments. By doing so, they will be able to understand their current threats as well as the type of probes attackers are using to find weaknesses in their infrastructure. Finally, they can use honeypots to enact countermeasures against attackers before they breakout of the honeypot and into the production environment. The Honeynet Project is a great resource to learn more about and deploy honeypots. The Honeynet Project's Web site is located at www.honeynet.org.

Encryption

Encryption must be implemented by the utility companies in order to safeguard data from successful compromises or insider threats. Obvious places for encryption implementations include transport layers that carry sensitive information such as customer data, but other implementations should include database, whole disk, and removable media. Sensitive information stored in the utility companies' databases should be encrypted using strong cryptographic standards such as AES. This will help prevent unauthorized access to data contained within the utility companies databases in the case of a successful compromise or insider threat. Extending encryption to whole disks on workstation and laptop systems as well as removable media will also aid in preventing unauthorized access to sensitive Utility Company data in the case of theft or misplacement.

Vulnerability Management

The utility companies must implement controls to ensure that properly manage the vulnerabilities present in their environments. A vulnerability management program will allow the utility companies to determine where their patching and configuration policies, processes, and procedures are effective, and where they are not. Vulnerability scanning, as part of a vulnerability management program, will identify weaknesses in the utility companies assets and provide them with valuable information that will be utilized in dealing with threats. By knowing where vulnerabilities exist within their environments, the utility companies will be able to operate an effective risk-based approach to managing their vulnerabilities. Without a vulnerability management program the utility companies, and in turn the smart grid, will have little chance to deal with the constant threats and attacks they attract.

Penetration Testing

One of the most commonly misunderstood practices in information security is penetration testing. Many confuse penetration testing with vulnerability scanning or vulnerability assessments. However, penetration testing differs from both vulnerability scanning and vulnerability assessments by attempting to validate the risk associated with identified vulnerabilities. Vulnerability scanning and vulnerability assessments simply identify, quantify, and rank the vulnerabilities within the tested environment. Penetration testing validates the risks identified by these other two practices by exploiting the identified weaknesses as well as the other controls in place. Utility companies should perform regular penetration testing against all of their environments, and more frequently against environments that contain sensitive information or critical infrastructure. Many organizations perform penetration testing on an annual basis, but as the threats facing the utility companies and the smart grid are constantly changing, the authors of this book believe that penetration testing should be performed at least quarterly against the aforementioned environments. In the ideal situation, utility companies would employ or contract penetration-testing specialists to constantly evaluate their critical environments.

TOOLS

The Metasploit Framework is an open-source testing tool that can be used to perform penetration tests against network devices, information systems, and Web applications. Originally developed by HD Moore and purchased by the vulnerability management firm Rapid7 in October of 2009, Metasploit provides a free alternative to commercial penetration testing tools such as Core Security's (www.coresecurity.com/) Core Impact and ImmunitySec's (www.immunitysec.com/) CANVAS.[10] In April of 2010, Rapid7 announced a commercial version of Metasploit, known as Metasploit Express. However, Moore and Rapid7 have consistently maintained that a free version of Metasploit will continue to be offered.[11] You can learn more about Metasploit and download the penetration-testing tool from www.metasploit.com.

Source Code Review

As part of a mature software development life cycle, organizations should perform reviews of their source code for vulnerabilities. Although vulnerability scanning attempts to identify vulnerabilities once they are introduced into an environment, source code reviews aim to identify vulnerabilities in software before the software is released. Utility companies must implement source code reviews for all of their software developed internally or by vendors that will be implemented in environments that will house sensitive information or critical infrastructure. By investing in source code reviews during the software development phase, the utility companies will recognize cost savings when compared with fixing vulnerable code once it is in production, while also being able to prevent vulnerabilities from being introduced into their environments.

Configuration Hardening

In a similar fashion, systems should be hardened before they are placed into production. Where applicable, a hardened system image should be used to build the systems as opposed to trying to harden systems from their vendor-supplied base configuration. Vulnerability scanning and penetration testing should be performed regularly on the hardened system images.

Standards have been created to harden common operating systems, and the majority of systems in a smart grid will be running one of these operating systems. One resource for these standards is the Center for Internet Security (CIS – http://cisecurity.org/), which provides benchmarks for numerous devices, applications, and operating systems. Utility companies should use the standards to ensure systems are secure as soon as they enter the production environment.

Strong Authentication

Strong authentication requires that in order to authorize access to a specific resource that at least two of three authentication categories be implemented. These categories are as follows:

- Something I know – Example: A password
- Something I possess – Example: A smart card
- Something I am – Example: A fingerprint.

Strong authentication aims to prevent unauthorized access to assets when one of the two authentication categories is compromised. For example, if the utility companies were to implement strong authentication requiring a password and smart card for remote access to their corporate networks, their security would not be compromised if the smart card were lost or the password was obtained by a malicious user. Utility companies should implement strong authentication to protect all environments that contain sensitive information and critical infrastructure. Strong authentication should also be extended to administrative actions on assets within these environments, rather than simply authenticating users a single time.

Logging and Monitoring

Logging and monitoring aim to provide information that can be used to identify attacks, as well as reconstruct events in the case of an incident. For example, the logging and monitoring of unsuccessful authentication attempts to a utility company's Web site can indicate that an attacker is trying to break into a customer's account. Likewise, if the attacker were able to successfully login into the customer's account, logging and monitoring can be utilized to see what actions the attacker performed. Utility companies should implement logging and monitoring on all devices within environments that contain sensitive information or critical infrastructure. Logging and monitoring should be extended to the application, operating system, and network levels and include the implementation and use of intrusion detection and intrusion prevention systems. Without logging and monitoring, the utility companies will be flying blind during and after attacks on their environments, including the smart grid.

SUMMARY

Developing and maturing an information security program is fundamental to the security of the utility companies and the smart grid. The process of developing and maturing information security programs cannot be performed in an ad-hoc fashion or be performed in a vacuum. Utilizing internationally recognized standards such as the ISO/IEC 27000 series standards of the Information Security Forum's Standard of Good Practice will ensure that the most critical aspects of an effective information security program are included.

While a standard-based approach to developing and maturing the utility companies information security program is fundamental, certain technical practices must also be in place to support them. Without these technical practices, the policies, procedures, and processes developed by any information security program will have little impact on the security posture of the utility companies and the smart grid.

Endnotes

1. International Standard ISO/IEC 27001 – Information technology – Security techniques – Information security management systems – Requirements. First Edition. ISO/IEC. 2005.
2. About the ISO27k Standards [document on the Internet]. Information 27001 Security; www.iso27001security.com/html/iso27000.html; 2010 [accessed 30.04.10].
3. International Standard ISO/IEC 27002 – Information technology – Security techniques – Code of practice for information security management. First edition. ISO/IEC. 2005.
4. About the ISF [document on the Internet]. Information Security Forum; www.security-forum.org; 2010 [accessed 30.04.10].
5. The standard of good practice for information security. 2007 Edition. London, UK: Information Security Forum; 2007.
6. Get Started: Threat Modeling Tool [document on the Internet]. Microsoft; www.microsoft.com/security/sdl/getstarted/threatmodeling.aspx; 2010 [accessed 1.5.10].
7. Payment Card Industry (PCI) Data Security Standard – Requirements and Security Assessment Procedures. Version 1.2.1. PCI Security Standards Council LLC. 2009.
8. Farrell N. Linux saves Aussie electrical grid [document on the Internet]. London, UK: The Inquirer; www.theinquirer.net/inquirer/news/1556944/linux-saves-aussie-electricity; 2009 [accessed 01.05.10].

9. IOActive's Mike Davis to Unveil Smart Grid Research at Black Hat USA [document on the Internet]. IOActive www.ioactive.com/news-events/DavisSmartGridBlackHatPR. html; 2009 [accessed 01.05.10].

10. Rapid7 Acquires Metasploit [document on the Internet]. Rapid7 LLC www.rapid7.com/ metasploit-announcement.jsp; 2009 [accessed 01.05.10].

11. Approaching Metasploit 3.4.0 and Metasploit Express [document on the Internet]. Rapid7 LLC; http://blog.metasploit.com/2010/04/approaching-metasploit-340-and.html; 2010 [accessed 01.05.10].

Third-Party Services

INFORMATION IN THIS CHAPTER

- Service Providers
- Attacking Consumers
- Attacking Service Providers
- Securing Third-Party Access to the Smart Grid

Utility companies will not play the only role in smart grids. They will rely on numerous third parties to provide core services and additional services that increase the effectiveness and functionality of smart grids. However, these third parties can also introduce new threats and attack vectors to smart grids.

The level of trust applied to third parties will influence the amount of risk they introduce to other entities within a smart grid. Reducing the number of security controls between business partners may make it easier to bridge networks and integrate applications; however, this may also increase your overall risk exposure. This chapter will describe attacks that abuse the inherent trust relationships between organizations and how to properly secure the shared connections, applications, and data with your business partners.

SERVICE PROVIDERS

Cutting costs and increasing functionality are just some of the goals that will entice utility companies to use third-party services. Although there are many different third-party services available, this chapter will use three examples to illustrate the security principles of integrating third-party services:

- Billing
- Consumer interfaces
- Device support.

Billing

The customer billing operations, or portions of it, can be outsourced to an organization that specializes in billing. The security impact of outsourcing billing will be based on how much of the billing operations are outsourced. A common approach is to use third parties, such as PayPal (www.paypal.com) and BillMatrix (www.billmatrix.com), to store, transmit, and process payment card data.

Compliance

One potential advantage to using a third-party payment gateway is providing consumers the option of paying with a credit or debit card without having to be responsible for compliance with the Payment Card Industry Data Security Standard (PCI DSS).[1] PCI DSS is a set of requirements for enhancing the security of payment account data and was developed by credit card companies including American Express, Discover Financial Services, MasterCard Worldwide, and Visa Inc. International.[2]

WARNING

It may seem like an easy choice to use a third party and wipe your hands of the responsibility for ensuring consumer payment card security. However, consumers may ultimately hold the utility company responsible if their payment card information is stolen from the third-party partner handling the payments. Ensuring the third party is compliant with the PCI DSS should only be the minimum requirement the third party must meet. Assessing the third party's overall security posture will be critical to ensuring your company's risk is minimized.

Required Access for Third-Party Payment Processors

In this example, which is illustrated in Figure 9.1, the payment card data is stored, transmitted, and processed by the third party. As shown by the data flow path in Figure 9.1, the utility company does not need access to the payment card data, and it should not need access to the third-party's internal network. If the utility company were to access the data, they would then be required to be PCI DSS compliant.

Additionally, the third party should only need limited access to consumer data in order to ensure the proper account is credited with the payment. The third party does not need to know consumer energy usage, payment history, or even balance information. Most importantly, there is no need for the third party to have access into the utility company's internal network. However, this particular example assumes the third party is only processing consumer payments. If the third party assumes additional roles, such as accounting, the required level of access may increase.

Consumer Interfaces

In order to provide the promised functionality of smart grids to consumers, utility companies will be installing new technologies into consumers' homes and businesses. Although utility companies could develop and manage their own products, numerous technology companies that provide these technologies already exist and present viable solutions.

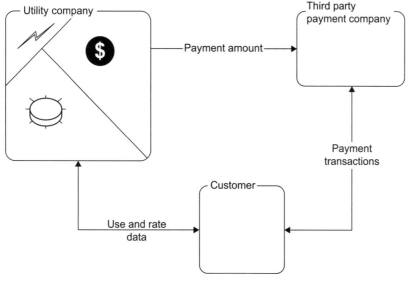

FIGURE 9.1

Example data flow path for third-party payment processor.

Viewing Energy Consumption

Let's consider energy consumption applications as an example of a third-party service. Instead of the utility company developing their own Web application, they could partner with a known service provider such as Google or Microsoft. Google and Microsoft have developed energy consumption Web applications called PowerMeter (www.google.com/powermeter/) and Hohm (www.microsoft-hohm.com/) that allow consumers to monitor their energy consumption and provide tips for reducing energy usage. These applications collect energy usage data either directly from utility companies or directly from smart devices and redisplay the data in a user-friendly format. Figure 9.2 illustrates the data flow in the scenario where the utility company sends the data to the third party.

Required Access for Energy Consumption Application Service Providers

So the questions then become, What data does Google or Microsoft need access to, and will they need direct access into the utility company's network to obtain the data? Google has released an application programming interface (API) to provide a convenient method of uploading usage statistics to their PowerMeter application[3] and in a similar fashion, Microsoft has developed an SDK for Hohm.[4] So, if the utility company has partnered with Google, the utility company could periodically (for example, every 30 minutes) send energy usage data to Google. The data would be transmitted in the form of an XML file that is sent to Google's servers through an encrypted HTTPS POST[3] transaction. This process presents

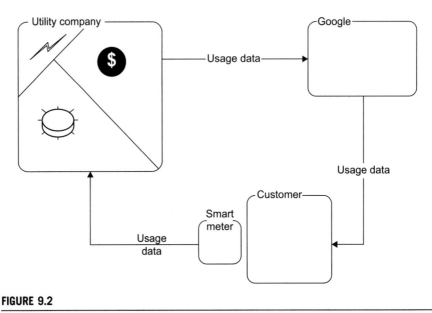

FIGURE 9.2

Example data flow path for third-party energy consumption application service provider.

minimal risk to the utility company due to the fact that Google does not need to access resources in the utility company's internal network. Additionally, the data is encrypted while in transit to Google's servers. Thus, there is minimal risk to the data being compromised … at least not yet. Later, in the section "Attacking Consumers" of this chapter, attacks against Google's and Microsoft's services to compromise usage data will be presented.

From a consumer's perspective, if their utility company has not yet partnered with a third party, there are still other options. Companies, such as The Energy Detective (www.theenergydetective.com), have created devices that directly interface with Google PowerMeter. These devices usually connect to the consumer's home or business network and use the consumer's Internet connection to transmit the data to Google. So, the utility company is now completely out of the picture and the risk falls on the consumer, Google (and/or other third parties that provide similar services), and the company that created the device.

Managing Smart Devices

Managing the risk of reporting energy usage will be a minor task compared with managing the risk of third-party services that allow consumers to remotely control their smart devices. Ranging from changing the temperature on thermostats to turning on/off the gas fireplace, these services will require network access to the smart devices. The network path that the command controls take will determine the risk to each entity involved in this scenario.

Required Access for Smart Device Control

Smart device management interfaces will require a completely different level of access than third-party payment processors or even energy usage reporting services. If you work for a utility company and you are asked to assess a third party that provides this type of solution, an important question to consider is: Will the third party need to use your operations network to access the smart devices? This scenario is depicted in Figure 9.3 and shows the increased access into the utility and third-party networks. Alternatively, does the third party provide consumers with a gateway that uses the consumer's Internet connection to communicate with the third party directly? From a utility company's perspective, requiring the third party and the consumer to communicate directly would appear to present the least risk. However, this would require the consumers to install another device on their network, thus increasing their risk, which may or may not sit well with the consumer.

NOTE

Have you caught on to the theme of this chapter yet? Access to data and network resources should be restricted as much as possible. If a third party does not have a valid business justification for access to a particular resource, do not allow access to that resource. Essentially, this means you should apply the Principle of Least Privilege, which is a simple concept in theory. How you react to a third party that demands a domain administrator account in order to provide their service is a different matter.

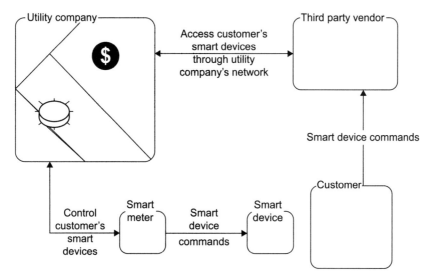

FIGURE 9.3

Example data flow path for third-party control of smart devices through utility company networks.

Device Support

When a utility company chooses a vendor from which to purchase devices, such as smart meters, they will usually be given the option of purchasing maintenance service as well. Smart meters are generally expected to have a 15 to 20 year life expectancy; however, the functionality that they are expected to provide will continually evolve. Additionally, security vulnerabilities will be identified in these devices and patches, or new firmware, will need to be pushed out to these devices. Fortunately, from an ease of use perspective at least, most smart meters provide the ability to remotely update the firmware.

Required Access for Remotely Managing Devices

Applying the patches or new firmware will most likely run through the utility company's operations network. Although connecting the smart meter to the consumer's network and directly communicating to the third-party service provider may be possible, this approach will most likely be the exception rather than the rule. If the service provider is responsible for administering the patches or new firmware, they will need a network path from their network enterprise into the utility company's operations network. The service provider will most likely utilize an existing file transfer protocol, such as file transfer protocol (FTP) or trivial file transfer protocol (TFTP), to upload the new firmware or patches to the device. Security professionals can hope for the use of more secure protocols such as secure file transfer protocol (SFTP) or secure copy protocol (SCP), but the reality is that unencrypted protocols will most likely be utilized. Depending on the third party, they may require a patch management system be placed in the operations network. The patch management system would grab the security patches or new firmware

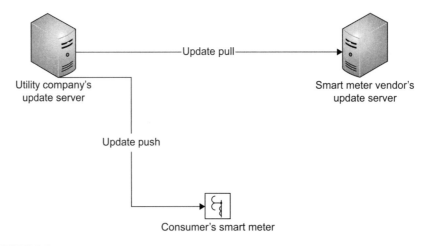

FIGURE 9.4

Example data flow path for remotely managing devices.

from the third-party's network, then push the security patches or new firmware to the devices. Thus, the utility company would need to allow a third-party server on the utility company's network and allow the server network access, which is illustrated in Figure 9.4.

ATTACKING CONSUMERS

Attacks targeting electricity consumers will become increasingly easier with the availability and further expansion of third-party services for smart grids. This should be no surprise considering the most difficult vulnerabilities to remediate are often the ones that target users. These vulnerabilities also tend to become the "acceptable risk" issues since the threat to an organization is not as obvious when discussing attacks against its users.

Functionality Undermines Security

Information security professionals are often accused of interfering with business operations, warning of unprotected and excessive functionality that may be abused by unknown malicious individuals; "hackers" as they are known in the media and general population. The fact of the matter remains, however, that the availability of useful functionality essentially translates into a higher level of risk to the confidentiality and integrity of the associated systems—electrical devices such as lights, thermostats, and refrigerators in the case of smart grid devices. Within the smart grid arena, functionality is expanding and evolving with smart grid devices, utility company applications and services, and third-party services.

Microsoft Hohm and Google PowerMeter

At the time of writing this book, the most visible third-party services such as Microsoft's Hohm and Google's PowerMeter are limited in functionality in that they collect and consolidate power usage data but do not offer functionality to manipulate the supply of power or the devices that use it. This limitation restricts the types of attacks that may be used against consumers as well as the potential effect of a successful attack. Specifically, an attacker would have to obtain access to a user's data and then devise physical attacks against the user's property— think robbery when no one is home. With essentially read-only functionality, an attacker cannot easily inflict the kind of damaging attacks described in Chapter 3, "Threats and Impacts: Utility Companies and Beyond," in a remote, automated, and widespread manner.

It should be expected that the more dangerous attacks against consumers will come into play when more useful functionality is made available to consumers. When users can remotely turn off electrical devices, attackers may be able to execute denial-of-service attacks by remotely turning off all electrical devices. When users can remotely manage their home area network (HAN), attackers may be able to remotely leverage HANs for attacks against the utility company or other targets. The attack possibilities will expand and evolve along with legitimate functionality. The following sections discuss specific aspects of third-party applications such as Microsoft Hohm and Google PowerMeter.

Single Sign-On

Single sign-on is one of the best examples of a double-edge sword in the information security industry. Edge 1: Without single sign-on, users are required to memorize several combinations of account credentials. For the purposes of this argument, disregard password database applications or at least keep in mind that most normal users will not be bothered to learn how to use one. The end result is typically one or a few very predictable or common user IDs and passwords, which will facilitate brute force authentication attacks. Edge 2: A vulnerability that leads to unauthorized access in one application enables unauthorized access to all applications. The same weak password idea may apply here, but one hopes the minimum password requirements in a single sign-on environment are configured such that brute force authentication attacks would result in very few compromises.

In the case of Hohm and PowerMeter, single sign-on means all of those publicly documented and privately exploited vulnerabilities in applications that utilize Microsoft Live or any other Google application may immediately become an issue for users. The converse of this statement is also true. That is, vulnerabilities in Microsoft Hohm and Google PowerMeter may immediately translate into unauthorized access to users' e-mail, RSS feeds, investments and other financial data, and other applications.

Persistent Authentication

Imagine, for a moment, the following common scenario: You get home from work and boot up your home PC, and open your favorite Web browser that automatically retrieves the latest e-mails. There are no new messages because you have already viewed them on your mobile phone. The next day at work you get a new desktop—presumably because the old one was infected with no less than three distinct viruses delivered from several hundred videos downloaded during lunch break—and you immediately connect and log in to Microsoft Live and/or Google accounts to ensure you can get access to e-mail, RSS feeds, stock tickers, and all the other wonderful tools offered to users. Then you buy a new car with Ford SYNC, which provides a wireless hotspot for you[5] and repeat the same process. Now any time you are within physical reach of these devices, you can access all of your data online. And now consider the eventual widespread implementation of wearable and embedded systems for humans that will offer access without the need for handheld devices. One thing that can make this scenario possible—in addition to the obvious hardware and software that is required—is persistent authentication, and it has some very powerful and attractive aspects. And now imagine that, in the same capacity, you can remotely manage all the electrical devices in your house, including the alarm system.

Persistent authentication in Web applications allows a user to authenticate once using the account credentials and then provide an authentication token as proof of identity in future requests. This token will remain valid until it is deleted or expired, neither of which may happen for a very long time. From an attacker's perspective, obtaining this token equates to impersonating the user for the associated application. Access to any of the devices storing this token could be obtained by physical or logical means and would lead to the same result. And to think you got angry when the company forced a 15-minute inactivity timeout on all desktops.

Possibly the most significant security issue related to persistent authentication for Web applications is the fact that many vulnerabilities have been and will be found that could allow an attacker to compromise the persistent authentication token with a malicious Web site. By enticing unsuspecting users to visit a malicious Web page, an attacker could obtain this token or utilize it in an automated attack. Refer to the section "Other Types of Attacks" in this chapter.

With persistent authentication comes ease of access, be it for a legitimate user or an attacker. The question of whether to implement it boils down to user acceptance: Will users still use the application if they have to enter their password just to turn off a light or reprogram the thermostat (and not complain about it constantly)? If not, then a dedicated attacker may be able to play chopsticks with the lights in your office building or the houses in your neighborhood. Or worse, of course.

Other Types of Attacks

Chapter 7, "Attacking the Utility Companies," described two very powerful attacks against Web application users, namely cross site scripting (XSS) and cross site request forgery (CSRF), that could be used by attackers to impact utility companies by way of their consumers. Although these attacks were discussed from the utility company's risk perspective, they may be applicable (of course) to any Web applications and thus any entity that implements or utilizes them. For users of third-party services from providers like Microsoft and Google, the risk lies almost entirely with the user since the provider has almost nothing to risk other than its reputation and maybe a temporary decline in stock value.

Smart Devices Gone Wild

The industry for smart devices is developing in a very decentralized manner, meaning that many different companies are producing products and hoping to become the standard by way of popularity among users. Though it should not have to be written again, this means that security controls will take a backseat for better and easier functionality and accessibility. One can only hope that security can stay in the car, rather than being stuffed in the trunk to be handled much further down the road. But one should hope that security is addressed some years down the road. Consequently, the reader should rest assured that security will be taken seriously and considered a "top priority" by these organizations once a major attack becomes public knowledge. The security professionals should rest assured that they will continue to enjoy job security as the smart grid industry continues to mature.

Consider the smart thermostat as an example. What could possibly go wrong with enabling users to remotely manage the thermostat settings? Consider the smart thermostat with knowledge of the attacks described throughout this chapter, and consider the risk versus the benefits. The benefit of remote thermostat management is a reduction of power use and increase in associated cost savings. The risk is unauthorized access and manipulation of the thermostat setting. At first consideration, this may not seem to pose a particularly significant risk. But what would happen if an attacker were able to turn off the thermostat at midnight for households in Wisconsin in the January timeframe? Consider how many people would become ill and have to call in sick during the following day or week. Hospitals may become overcrowded, consumers unwittingly flood the utility company's customer support numbers, and the whole process restarts every week until someone figures out the real cause of the problem.

A thermostat prank is one thing, but consider the fact that every electrical device in the home will soon be equipped with "smart" functionality … which of course simply means programmability and remote access via Web server/application. For office buildings and organizations with less-than-stellar remote access security, attackers may be able to execute similar attacks. If power supplies, alarm systems, and physical security devices are configured with similar smart functionality, the phrase "taking candy from a baby" may make a resurgence in popularity. Without spreading too much fear, uncertainty, and doubt, it suffices to say that a well-planned attack could actually impact the daily lives of thousands or millions of people and organizations.

ATTACKING SERVICE PROVIDERS

One of the most over-looked or disregarded risks associated with any organization is the threat from trusted third parties. Organizations are often left at the mercy of the third party: either accept the risk of providing remote domain administrator access or find another vendor to supply the needed service or product. Admittedly, domain administrator access may be a stretch and not very common, but is rather an example of the general problem: An organization that utilizes a third-party service will either outsource sensitive data for processing or lessen the security defenses to enable operations … or both in some cases. The overlooked risk involves both scenarios in that the third party is inherently trusted to protect sensitive data and to not enable or instigate attacks against the purchasing organization. Security professionals know this, and attackers can exploit it to get to the utility company through the service provider.

SECURING THIRD-PARTY ACCESS TO THE SMART GRID

Regardless of the environment, when discussing third-party access to your resources, the Principle of Least Privilege is the golden rule. Limiting access to only what is necessary for valid business functionality will minimize the risk. The first step in this process is evaluating the trust in the relationship.

Trust

Security professionals are stereotypically paranoid. They are kept awake at night thinking of their organization getting attacked through zero-day vulnerabilities, massive botnets executing a distributed denial of service (DDoS), and for countless other reasons. So when the business units of an organization broker a partnership with a third party that wants access to sensitive resources, the immediate response from the security department is usually a string of four letter words that cannot be repeated in this book. However, the security department must walk a fine line due to the trust placed by other parties in the company. For example, consider a third party whose CEO (Alice) is a very close friend of the utility company CEO (Bob). Alice and Bob may have come to an agreement based on their mutual trust of each other, but Bob did not consult with his security department before agreeing to use Alice's Web application for remotely controlling smart devices. Thus, the security department did not have a chance to tell Bob why transmitting credentials over HTTP is a bad thing.

The security department screaming expletives at Bob, or even politely criticizing Alice's security posture, is probably not the best approach for dealing with this situation. Taking a combative attitude toward these situations will only drive a rift between the security department and the rest of the company, which will only make the security department's job that much harder. The best approach will most likely be to work with Alice's company to address any issues before the integration process is complete. Ensuring that Alice's company has implemented similar security controls will help the security department deal with the new trust relationship.

When creating the agreement with the third party, usually in the form of a Service Level Agreement (SLA) or functional requirements document, explicitly define all of your security requirements in the agreement. Including the security requirements in the contract will make the third party contractually obligated to implement those security requirements.

Daisy-chaining Trust

Another consideration is the third-party's business partners. So maybe the third party has a solid security management program, but do you trust their third-party business partners? For example, at the time of the writing of this book, Microsoft currently limits access to the Hohm SDK to their partner utility companies. Additionally, Microsoft lists in their Online Privacy Statement that they do not sell, rent, or lease their customer lists to third parties,[6] which is commendable.

However, they do provide information to other companies that work for Microsoft.[6] Understanding the third-party's privacy policy and specifying how access is granted in the partnership agreement will largely dictate the trust relationship.

Additionally, the third party will most likely have more than one customer. So, will your company trust the third party to protect your information from their other clients? This question will be covered in more detail in the sections "Assessing the Third Party" and "Securing the Third Party."

Data Access

In the section "Billing" of this chapter, the scenario of using a third party to process payment card transactions was discussed. In particular, it was noted that the utility company has no need to access the payment card data and the third-party payment processor should not need access to consumer data, such as energy consumption or payment history. Access to sensitive data should be reviewed and linked to a specific functionality that requires access to the data.

TIP

Third parties will often request more access than what they really need. Sometimes this happens because they honestly do not know or do not have a complete understanding of what data they really need access to. Alternatively, they could be asking for access to more data to help their marketing departments. Sometimes they will ask for more access because they are anticipating that your company will reject their first request, and then "mitigate the risk" by granting less access than what was requested. Regardless, your company should respond to their access requests with the same question: Why? You should force the third party to provide justification for the requested access.

Data Classification

In order to properly protect access to data, the data needs to be assigned a criticality rating. Unfortunately, this will be a lengthy and difficult process. One of the first steps will be to define the criticality labels. For example, the following labels are commonly used:

- Confidential
- Proprietary
- Official use only
- For public distribution.

The actual label titles matter less than having a clearly defined definition for each label and educating employees on how to use the classification system.

Classifying certain data, such as payment card data or social security numbers, will be relatively easy. Everyone knows this is sensitive information and should be kept confidential. Unfortunately, not all data is so easily classified, especially when you consider data aggregation and combination. As an overly simplified example, consider that by itself, a consumer's total energy consumption for one hour could be considered nonsensitive. So, if your company were to disclose that Tony Flick used two kilowatts from 8:00 A.M. to 9:00 A.M. today, this would probably not cause too much concern from Tony. However, if you were to release his hourly energy consumption for one week, a quick analysis would probably reveal his daily schedule, such as when he wakes up, leaves for work, returns from work, and goes to sleep. Thus, allowing people to know the best time to rob him. In order to properly classify data sensitivity, an evaluation should determine the risk of disclosing just that particular data, an aggregation of that data over time, and how attackers could use the data in combination with other data.

Data Segmentation

Data segmentation should be implemented by the third party to prevent their clients from accessing each other's data. Third-party service providers will have multiple clients. These clients will most likely share the same application interfaces, network gateways, and potentially data storage. If at all possible, storing data on the same system(s) with other client data should be avoided. Although physical separation would be ideal, virtualization is used in just about every organization these days. So, virtual and logical segmentation will be the most likely scenarios.

If data segmentation is not possible, and your organization absolutely must partner with that third party, your organization should evaluate their authorization security controls to mitigate the risk. Strong authorization security controls will help prevent other organizations from accessing your data. Authorization security controls will not completely eliminate the risk; however, the risk will be more acceptable.

Network Access

Business-to-business (B2B) connections are often accepted for business reasons without considering the security implications. In Chapter 7, "Attacking the Utility Companies," the incident at the Davis-Besse nuclear power plant was illustrated. To recap the incident, the Slammer worm was able to infect internal systems at the power plant. Although the power plant's external firewall would have blocked the worm, a connection between a contractor's network and the power plant that bypassed the firewall allowed the worm to propagate from the contractor's network to the power plant's internal systems.[7] This provides just one example of why network traffic from third parties should go through the same security controls as any other network traffic.

TIP

B2B connections are usually allowed to bypass external security controls, which results in an unfiltered connection between the two organizations. As illustrated in the Davis-Besse nuclear power plant example, a vulnerability in the third-party's network will affect the security posture of your organization and potentially vice versa. From an external perspective, the B2B connection between the two organizations should be restricted by which ports, protocols, and systems are allowed to communicate.

Some third-party vendors will require domain credentials for their service or product to operate appropriately. Although providing domain administrator access will make the implementation easier, the level of risk obviously increases with this decision. If the service is compromised by an attacker, the attacker will be able execute commands with the same level of privileges. Thus, if the service is running under a domain administrator account, the attacker will be able to execute commands with the permissions of a domain administrator. If a domain account is required, an account with the least privileges as possible will be ideal. Additionally, this account should be required to adhere to corporate password policies.

Segmentation

In most cases where network access is required, the third party will most likely not need access to the entire network(s). So, for example, a service provider that performs patch management for smart meters will not need access to human resources network subnets or systems. Even if your organization does not use any third-party services, the network architecture should not be a flat design, which allows network access to and from any system on the network. Appropriate access controls should be configured in firewalls and other network devices to restrict unnecessary access between networks and subnets. Restricting access to specific network segments will limit your organization's risk exposure to an attack that comes through the third party.

Monitoring

If your organization has already implemented a security monitoring solution, such as an Intrusion Prevention System (IPS) or Intrusion Detection System (IDS), any third-party traffic should be analyzed by these monitoring systems. A common request from third parties is to be white-listed on monitoring systems, which essentially allows any traffic from the third party be allowed to pass through the monitoring devices without being analyzed first. Of course, this request may also come from within the prime organization when the personnel responsible for reviewing the alerts from these monitoring systems keep getting alerts everyday at 2:00 A.M. The network traffic from third parties should be treated as untrusted and analyzed accordingly.

Secure Transport

Sensitive data should be encrypted at all times, which includes while in transit. Although this rule is more important when the data is transmitted across untrusted networks, this rule should still be applied when the data is transmitted across a trusted network. Common clear-text protocols used to transmit data and their more secure alternatives are listed in Table 9.1. Replacing clear-text protocols with more secure alternatives should not come as a shock and may seem like an easy policy to implement; however, certain devices will pose problems to encrypting sensitive data in transit. Encryption is computationally expensive and as a

Table 9.1 Clear-text protocols and their secure alternatives

Clear-text protocol	Secure alternatives
FTP	Secure File Transfer Protocol (SFTP)
	Secure Copy (SCP)
TFTP	SFTP, SCP
Telnet	Secure Shell (SSH)
Rlogin	SSH
RSH	SSH
HTTP	HTTPS (SSL/TLS)

result, increases the power consumption of the device. This could dramatically decrease the battery life of the device and the lifetime of the device.

A common approach is to implement a site-to-site virtual private network (VPN) between the organization's network and the third-party network. This will result in all data transmitted between the two networks to be encrypted. However, there is a catch. Let's consider as an example, a utility company (FakeUtility) sending consumer usage data to a third party (FakeAnalysisCompany) for analysis. FakeAnalysisCompany has an anonymous FTP server that allows anyone to write data to the FTP server, but restricts read access. So, anyone can upload data to the FTP server, but only the third party can access it once it has been uploaded. This is a common approach to make it simpler for clients to create scripts to automatically transmit the data. To follow the data path, FakeUtility initially transmits the data unencrypted across their network via FTP and is encrypted right before it leaves the network by the VPN. The data is transmitted encrypted to FakeAnalysisCompany's network and is unencrypted at their VPN. Once inside FakeAnalysisCompany's network, the data is decrypted and transmitted unencrypted to the FTP server. This approach may be acceptable to your organizations since it mitigates the risk of transmitting sensitive data unencrypted across untrusted networks. However, there is still risk while the data is transmitted inside FakeUtility and FakeAnalysisCompany's internal networks.

> **TIP**
>
> During audits, systems will be checked for clear-text authentication protocols, such as Telnet and FTP. Even if the clear-text services are unused, the auditors will still report them as vulnerabilities. Either remove or disable the clear-text services to prevent port scanners and network vulnerability scanners from reporting them as vulnerabilities.

Assessing the Third Party

Before agreeing to partner with a third party, your organization should assess their security posture since their security posture will soon affect your organization's security posture. As a minimum baseline, the third party should be required to implement the security controls that your organization has implemented. If your organization has a policy that explicitly disallows the use of clear-text protocols, the third party should not allow them either.

If possible, a security assessment of the third party should be performed to determine the level of risk that they will introduce to your organization. Although this request is not accepted very often, it never hurts to ask. Assuming your organization and the third party have executed a Non-Disclosure Agreement (NDA), the third party may be willing to provide the results of their last security assessment. However, keep in mind that the report you receive may be the fifth version where the vulnerabilities listed in the first version were remediated and subsequently removed from the report by the fifth version.

SAS 70

Statement on Auditing Standards No. 70 (SAS 70) is commonly used by third-party service providers to answer their client's questions regarding security. When the third party is asked a security-related question, the third party will usually refer their clients to their SAS 70, regardless of whether the answer is in the SAS 70 or not. SAS 70s can provide useful information to reassure your organization that the third party has implemented at least some security controls. However, you should keep in mind that SAS 70s are essentially marketing tools for the third party and they are generally written to convince you of how great that third party is.

SAS 70 is an audit performed by an independent certified public accountant (CPA) or firm, where the auditor issues an opinion on the internal controls of a service organization.[8] The important thing to note here is that an SAS 70 report will only provide analysis on the service organization's internal controls. A SAS 70 audit does not perform a gap analysis between the service organization's internal controls and a set of respected standard controls.[8] Thus, it still falls on the service organization's clients to determine whether the controls specified in the SAS 70 report cover all their expected security control requirements.

Securing the Third Party

The majority of the scenarios in this chapter refer to the third-party service provider introducing risk to an organization, usually a utility company. However, the utility company can provide just as much risk, if not more to the third party if that third party has not designed a secure enterprise. Third parties should treat their clients' networks as untrusted entities as well. Attacks can originate from their clients and they should be prepared to protect against that threat.

As a third party, you will most likely have more than one client (hopefully) and have a duty to protect your customers from each other. If a shared environment exists, which is highly advised against, the proper security controls should be in place to prevent clients accessing each others' data or clients gaining access to each others' networks. Specifically, access control, data segmentation, and authorization security controls must be implemented to ensure your client's protection.

SUMMARY

Third-party service providers can play a huge role in assisting utility companies and consumers achieve their goals with smart grids. In some cases, their services and products will make smart grids more secure. However, they may also increase the risk to each entity involved in the smart grid. Although personal relationships and business justifications may warrant a trusting relationship, the proper security controls must be in place to protect the utility company, the third party, the consumer, and any other entity involved.

Attackers are aware of third parties and will seek to abuse the trust between business partners. Companies often include their new relationships on the news sections of their Web sites, which allows for easy identification. If a determined attacker has been unsuccessful in obtaining direct access to their target, they will attempt to use the third parties as alternate routes to get to their original target.

Endnotes

1. PayPal. Mandatory PCI Compliance: with PayPal, it's easy [document on the Internet]. https://www.paypal.com/pcicompliance; [accessed 03.04.10].
2. PCI Security Standards Council, LLC. About the PCI Data Security Standard (PCI DSS) [document on the Internet]. https://www.pcisecuritystandards.org/security_standards/pci_dss.shtml; [accessed 03.04.10].
3. Google. Google PowerMeter API [document on the Internet]. http://code.google.com/apis/powermeter/; [accessed 03.04.10].
4. Microsoft. Microsoft Hohm Partner SDK Overview [document on the Internet]. http://msdn.microsoft.com/en-us/library/ee724276.aspx; [accessed 03.04.10].
5. Ford. FORD SYNC CONNECTS CAR WITH INTERNET: NEW WIFI RECEIVER, BUILT-IN WEB BROWSER, MOBILE HOTSPOT [document on the Internet]. http://media.ford.com/article_display.cfm?article_id=31705; [accessed 03.04.10].
6. Microsoft. Microsoft Online Privacy Statement [document on the Internet]. http://privacy.microsoft.com/en-us/default.mspx; [accessed 04.04.10].
7. Security Focus. Slammer worm crashed Ohio nuke plant network [document on the Internet]. Kevin Poulsen; http://www.securityfocus.com/news/6767; 2003 [accessed 08.02.10].
8. SAS 70 FAQ'S [document on the Internet]. Scott Coolidge; http://sas70.com/sas70_faqs.html; [accessed 20.05.10].

Mobile Applications and Devices

INFORMATION IN THIS CHAPTER

- Why Mobile Applications?
- Platforms
- Trust
- Attacks
- Securing Mobile Devices
- Secure Mobile Applications

From providing data access to allowing remote control of systems, mobile applications will play a large role in the smart grid. As mobile devices continue to grow in popularity, consumers and utility personnel alike will integrate mobile devices more with their daily lives and use them to interact with smart grids. As a result, attackers view mobile devices as higher value targets.

Mobile devices will access smart grid resources through mobile applications designed specifically for mobile devices. However, these mobile applications will be attacked by every type of device capable of accessing the applications. Since most of the mobile applications will be accessible via the Internet, attackers will be able to use any type of device to attack these applications. This chapter will describe the possible attacks against mobile applications and mobile devices, and then explore how to protect these applications and devices.

WHY MOBILE APPLICATIONS?

Cell phones and other mobile devices have become prevalent in today's society. At the end of February 2010, comScore (www.comscore.com) estimated that roughly 234 million Americans (aged 13 years or older) were mobile subscribers.[1] Thus, mobile devices provide a convenient platform that utility companies can utilize to distribute energy consumption information to their consumers in a manner that consumers are comfortable with. Additionally, mobile devices will allow consumers to rapidly adapt to consumption information by enabling consumers to change their energy consumption from anywhere.

Although smart grid functionality will allow utility companies to remotely diagnose and fix most problems in electric grids, there will still be situations that require employees to physically visit the location of the problem. Mobile devices will enable these employees to stay connected with their organization's network and resources while out in the field diagnosing and fixing issues. Some of these devices will be able to interact flawlessly with existing applications; however, some devices will require applications specifically designed to allow access from mobile devices.

PLATFORMS

Mobile application developers seeking to reach the broadest audience will have to support multiple platforms. The following list contains some of the more common mobile platforms:

- Cell phones (smart and regular)
- Mobile Internet devices (MID)
- Portable media players (PMPs)
- Laptops
- Netbooks
- Ultra mobile personal computers (UMPC)
- Tablet PCs

From a functionality standpoint, developing mobile applications for mobile platforms is traditionally difficult due to how varied the devices are. The application will need to display correctly on devices ranging from smart phones with three-inch screens to laptops with 17-inch screens. Similarly, the security requirements for these platforms will vary depending on the specifications for each supported mobile device.

TRUST

Chapter 9, "Third-Party Services," discussed the trust relationships between utility companies and third-party service providers, and this chapter will describe the trust relationship between the application developers and the consumers. However, in this case, the consumers will be taking a further leap of faith when using the mobile applications. For the most part, the consumers will just click the **I Agree** button and blindly accept the developer's terms of service.

EPIC FAIL

Have faith in consumers spending the time to make informed decisions regarding what applications to install? Consider the Lose/Lose video game (www.stfj.net/art/2009/loselose/), developed by Zach Gage, as an example. The video game closely resembles Space Invaders, but with one important difference. For every alien space ship the user destroys, the video game deletes a file in the user's home directory.[2] On his Web site, Zach clearly warns that the application will permanently delete files. Additionally, when you start the video game, it will warn the user that killing the alien ships will permanently delete files on the hard drive. Yet, on the video game's Web site, the list of high scorers contains over a thousand players.

Trusting Strangers

Would you trust a stranger with your online banking password? If not, why would you trust an application developed by a stranger with your online banking password? Without performing a source code review of the application, how can a consumer be assured their information will not be compromised? The application could provide a back door that allows the malicious developer to access the consumer's mobile device remotely or the application could be sending data to the developer's malicious server. From a smart grid perspective, would you provide a stranger with a key to your house to adjust your thermostat's setting to reflect changing electric prices? If not, why would you trust an application developed by a stranger with the password to control smart devices in your home?

One argument to trust the application is that you trust the parent company to provide the proper oversight, as well as the dozens of strangers who have posted reviews. Let's take Apple's iTunes (www.apple.com/itunes/) App Store as an example, although Google's Android Market (www.android.com/market/) and BlackBerry's App World (http://na.blackberry.com/eng/services/appworld/) could be used in this example as well. Most consumers have grown to trust Apple through using iTunes to download music, movies, and television shows. With the tremendous success of their iPhone, iPod Touch, and iPad, developers have created an overwhelming number of applications for these mobile devices. However, Apple does not blindly allow any application to be distributed through their App Store. For example, Apple has prohibited applications that include sexual content and has pretty thoroughly rejected or removed most applications with sexual content on that basis.[3] So how thoroughly has Apple screened the applications to prevent malicious applications from being distributed in the App Store? Although consumers can rest assured that any respectable company would remove malicious applications, finding sexually explicit material in an application is a lot easier than finding back doors in an application. Performing a thorough security assessment of each application would be too time consuming and thus unrealistic. So the question then changes from is there an app for that to is that app secure, and should you trust the new smart grid mobile applications on your device?

Code Signing

Code signing is one method the software industry has used to address the issue of trust with applications downloaded from the Internet. Code signing uses digital signatures to confirm the authenticity and integrity of the application. Specifically, the author of the application will digitally sign the executable(s) using their private encryption key, or signing key, and any recipients of the executable can use either the author's public key or a certificate authority (CA) to validate the signature. Theoretically, this method would prevent anyone from tampering with the application, which should instill trust in the user.

> **NOTE**
>
> A digital signature is a cryptographic transformation that allows the verification of origin authentication, data integrity, and signatory nonrepudiation.[4] For more information on digital signatures, NIST FIPS PUB 186-3 provides a very detailed perspective on how digital signatures work. If you are unfamiliar with digital signatures, or public key infrastructure (PKI) in general, a beginner's guide to PKI can be found at: http://articles.techrepublic.com. com/5100-10878_11-5839988.html.

Although code signing can help mitigate the risk involved with downloading applications from the Internet, the risk is not completely eliminated. It is important to note that code signing does not prevent the original developer from inserting malicious code into their application. Additionally, the user needs to trust that the developer has protected their private encryption key. If a third party has compromised the developer's private key, then that third party would be able to tamper with the application and digitally sign the executable as the original developer.

As a real-world example of code signing, iPhones require all applications to be signed by Apple.[5] Thus, developers will need to request a signing certificate from Apple before their application can run on iPhones and be distributed in the App Store. So in this scenario, Apple acts as the CA, who can issue and revoke signing certificates. If an application is later determined to be malware, Apple could revoke the signing certificate for that developer and application to prevent their application from further spreading. Additionally, Apple could refuse to issue further signing certificates to that developer, effectively banning that developer from distributing more malware through the App Store.

Apple's code signing technique is susceptible to attacks, though. At the 2010 CanSecWest conference, Halvar Flake compromised an iPhone in the Pwn2Own contest on the first day using an exploit developed by Vincenzo Iozzo and Ralf-Philipp Weinmann.[5] The attack was performed by browsing a malicious Web site on the iPhone, which forced the iPhone to disclose the contents of its SMS database.[5] The exploit circumvents the code signing security control by using return-oriented programming techniques, which manipulate the function call stack to convert valid code into a malicious payload.[5]

ATTACKS

Mobile applications and devices will be targets in the smart grid. Attackers generally take the path of least resistance to achieve their goal, and mobile applications provide an easily accessible target. Attacks against certain mobile devices, such as cell phones and PMPs, have been limited in the past; however, this will dramatically change as their integration into society and level of connectivity continue to increase.

Why Attack the Handset?

Mobile devices, such as laptops, netbooks, and tablet PCs, generally run traditional operating systems, applications, and share the same connection speeds as their nonmobile variants. Thus, the reasons for attacking these devices should not be a surprise. Cell phones, MIDs, and PMPs have only recently become major targets for attackers. Faster Internet connections and the sensitive data now stored on these types of devices will compel attackers to consider them as better targets.

Cell phones used to store a very small amount of information, including names and phone numbers, which provided little to attackers. The same can be said for PMPs, which would traditionally store media files and maybe some personal information about the owner. However, these devices have been transformed into multipurpose computers that can perform the same functions as other mobile devices such as laptops. The following list contains examples of what can be found on mobile devices:

- VPN keys
- Corporate e-mail passwords
- Authentication tokens
- GPS location
- Sensitive information cached by applications

Additionally, most cell phones and PMPs will sync with other devices, such as laptops or desktops. So, if an attacker compromises a cell phone or a PMP, they could use that compromised device to attack the system it syncs with.[6] When the user plugs in the device or connects it to the host system wirelessly, the device could compromise the host system's operating system.[6] As a recent example, consider the incident where Vodafone was shipping HTC Magic cell phones with malware pre-installed.[7] Specifically, when a user connected their new phone to their computer, the phone would attempt to install a Mariposa bot client, as well as a Confiker and Lineage password stealing program onto their computer.[7]

SMS

Short Message Service (SMS) messages are often seen as harmless text messages; however, attacks can be carried out through the SMS messaging systems on cell phones. For example, Charlie Miller and Collin Mulliner demonstrated at the Black Hat (www.blackhat.com) USA 2009 conference an attack against iPhones using malicious SMS messages.[8] By sending specially crafted SMS messages, an attacker could obtain complete control over the iPhone.[8] Additionally, further research showed that other cell phones were also partially vulnerable to this same attack.[8]

E-mail

If an attack can occur via SMS, then attacks will also occur over e-mail. E-mail attacks targeting mobile devices may take the same form as the example SMS attack; however, they will also take other forms, such as phishing attacks that attempt to spoof messages from the utility companies in order to get sensitive information out of their targets.

NOTE

Other variants of phishing attacks include spear phishing and whaling attacks. Spear phishing refers to phishing attacks that are targeted at certain groups. So, for example, the attacker would first attempt to identify a group of e-mail addresses for a specific utility company and then craft an e-mail that spoofs that particular utility company, thus, improving the likelihood of success in their attack. Whaling attacks are similar to spear phishing except that they further refine the target list to senior executives or other high-profile targets.

As an example, consider a two-vector attack that targets a business for ransom or blackmail. The attacker initially compromises the smart meter that controls various smart devices (such as HVAC, cooling, and of course, power for the company's servers) within the company's data center. The attacker then sends e-mails to each member of the board of directors for the company, whose e-mail addresses are listed publicly on the company's Web site. The e-mails state that if the company does not pay the attacker $5 million (or some appropriate amount), the attacker will turn off power to the mission critical systems, increase the temperature to unsafe levels, and wreak havoc with the HVAC. The company's backup power generators may provide temporary support, but will the board want to risk the company's business operations on that chance?

Malicious Web Sites

Mobile Web browsers can be attacked just like traditional Web browsers, thus, following links sent via e-mail on your cell phone does not provide any more protection than on your desktop. Most attackers will create malicious Web sites that target the broadest audience, which usually ends up being desktop Web browsers such as Internet Explorer or Safari. However, an attacker who is determined to target your mobile device will be able to setup a malicious Web site to compromise mobile Web browsers.

Physical

When discussing threats to mobile devices, the physical security threat usually rises to the top of the list. By their very nature, mobile devices will go outside the protective physical security layers of fences, security guards, and security cameras. Thus, these mitigating controls will cease to reduce the risk of physical security threats.

The primary physical security threat to mobile devices will be theft. Mobile devices are already seen as a target for thieves for their resale potential, but attackers will also view these devices as methods to bypass perimeter security controls. As an example, consider utility company maintenance workers who spend most of their days out in the field-fixing issues that cannot be fixed remotely, such as a downed power line. The maintenance worker carries around a laptop with an internal 3G wireless card that provides Internet access over a cellular network. The maintenance worker connects to the utility company's network through the corporate VPN to check their e-mail and check the sensor networks that detect when there is a problem within the electric grid. When the maintenance worker arrives at the downed power line, he leaves the laptop in the car. If an attacker can steal the laptop that is still connected to the VPN, then he has most likely gained initial access to internal resources in that organization. Hopefully, the organization has compensating controls that would prevent unrestricted access to the internal network from a VPN connection, but the attacker would still have gained an access point to that organization.

From a consumer perspective, consider the upcoming Chevy Volt OnStar mobile application as another example. Mobile phone applications are currently being developed for the iPhone, BlackBerry, and Android platforms, in addition to a Web interface.[9] These mobile applications will allow Chevy Volt owners to remotely control the following features:

- Display charge status
- Provide flexibility to "Charge Now" or schedule charge timing
- Display percentage of battery charge level, electric, and total ranges
- Allow owners to manually set grid-friendly charge mode for off-peak times when electricity rates are lowest
- Send text or e-mail notifications for charge reminders, interruptions, and full charge
- Show miles per gallon, EV miles and miles driven for last trip and lifetime
- Remotely start the vehicle to precondition the interior temperature
- Unlock/lock the car doors[9]

The application integrates nicely into the smart grid goal to reduce consumer energy consumption during peak times by allowing the owner to set the charging schedule to off-peak times. If an attacker were able to steal the device, they could wreak havoc on the owner. Consider the example of a Chevy Volt owner who lives in a warm place, such as Florida. During the summer, cars that are parked outside can reach unbearable temperatures that exceed 100 degrees Fahrenheit. So, the natural elements alone can cause damage to items inside the car. Then, consider if the attacker were to turn the car on remotely. The car will try to adjust the temperature to be comfortable, thus causing the battery and gas tank to drain. The attacker could continue to drain the battery by repeatedly turning on the car until the mobile application informs the attacker the battery is empty. Alternatively, the attacker could just use the mobile application's ability to unlock the doors and steal the car.

Mobile devices are often recycled, resold, or thrown away without properly removing sensitive information. EBay (www.ebay.com) has made selling these devices an easy transaction but if the information is not removed properly, the buyer could become access to the information and resources stored on the mobile device. According to a recent research survey, 40 percent of hard drives bought on eBay

Table 10.1 Sample secure deletion resources[12]

Tool	Device support	License type
Dariks boot and nuke (DBAN – www.dban.org/)	ATA/IDE, SATA	Free
Roadkill's datawipe (www.roadkil.net/)	ATA/IDE, SATA Flash	Free
Secure erase 4.0 http://cmrr.ucsd.edu/people/Hughes/SecureErase.shtml)	Solid-state drives (SSD)	Free
Wireless recycling (www.recellular.com/recycling/data_eraser/)	Cell phones	Free

contain sensitive information from their previous owners, including corporations and government agencies.[10] In 2009, data for a U.S. missile air defense system were discovered on a hard drive bought on eBay.[11]

TIP

The process to securely erase flash memory is different than erasing traditional storage devices and will most likely require different applications.[12] Alternatively, degaussing or physically destroying the device memory can also achieve the same goal. See Table 10.1 for a list of several examples of secure deletion tools.

SECURING MOBILE DEVICES

Mobile applications will mainly be developed to support access through two mediums: a mobile Web site and a client application installed on the mobile device. In either case, the mobile device will need to be protected to prevent unauthorized access to the mobile application. Traditional security controls can be extended to protect many mobile devices; however, new issues that arise from mobile devices will need to be addressed by additional security controls.

The following best-practice guides and tips have been developed for mobile device security:

- US-CERT Cyber Security Tip ST06-007: Defending Cell Phones and PDAs Against Attack – www.us-cert.gov/cas/tips/ST06-007.html
- US-CERT Cyber Security Tip ST05-017: Cybersecurity for Electronic Devices – www.us-cert.gov/cas/tips/ST05-017.html
- US-CERT Cyber Security Tip ST04-020: Protecting Portable Devices: Data Security – www.us-cert.gov/cas/tips/ST04-020.html
- NIST SP 800-124: Guidelines on Cell Phone and PDA Security – http://csrc.nist.gov/publications/nistpubs/800-124/SP800-124.pdf
- NIST SP 800-101: Guidelines on Cell Phone Forensics – http://csrc.nist.gov/publications/nistpubs/800-101/SP800-101.pdf

Traditional Security Controls

Most mobile devices can utilize the same controls as nonmobile devices, especially laptops and tablet PCs. Firewalls, host-based IDS/IPS, antivirus programs, and patch management programs can be extended to mobile devices to provide host-based protection; however, not every device will support these traditional security controls. Thus, additional security controls will need to be implemented to fill in the gaps where appropriate.

Secure Syncing

Certain portable devices, such as PMPs and cell phones, can be synced to a host system, which allows the user to manage the device via a management interface. As discussed earlier in the section "Why Attack the Handset" of this chapter, the device can be used to attack the host system or conversely, an infected host system could attack the mobile device. In order to carry out this type of attack, an attacker would exploit the automatic actions that occur when a user connects their mobile device to the host system. In Microsoft Windows, these features are called Autorun and AutoPlay. Autorun starts programs automatically when a device is inserted or connected to a computer, and AutoPlay can be configured to automatically select a program to start based on the type of media inserted into a computer.[13] Generally speaking, these features should be disabled in a corporate environment, especially considering Conficker and other malware have recently exploited this functionality.[14] Instructions on how to disable these features are provided in the following Microsoft Support article: http://support.microsoft.com/kb/967715. Other operating systems have similar features and should be disabled if at all possible.

Disk Encryption

Sensitive data, such as credit card numbers or social security numbers, should always be encrypted. It does not matter if the data is sitting on a desktop inside the utility company's office building or on a laptop that is taken home by an employee every night. However, since mobile devices tend to leave the physical security barrier of most office buildings, the need for full disk encryption on mobile devices is greater. Unfortunately, there is not a full disk encryption solution for every mobile device. So, mitigating controls such as requiring any sensitive data to be stored inside an encrypted file container or prohibiting the storage of sensitive data on mobile devices, such as cell phones, can help mitigate the risk.

TOOLS

TrueCrypt (www.truecrypt.org) is a free, open-source tool that provides support for encrypted file containers, partitions, and full disk encryption. The full disk encryption is only supported on Windows; however, the other features are supported on Windows, Mac OS X, and numerous Linux distributions.

Screen Lock

Most mobile devices can be configured to require a username/password combination, PIN, or some other form of authentication credential to be entered before granting access to the device. From an organization's perspective, mobile devices should follow the policy that covers screen locking. Typically, this policy dictates the following:

- Screen is automatically locked after 5 to 15 minutes of inactivity
- User will manually lock the screen when leaving the system unattended
- Authentication is required to unlock the screen

For mobile devices, such as cell phones and handhelds, these settings are usually configurable; however, the management is more difficult. On Windows systems, group policy can be set to automatically configure the device to implement the screen lock policy. Other devices do not support centralized management and must be configured manually. Additionally, some devices are hard to type on and will frustrate users who need to type in a complex password. Thus, some users may choose a password/PIN that is easier to type ... and of course easier to guess.

Screen locking on mobile devices can be defeated by attackers in multiple ways and should not be solely relied upon. For example, some touch screen mobile devices pose a risk due to finger smudges. Oil from the user's fingers can create a fingerprint trail that reveals the characters of the password/PIN. An attacker could then try the different combinations of the characters to unlock the device. If the device is configured to use an unlock pattern to unlock the screen, then it can be even easier for the attacker. For example, Android phones can be configured to use an unlock screen that displays nine dots on the touch screen, and the user must draw a pattern with the nine dots to unlock the screen.[15] The pattern can be any series of lines with the following constraints:

- Between four and nine dots must be used
- A dot can only be used once
- A dot cannot be crossed, unless it has already been used
- A line between dots can be horizontal, vertical, diagonal, or similar to the way a chess knight piece moves[16]

Figures 10.1 through 10.4 provide example unlock patterns that comply with these constraints. Considering users routinely choose poor passwords, the pattern chosen will most likely be a simple line that has two distinct end points, which is illustrated in Figures 10.1 and 10.2. For the examples in this chapter, consider an end point to be a point with only one line connected to it. In Figure 10.1, the points in the upper left corner and the bottom right corner would be considered end points. If drawing the pattern leaves a smudge trail on the screen, there will only be two possible unlock combinations for Figures 10.1 and 10.2. In this scenario, the attacker simply needs to start at one end point and traverse the line, or smudge trail, until they have reached the other end point. If that does not work, the only other possible combination is to follow the line in reverse. Even if the user chooses a more complex pattern, such as those

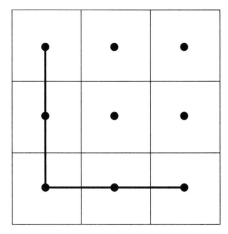

FIGURE 10.1

Simple android unlock pattern.

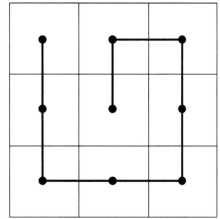

FIGURE 10.2

Simple android unlock pattern using all nine points.

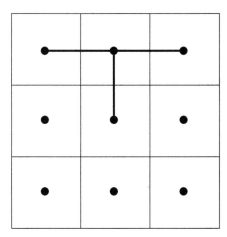

FIGURE 10.3

More complex android unlock pattern with three potential end points.

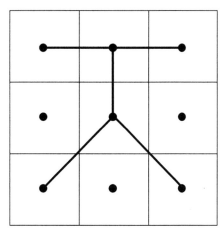

FIGURE 10.4

More complex android unlock pattern with four potential end points.

illustrated in Figures 10.3 and 10.4, the number of distinct end points will not increase significantly. For example, the pattern in Figure 10.3 has three potential end points and has only six possible unlock patterns. Thus, drawing the pattern may leave a smudge trail that has only a few different combinations. The pattern in Figure 10.4 is a little more complex with 4 potential end points and 24 possible unlock patterns; however, performing 24 combinations would still not take a very long time.

Wiping the Device

Mitigating the attacks described in the section "Screen Lock" can be done by securely erasing all the data on the mobile device after a defined number of unsuccessful authentication attempts. This number is usually set to be between five and 10. Setting this number to less than five would be ill advised since users tend to mistype their password on the smaller keyboards of mobile devices.

Additionally, the ability to remotely wipe the mobile device will help mitigate the risk of theft. Several commercial solutions exist that will enable administrators to remotely wipe the mobile device after it has been reported lost or stolen. Additionally, some of these solutions also provide a phone-home function that attempts to alert the owners of the device's location via coordinates provided by a GPS signal.

WARNING

Wiping the device can help mitigate the risk of several attack vectors, but should only be considered a last resort security control. In the situation where the device is remotely wiped, the attacker will have time between when they stole the device and when the owner reports the device stolen to obtain the sensitive information stored on the host. Thus, wiping the mobile device may only remove that copy of the sensitive information. Each security control discussed in this chapter should be part of a defense in depth approach to security.

Recovery

Some attackers may not be interested accessing the sensitive information and only want to cause damage by taking their anger out on your property. Additionally, the attacker may be the mobile device owner's dog that causes the owner to trip and smash the mobile device. In a more common scenario though, utility company maintenance workers may need to work during harsh weather storms that batter the mobile devices with rain and debris.

Regardless of the scenario, there will be instances where the data on the mobile device becomes inaccessible. Recovering the data may be possible, but if the organization or consumer was maintaining backups of the mobile devices, they may not need to go through the often-painstaking process of trying to recover data from a corrupt storage disk. For cell phones and PMPs, most syncing applications provide the functionality to backup the mobile device to the host system. Users who take advantage of this functionality will be grateful when their mobile device's data is deleted or becomes inaccessible.

Forensics

Forensics is a difficult process on even nonmobile systems, but one thing that can help an investigation process is by keeping detailed logs. Access to sensitive data should be logged to assist the forensics process in the case of an incident.

Although not every mobile device will have logging capabilities, those that do should be enabled. For more information on forensics for mobile devices, please see NIST SP 800-101: Guidelines on Cell Phone Forensics.

Education

Users are almost always the weakest link in security, which is why educating mobile device users is so important. Mobile devices are stolen frequently when an owner leaves them in the car to buy a cup of coffee or go to the bathroom. Thus, regular training on at least an annual basis should be done to reinforce the importance of security awareness, which includes the following:

- Never leave the mobile device out of reach or sight in an untrusted environment
- Manually lock the screen, logout, or shut down the mobile device
- Do not visit untrusted Web sites on the mobile device or open messages from unknown e-mail addresses or phone numbers
- Backup the device regularly

SECURE MOBILE APPLICATIONS

In most cases, mobile applications are developed to be an interface to the standard application. The mobile application sits between the standard application and the mobile client, and it handles communications between the mobile client and the standard application. There are, of course, exceptions where a mobile application is developed independently, but the security controls will remain the same.

Mobile Application Security Controls

One of the biggest mistakes that mobile application developers make is assuming that only mobile devices will interact with the mobile application. Assuming the mobile application server is network accessible, any system with access to the network will be able to attack that application server. So, for example, let's consider the Chevy Volt OnStar mobile applications again. Users will be able to use an iPhone, Black-Berry, Droid, or most mobile Web browsers to remotely control certain functions in their Chevy Volt car from anywhere.[9] In order to provide this level of access, the mobile application server(s) will be Internet accessible. Thus, any system with an Internet connection will be able to attack that application server.

Mobile applications will need to be able to defend against traditional application attacks, including those described in Chapter 7, "Attacking the Utility Companies." The following resources provide detailed information regarding how to develop secure applications:

- Open Web Application Security Project (OWASP) – www.owasp.org
- Web Application Security Consortium (WASC) – www.webappsec.org

> **WARNING**
>
> The OWASP Top 10 (www.owasp.org/index.php/Category:OWASP_Top_Ten_Project) can be used as a good starting point to understand the types of attacks that the mobile applications will face. Many organizations use the OWASP Top 10 as the only criteria for assessing their application security posture and only concern themselves with the ten items in the list. The OWASP Top 10 is intended to provide awareness on the top 10 Web application security flaws,[17] thus it is not intended to be a comprehensive list.

Encryption

When developing mobile applications, it is tempting to offload encryption to the network provider. So, for example, if the developers intend to support only cell phones, they may make the justification that the cellular network will encrypt the data in transit, thus implying that SSL will be a waste of resources. However, Chapter 7, "Attacking the Utility Companies," discussed attacks against encryption used in GSM networks. Additionally, a large number of cell phones now include Wi-Fi radios, so there is no assurance that cell phones will even be using the cellular networks to communicate with the mobile application server. Making these types of assumptions can lead to critical vulnerabilities in applications.

SUMMARY

Mobile applications and devices will be used extensively to increase the functionality and reach of smart grids, which is also why they will introduce greater risk to smart grids. They provide a conduit for attackers to easily bypass an organization's physical and virtual perimeter security controls. Additionally, they will provide attackers with another attack vector to compromise user's security.

Due to the extensive variety of platforms, applications, and inherent mobility, mobile devices are more difficult to manage and oftentimes lack centralized management capabilities. This leads to a greater reliance on individual users to implement secure practices, such as screen locking and regularly making backups. However, the applications will face familiar attacks that organizations should already be prepared to face. By implementing the security controls discussed in this chapter, organizations can greatly reduce the risk that mobile applications and devices present to their security posture.

Endnotes

1. comScore. comScore reports February 2010 U.S. Mobile subscriber market share [document on the Internet]. www.comscore.com/Press_Events/Press_Releases/2010/4/comScore_Reports_February_2010_U.S._Mobile_Subscriber_Market_Share; 2010 [accessed 11.04.10].

2. Raywood D. Secure Computing Magazine. Online game disguised as space invaders hits mac users with trojan [document on the Internet]. www.securecomputing.net.au/News/159811,online-game-disguised-as-space-invaders-hits-mac-users-with-trojan.aspx; 2009 [accessed 19.05.10].

3. VanHemert K. Gizmodo. Apple says no more titillating apps, period [document on the Internet]. www.gizmodo.com.au/2010/02/apple-says-no-more-titillating-apps-period/; 2010 [accessed 12.04.10].

4. NIST. FIPS PUB 186-3 Digital Signature Standard (DSS) [document on the Internet]. http://csrc.nist.gov/publications/fips/fips186-3/fips_186-3.pdf; 2009 [accessed 20.05.2010].

5. Goodin D. The Register. iPhone, IE, Firefox, Safari get stomped at hacker contest [document on the Internet]. www.theregister.co.uk/2010/03/25/pwn2own_2010_day_one/; 2010 [accessed 20.05.10].

6. Garfinkel S. CSO. Attack of the iPods! [document on the Internet]. www.csoonline.com/article/220868/Attack_of_the_iPods_; 2006 [accessed 12.04.10].

7. Zorz Z. HelpNet Security. Mariposa bot distributed by Vodafone's infected phone [document on the Internet]. www.net-security.org/secworld.php?id=8991; 2010 [accessed 20.05.10].

8. Mills E. CNET. Researchers attack my iPhone via SMS [document on the Internet]. http://news.cnet.com/8301-27080_3-10299378-245.html; 2010 [accessed 29.07.10].

9. General Motors. Chevrolet and onstar give volt owners 24/7 connection and control via wireless smartphone application [document on the Internet]. http://gm-volt.com/p/OnStar%20Mobile%20release%20CES.pdf; 2010 [accessed 05.04.10].

10. Mearian L. Computerworld. Survey: 40% of hard drives bought on eBay hold personal, corporate data [document on the Internet]. www.computerworld.com/s/article/9127717/Survey_40_of_hard_drives_bought_on_eBay_hold_personal_corporate_data; 2009 [accessed 20.05.10].

11. Llewellyn G. The Independent. US missile data found on eBay hard drive [document on the Internet]. www.independent.co.uk/news/world/americas/us-missile-data-found-on-ebay-hard-drive-1680529.html; 2009 [accessed 20.05.10].

12. Soper M. MaximumPC. Leave No Trace: how to completely erase your hard drives, ssds and thumb drives [document on the Internet]. www.maximumpc.com/article/howtos/how_complete_destroy_your_data; 2010 [accessed 12.04.10].

13. Microsoft. How to disable the AutoRun functionality in Windows [document on the Internet]. http://support.microsoft.com/kb/967715; 2009 [accessed 13.04.10].

14. Microsoft. Autorun changes in Windows 7 [document on the Internet]. http://blogs.technet.com/srd/archive/2009/04/28/autorun-changes-in-windows-7.aspx; 2009 [accessed 13.04.10].

15. Arrington M. TechCrunch. Android's Login Is Cool, But Is It Secure? [document on the Internet]. http://techcrunch.com/2008/10/12/androids-login-is-cool-but-is-it-secure/; 2008 [accessed 13.04.10].

16. Beust C. Otaku, Cedric's weblog. Android's Locking Pattern [document on the Internet]. http://beust.com/weblog2/archives/000497.html; 2008 [accessed 20.05.10].

17. OWASP. OWASP Top Ten Project [document on the Internet]. www.owasp.org/index.php/Category:OWASP_Top_Ten_Project; 2010 [accessed 13.04.10].

Social Networking and the Smart Grid

11

INFORMATION IN THIS CHAPTER

- The Smart Grid Gets Social
- Social Networking Threats
- Smart Grid Social Networking Security Checklist

With Facebook reaching the level of the second most visited site on the Internet, it was a foregone conclusion that the smart grid would find a home on social networking Web sites.[1] Ranging from Twitter.com to Blogger.com, the smart grid is already leveraging benefits of social networking. In this chapter, we will take a look at how smart grid technologies have integrated with social networking sites, as well as discuss any associated security risks.

THE SMART GRID GETS SOCIAL

The push for using social networking in the smart grid comes from several factors. One of the goals of smart grids is to keep customers constantly informed of how much energy they are using. With more and more people using social networking services, social networking will provide a medium that customers are comfortable with. There are also business drivers for utilizing popular social networking sites. Marketing departments for technology vendors will be able to advertise broad functionality support and utility companies will be able to advertise their use of social networking.

By far, Twitter and Facebook have become the social networking sites of choice amongst smart grid technologies. Facebook provides a massive user base while also allowing for custom application development, while Twitter provides the perfect platform for micro updates. Let us now evaluate some of the current uses of both Twitter and Facebook by smart grid technologies.

Twitter

For the three of you reading this book who are unaware of what Twitter is, here is how it present itself to the world:

> *Twitter is a real-time information network powered by people all around the world that lets you share and discover what's happening now.*[2]

Twitter is a micro-blogging Web site that allows users to "tweet" messages of up to 140 characters at a time. Tweets can be made from nearly any type of device that is connected to the Internet via countless client applications or directly via Twitter's Web site. Users of Twitter can follow specific individuals, organizations, groups, or search for specific terms within tweets. Hash tags (#) are used to associate tweets with specific events. For example, #syngress is the hash tag for the publisher of this book.

Part of the reason for Twitter's success has been the ability for its users to follow events in real time via the information posted by other users. Such real-time information sharing makes Twitter a perfect tool for smart grid technologies.

Tweeting Energy Usage

At the time of writing this chapter, a simple Google query of "site: twitter.com kWh usage" produced over 128 unique results. I am sure that by the time you are reading this book that number will significantly increase. Let's take a look at some of the individuals and businesses who are utilizing Twitter to broadcast their energy consumption.

Andrew Jones, Managing Director of Alquist Consulting Ltd, has decided to utilize Twitter to demonstrate his organization's commitment to reducing their carbon footprint. Via their Twitter page, located at http://twitter.com/AlquistARJ, individuals can monitor Alquist's buildings' energy usage. Unlike many others who post tweets about energy consumption in kWh, Alquist's Twitter feed provides usage data based on costs. Alquist's tweets also take the consumption data available via the tweets to the next level by providing costs data via graphical representations posted to TwitPic.com. Figure 11.1 is a sample of Alquist's graphical representation of their energy consumption data.

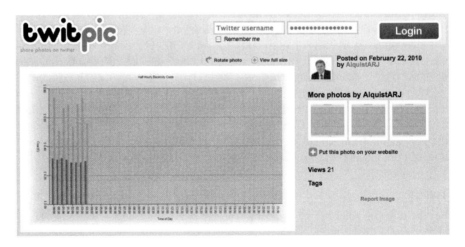

FIGURE 11.1

Alquist's energy consumption data in graph form.

Andy Stanford-Clark of IBM has utilized Twitter to provide real-time information on his home's energy usage. Beyond simply tweeting whether or not Andy has turned his outside lights on or off, his home posts other energy-related information such as the current electric meter reading, as shown below in Figure 11.2. But why stop at simply posting information? Andy certainly did not. Through custom software, Andy can actually turn the lights on or off through issuing commands online.

Andy's particular setup is more advanced than other smart grid social networking solutions, but provides a quick glimpse into the future of social networking and the smart grid. Simpler, more user-friendly solutions are currently available to the masses that allow them to tweet their energy usage. For more information, you can visit Andy's Web site located at http://stanford-clark.com/andy_house.html.

FIGURE 11.2

Andy Stanford-Clark's home Twitter feed.

Tweet-a-Watt

One of these solutions is called the "Tweet-a-Watt," shown in Figure 11.3. Although Tweet-a-Watts currently require some hardware hacking, they are relatively simple to build and set up. A Tweet-a-Watt consists of a P3 International "Kill-a-Watt" device, modified with XBee wireless adapters. The XBee wireless adapters utilize the Zigbee wireless technology and require the receiver to be plugged into an Internet-connected device. The XBee transmitter is connected to the Kill-a-Watt and sends energy usage data, in Kilowatt-hour, to the receiver. The receiver then uses the Internet-connected device to tweet the energy consumption information to Twitter.

> **NOTE**
>
> You can purchase a Do-It-Yourself Tweet-a-Watt kit from: www.adafruit.com/index.php?main_page=product_info&cPath=32&products_id=143&zenid=6d1306727167af57a11c948993e0bedc. Note that a Kill-a-Watt is not included in the kit. Kill-a-Watts can be found at your local hardware store or online at your favorite electronics store.

Not everyone is keen on the idea of the Tweet-a-Watt. Graham Winfrey of The Business Insider included the Tweet-a-Watt in his "Ten Dumbest Green

FIGURE 11.3

P3 International's Kill-a-Watt.

Courtesy of GadgetGrid.com

Gadgets"[3] list in December 2009. Winfrey does not elaborate on why he included the device in his list, but alludes to the fact that it is simply a way to brag about your green living. Perhaps he should have mentioned the privacy aspects of tweeting your energy consumption.

Smart Meter and Broadband Integration

In deregulated energy markets, consumers can choose from multiple utility companies for their energy needs. Usually, customers will choose their energy provider based on pricing and reliability. However, some companies are trying to use popular trends to compete in the energy market. One such utility company in Germany, Yello Strom (www.yellostrom.de/), has developed and sell its own smart meter that utilizes the consumer's home broadband connection.[4] This has allowed Yello Strom to develop consumer-centric applications, such as their Twitter application.

Essentially, the application works by creating a Twitter account for the smart meter. Then on a periodic basis (for example, every 10 minutes), the smart meter tweets the energy usage via the consumer's home broadband connection.[4] Most utility companies will send the data to the back office for processing first before being sent to service providers, which can lead to a significant delay.[4] Directly connecting the smart meter to the consumer's broadband connection will provide the information to the consumer much quicker.

Facebook

If only three of you reading this book have not heard of Twitter, then I suppose two of you do not know about Facebook. For those who do not know, Facebook is the Internet's top social networking site, according to Compete.com.[5] Since May 24, 2007, Facebook has allowed third parties to develop applications for its Web site that allow Facebook users to play games, share information, or even track energy usage.[6]

PICOwatt

Tenrehte Technologies, a Rochester, New York-based startup, is one of the first to develop a Facebook application that will allow users to remotely monitor and control their energy usage. Tenrehte's application will utilize their PICOwatt technology, which consists of consumer products poised to hit the market before the utility companies deploy smart meters to the masses.

PICOwatts, shown in Figure 11.4, are Wi-Fi-enabled smart plugs that augment consumer's traditional power outlets. These smart plugs are essentially software-powered devices that provide real-time energy usage monitoring and device control. Theoretically, consumers will install PICOwatts throughout their homes and aggregate the data via PICOwatt's built-in Web server or via Tenrehte's Facebook application. PICOwatt users can then determine how much energy devices are using and decide when to turn devices on and off, in an attempt to lower their electric bills. At the time of writing this book, Tenrehte plans to release their PICOwatts in April 2010 at an anticipated price of under $125.[7]

FIGURE 11.4

Tenrehte Technologies PICOwatt.

> **NOTE**
>
> You can get a sneak peak at the monitoring and control capabilities of PICOwatts by visiting Tenrehte's demo Web site at http://airlock.tenrehte.com/aps/watt/PICOwatt.cgi?btnG=PICOstatus. Here, you will be able to view such information at device status, energy usage, pricing information, as well as interface with the command and control options that would allow device startups and shutdowns, as well as other potential event operations.

SmartSync

SmartSync, Inc, a Jackson, Mississippi-based smart grid infrastructure company, is also utilizing social networking to provide energy usage monitoring to the masses. In a partnership announced on August 27, 2009, SmartSync and the University of Mississippi will utilize SmartSync's Smart Meters to "reduce the power consumption of campus buildings while publishing real-time results for the general public on Facebook, Twitter and RSS feeds."[8]

In its press release, SmartSync stated that each building at the University of Mississippi to be equipped with SmartSync Smart Meters will have its own Facebook profile page. These profile pages will provide interested parties with information such as energy consumption, complete with comparative analysis. The initial deployment of SmartSync's Smart Meters at the University of Mississippi included 16 smart meters. Additional deployments are being considered. Figure 11.5 shows the University of Mississippi's Lyceum building's Facebook profile page, complete with daily energy consumption data and address.

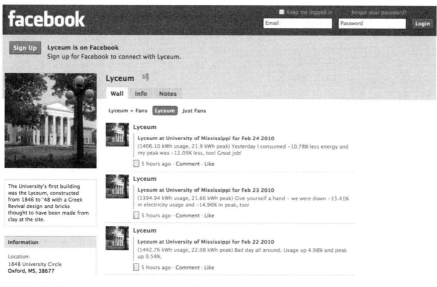

FIGURE 11.5

The University of Mississippi's Lyceum Building's Facebook profile page.

Source: www.facebook.com/pages/Oxford-MS/Lyceum/117754575778. Shown for educational purposes.

In their press release, SmartSync noted that

Once registered online at www.olemiss.edu/green, students, faculty, building administrators and others will be able to access UM's smart meter data and receive updates on UM's energy usage …[8]

As you can see by the screenshot in Figure 11.5, this information is available to anyone, not just "registered users." You can view the University of Mississippi's Lyceum building's Facebook profile page yourself by visiting www.facebook.com/pages/Oxford-MS/Lyceum/117754575778.

The University of Colorado has also jumped on the Facebook bandwagon by creating a profile page for its Fiske Planetarium. This profile page, located at www.facebook.com/pages/Boulder-CO/Fiske-Planetarium/138531010808, is very similar to the University of Mississippi's Lyceum building's profile page. Although no information validating that the Fiske Planetarium utilizes SmartSync's technologies was available to the authors of this book, we will let you make your own decision by comparing a screenshot of the University of Colorado's Fiske Planetarium's Facebook profile page, shown in Figure 11.6, to the University of Mississippi's Lyceum building's Facebook profile page, shown in Figure 11.5.

WattsUp

Other consumer-based Facebook applications exist, including Derek Foster's WattsUp. WattsUp allows Facebook users to share their home's energy usage

FIGURE 11.6

The University of Colorado's Fiske Planetarium's Facebook profile page.

Source: www.facebook.com/pages/Boulder-CO/Fiske-Planetarium/138531010808.

Shown for educational purposes.

with other WattsUp users. Foster developed the application in order to "raise awareness of energy consumption in the home which can have a positive impact on climate change. (The concepts driving creation of WattsUp are) social psychology elements such as peer-pressure and normative measurement between friends."[9]

Figure 11.7 is a screenshot of Derek's WattsUp energy usage. Ironically, it appears as though Derek is no longer using his WattsUp application to publish his home's energy usage.

WattsUp was designed to use DIY KYOTO's Wattson energy usage monitoring device. Wattson (Figure 11.8) consists of a transmitter and receiver (referred to by DIY KYOTO as the Display). The transmitter comes with a sensor clip that is connected to the main cables between your home's meter box and fuse box. Energy consumption information is then wirelessly transmitted to the receiver, which displays the information in both watts and monetary values. The receiver will change colors depending on your usage; blue for low energy usage, purple for average energy usage, and red for very high energy usage. Historical information, as well as the ability to send usage data to the WattsUp Facebook application, is captured via a USB connection to the receiver and DIY KYOTO's Holmes software. More information on the Wattson is available from www.diykyoto.com/uk/wattson/about, while the WattsUp Facebook application is available at www.facebook.com/apps/application.php?id=50473167243.

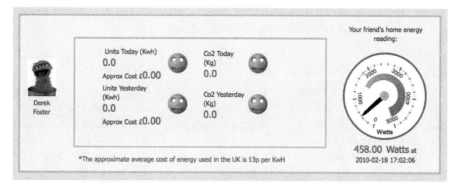

FIGURE 11.7

Derek Foster's WattsUp Facebook application.

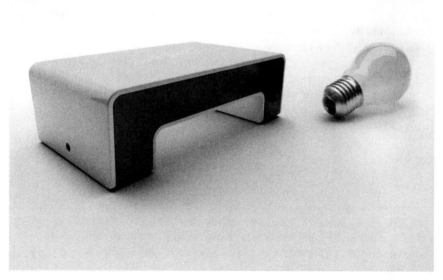

FIGURE 11.8

DIY KYOTO's Wattson.

SOCIAL NETWORKING THREATS

Now that we have discussed the use of social networking sites by some of the latest smart grid technologies, let us focus in on their associated threats. Ranging from simple information disclosure to the complete loss of control of a connected device, the use of social networking by smart grid technologies presents a wide range of threats with an equally large impact variance.

Information Disclosure

As we discussed in Chapter 2, "Threats and Impacts: Consumers," information disclosure is one of the largest threats associated with the smart grid. The integration of social networking sites simply increases this risk, as by their sheer nature, social networking sites were developed as a way to share information with others. Several recent social networking blunders have direct implications for smart grid technologies that utilize social networking.

On February 17, 2010, the Web site www.pleaserobme.com hit the blogosphere, opening the eyes of the masses to what the security community was already concerned about. Conceptualized and run by the folks at FortheHack.com, Please Rob Me aggregates Twitter information that suggests when people are not home. Specifically, the site relies on tweets of users of the Internet phenomena known as Foursquare (http://foursquare.com). Foursquare allows users to let their friends know their current location via smart phones that post to Twitter and Facebook. Figure 11.9 provides a sample of Foursquare users whose information has been captured by Please Rob Me.

Coincidently, the authors of this Web site had a similar idea to Please Rob Me, but ours was specifically tailored to people who tweet their energy usage on Twitter. As an experiment, Tony purchased three Tweet-a-Watt devices for his apartment, and Justin wrote a couple of perl scripts, utilizing Twitter's API, that would capture Tony's energy usage. The goal of the experiment was for Justin to be able to accurately determine when Tony was home, and when he was not, solely based on his energy usage. To determine the outcome of the experiment, Justin would call Tony when Justin believed that Tony was not home. Justin would only be able to call Tony five times over the course of one week. Before proceeding with the experiment, Justin believed that he would be 100 percent successful, or five correct out of five attempts, in determining when Tony was home or not. Tony, while believing that 100 percent accuracy was not unattainable, believed that Justin would be 80 percent successful, or four correct out of five attempts, in successfully identifying when Tony was not home. Justin reminded Tony that he could not alter his energy usage in an attempt to get Justin to wrongly identify when Tony was not home. Tony begrudgingly agreed.

To accomplish the task, Tony modified his three Tweet-a-Watts to send information to a local server running at his house. The server would capture the information from the three Tweet-a-Watts, aggregate them, and then post the information to Twitter in five-minute intervals. Unlike many of the previously noted examples of tweeting energy usage, Tony protected his apartment's Twitter account so that only Justin's server account could access the information.

Recent Empty Homes

<u>29 new opportunities</u>

 left home and checked in **about a minute ago**:
Monday, prepare for a beat down. (@ BURN World Headquarters)
http://4sq.com/6jvJ2v

 left home and checked in **about a minute ago**:
I'm at 古本市場 西大島駅前店. **http://4sq.com/9rhuP7**

 left home and checked in **about a minute ago**:
I'm at Admium (Computerweg 37, Amersfoort). **http://4sq.com/dgfthQ**

 left home and checked in **about a minute ago**:
... Four kids four unlawful one family. Good grief. (@ Gateway School for
Communication and Technology) **http://4sq.com/4RFvHI**

 left home and checked in **about a minute ago**:
I'm at ████████ (Lorraine St, Ann Arbor). **http://4sq.com
/cDgo6n**

 left home and checked in **about a minute ago**:
I'm at Caribou Coffee - Bloomington (Normandale Office Park) (8000
Norman Center Dr - Ste 140, Bloomington). **http://4sq.com/77m7bc**

FIGURE 11.9

PleaseRobMe.com sample screenshot.

Source: www.pleaserobme.com. Shown for educational purposes.

TIP

If you plan on jumping on the social networking/smart grid bandwagon, we recommend
creating a separate Twitter account for the dwellings or devices that you utilize. Then, just
like Tony did, protect the account to only allow those accounts you want to be able to
monitor your energy usage to do so. This will eliminate the risks we are highlighting here,
as well as those that gave rise to Please Rob Me.

Over the period of three weeks, Justin's perl scripts captured Tony's tweets, and massaged the data via several simple MySQL queries. Utilizing the information, Justin was able to determine profile estimates of Tony's energy usage. These profiles were as follows:

- **Home** – Energy usage was clearly above the mean energy usage, suggesting that Tony was using such high-energy devices as his heater, washer and dryer, dishwasher, and televisions.
- **Not Home** – Energy usage was clearly below the mean energy usage, suggesting that Tony was not using any high-energy devices as his heater, washer and dryer, dishwasher, or televisions.
- **Sleeping** – Energy usage was below the mean, but above the basement of his usage. This profile suggested Tony was only using the "bare" essentials of his house, such as his heater.
- **Unknown** – Energy usage was close to or at the mean of Tony's energy usage.

Simply having a reported energy usage that fell within one of the four aforementioned energy profiles did not simply mean that Tony was or was not home. Rather, in developing the experiment, we decided that we should include several additional criteria that should be met before Justin called Tony for one of his five attempts. The first additional criteria were that Tony's energy usage should fall into the same energy profile for more than 30 minutes. In other words, since Tony's setup would tweet his energy usage every five minutes, Justin's scripts should only alert him after six sequential tweets that fell within the "Not Home" energy profile. The second additional criteria would be the "common sense" factor. When Justin's scripts would alert him that Tony was potentially not home (meaning that Justin's server observed at least six sequential tweets that fell within the "Not Home" energy profile), Justin would manually review Tony's energy usage for the past hour or so. This previous information was reviewed to determine if there were any anomalies in Tony's energy usage that would suggest this was a false positive. Justin would also take into account the time of day and day of the week. During the day on weekdays and during the night on weeknights, were, for obvious reasons, the most likely times when Tony would not be home. If an alert was triggered during these times, Justin believed the likelihood that Tony was not home was high.

As a result of the experiment, Justin was able to successfully identify when Tony was not home five out of five times, or 100 percent, of the time. Tony believed that Justin may have chosen the most opportune times, that is, Friday nights and Sunday mornings, to make his five attempts, but Justin argued that a malicious person would capitalize on the same opportunities. Justin continued to argue that monitoring Tony's energy usage simply provided supplemental information that when aggregated with common sense (or the third criteria we previously covered) would increase the likelihood of success.

So what exactly can be learned from the author's experiment? Does tweeting your energy usage make you more vulnerable to robbery or other crimes? The authors believe that insecurely doing so does indeed make you more vulnerable;

however, the risk of someone using this information is very low. Although, this risk could be increased if someone like the folks at Please Rob Me integrate this type of monitoring. All said, the authors of this book do see the benefits of tweeting your energy usage, but want to reinforce the tip previously mentioned in this chapter: Make sure you protect your tweets and only allow users who you want to see this type of information to see it.

> **WARNING**
>
> A simple warning about using Twitter and Facebook. By default, many third-party Twitter and Facebook applications have you login using an insecure connection, such as HTTP. If you use any of these third-party applications to connect to Twitter or Facebook, make sure you are using a secure protocol to transmit login credentials or contact the application's author and request this functionality. Additionally, social networking sites are not without their own vulnerabilities and attackers see these sites as large targets. For more information on securing third-party services, Chapter 9, "Third-Party Services," describes how to mitigate the risk with third-party services.

SMART GRID SOCIAL NETWORKING SECURITY CHECKLIST

In an effort to safeguard end users who will utilize smart grid devices that integrate with social networking sites such as Facebook and Twitter, the authors of this book have developed a smart grid Social Networking Security Checklist. This checklist aims to provide end users with a set of basic controls that when implemented will provide end users with a security baseline. The smart grid Social Networking Security Checklist will continue to evolve, and the authors of this book recommend visiting this book's companion site, located at www.fyrmassociates.com/securingthesmartgrid, to view the latest version.

Before You Begin

Before you begin your smart grid/Social Networking device implementation, you must first understand what you attempt to gain from your implementation. Do you want to simply remotely monitor and control your devices or do you want to share your information with your friends, colleagues, or everyone. Determining what you hope to accomplish with your implementation will guide you in implementing the following controls.

Basic Controls

The smart grid Social Networking Security Checklist contains five categories for implementing basic security controls. These categories are as follows:

1. Identity
2. Authentication

3. Information sharing
4. Networking
5. Usage

Identity Controls

The following controls should be implemented to safeguard your smart grid/social networking device deployment.

- **Account Name** – Utilize an account name that does not easily identify you or your device. For example, if you setup a PICOwatt device, do not name your device "Justin-BedRoom-PicoWatt." Choose something less obvious like "JsPi1." Although this is a classic example of security through obscurity, it will prevent you from being identified by simple Google queries looking for smart grid devices that integrate with social networking sites. Additionally, avoid using your user e-mail address account ID. For example, if your e-mail address is jtothemototheho@gmail.com, do not name the device jtothemototheho.
- **Personal Information** – Do not post unnecessary information to the account. In particular, avoid entering location-based information into the account. If a Facebook page is setup for your smart device, you probably do not need to enter the city, state, or post a picture of the device.

Authentication Controls

- **Secure Login** – When your smart grid device connects to social networking sites, make sure that it is utilizing a secure protocol, such as HTTPS. A warning earlier in this chapter called out that some third-party applications utilize HTTP and not HTTPS to transmit your login credentials. Ensuring that you are utilizing a secure protocol when providing login credentials to social networking sites will help protect your device's social networking account. Additionally, ensure that the application transmits your session credentials securely as well. As long as your current login session is valid, your session credentials, such as a session cookie, are your login credentials.
- **Unique Password** – In addition to the standard complexity requirements, choose a unique password for each of the social networking accounts. Avoid using passwords that you use for other accounts, such as your e-mail account. If someone is able to compromise your e-mail account, they would then be able to access your social networking account.
- **Password Sharing** – Although the traditional recommendation of not sharing your password with other persons still applies, you should also not share your other account passwords with the social networking site. For example, Facebook allows you to enter your e-mail address and e-mail account password to automatically identify friends in your e-mail account's address book.
- **Security Questions** – Apply the same password security controls to the security questions. Some social networking sites will utilize security questions,

such as what is your mother's maiden name or what is your favorite restaurant, to provide an additional layer of security or to change your "forgotten" password. The problem is that this information can usually be obtained by reading your social networking profile. By choosing complex and unique answers (that are factually incorrect), you will be able to prevent someone from intelligently guessing the answer.

Information Sharing Controls

- **Privacy** – When you setup your smart grid device's social networking profile, make sure that you set it to "private." This will prevent anyone from viewing your smart grid devices information updates. Once you have configured the profile as "private," allow only the users (or accounts) you want to be able to view your smart grid device's information. For Facebook and Twitter, requests must be sent from the user account that would like to be able to view the smart grid device's updates.
- **Third-Party Application Sharing** – Avoid using any unnecessary third-party applications. Social networking sites highly encourage the development of application add-ons. When you attempt to use these add-ons, the applications will try to access the information in your profile, which may make your information accessible to the third party.

Networking

- **Segmentation** – When installing your smart grid device on your local area network, segment it from the rest of your home's network devices. This can be done through firewall access control lists or via switch virtual local area networks with access control lists. Segmenting your smart grid device will help prevent unauthorized access to the rest of your devices in the case that smart grid device is compromised.

Usage

- **Browsing** – When you are logged into the social networking account, avoid browsing to other social networking profiles or Web sites. Additionally, explicitly log out and close the browser before browsing to other Web pages. Restricting your browsing habits while logged in will help avoid cross-site request forgery attacks against your device's social networking profile.

SUMMARY

Social networking sites like Facebook and Twitter have forever changed the way that we use the Internet. Ubiquitous access to social networking sites has also forever changed the way that we utilize social networking sites. The marriage between smart grid devices and social networking sites is one that does make sense. However, precaution and constant monitoring of new and emerging threats must take precedence to ensure their marriage is a healthy one.

As with using social networking sites for the primary purpose, sharing information with other people, maintaining much of privacy and security is dependent on the end user. Utilizing smart grid devices that integrate with social networking sites will require additional maintenance and vigilance of end users in order to limit the risk associated with using these devices and services.

The risks associated with the smart grid and social networking sites are continually evolving. However, implementing basic controls will provide end users with a baseline security level. The authors of this book believe that the aforementioned smart grid Social Networking Security Checklist will enable end users to implement these basic controls and attain a baseline security level. However, as new functionality is added to smart grid devices and social networking sites, new threats and attacks will undoubtedly be introduced. Thus, the end user must remain vigilant by understanding these new threats and attacks and implementing the appropriate controls.

Endnotes

1. Alexa Internet, Inc. Alexa Top 500 Global Sites [document on the Internet], www.alexa.com/topsites; 2010 [accessed 01.03.10].
2. Twitter. About Us [document on the Internet], http://twitter.com/about; 2010 [accessed 01.03.10].
3. Business Insider, Inc. Ten Dumbest Green Gadgets [document on the Internet], www.businessinsider.com/the-ten-dumbest-green-gadgets-2009-12/wind-n-go-freedom-shaver-1; 2009 [accessed 01.03.10].
4. Earth2tech. The World's Coolest Utility: Yello Strom's Got Smart Meters That Tweet [document on the Internet], http://earth2tech.com/2009/07/02/the-worlds-coolest-utility-yello-stroms-got-smart-meters-that-tweet/; 2009 [accessed 01.03.10].
5. Compete, Inc. Social Networks: Facebook Takes Over Top Spot, Twitter Climbs [document on the Internet], http://blog.compete.com/2009/02/09/facebook-myspace-twitter-social-network/; 2009 [accessed 01.03.10].
6. TechCrunch. Facebook Launches Facebook Platform; They are the Anti-MySpace [document on the Internet], http://techcrunch.com/2007/05/24/facebook-launches-facebook-platform-they-are-the-anti-myspace/; 2007 [accessed 01.03.10].
7. CNET. Picowatt does smart grid without smart meter [document on the Internet]. CBS Interactive, http://ces.cnet.com/8301-31045_1-10429865-269.html; 2010 [accessed 01.03.10].
8. SmartSync, Inc. SmartSync Partners with the University of Mississippi to Lower Campus Power Consumption with Smart Meters and Social Networking tools [document on the Internet], www.smartsynch.com/news/082709.htm; 2009 [accessed 01.03.10].
9. Windows Developer Center. Facebook Developer Toolkit [document on the Internet]. Microsoft Corporation, http://msdn.microsoft.com/en-us/windows/ee384421.aspx; [accessed 01.03.10].

Attacking Smart Meters

12

INFORMATION IN THIS CHAPTER

- Open Source Security Testing Methodology Manual (OSSTMM)
- NIST Special Publication 800-42: Guideline on Network Security Testing

One of the strongest arguments made for securing smart meters is that consumers will have physical, and potentially logical, access to the smart meters. Although consumers had physical access to previous utility meters, these meters did not operate using technologies that consumers were familiar with or had ready access to. Because of the prevalence of these familiar technologies, smart meters can be treated like any other traditional target when applying security-testing methodologies to it.

In this chapter, we will review two of the most common security-testing methodologies and discuss how they can be applied to testing smart meters.

OPEN SOURCE SECURITY TESTING METHODOLOGY MANUAL (OSSTMM)

The first methodology that we will discuss and apply to testing the security of smart meters is the Institute for Security and Open Methodologies' (ISECOM) *Open Source Security Testing Methodology Manual* (OSSTMM). The Institute for Security and Open Methodologies was founded in January of 2001 as a nonprofit organization in the United States and Spain.[1] ISECOM aims to provide security awareness, research, certification, and business integrity solutions that are practical.[1]

ISECOM's *Open Source Security Testing Methodology Manual* provides its users with a peer-reviewed methodology for performing security testing.[2] The OSSTMM contains six sections that review myriad security aspects including networks, wireless devices, and physical security. For these security aspects (networks, wireless devices, and physical security), it is easy to apply OSSTMM while security testing smart meters. However, other aspects covered by OSSTMM such as personnel security awareness levels, apply to the utility companies' overall security posture, but those will not be covered in this chapter because of their indirect relationship to smart meter security.

NOTE

As of the authoring of this chapter, the current version of ISECOM's OSSTMM is version 2.2. However, version 3 of the *Open Source Security Testing Methodology Manual* was currently under development. The authors of this book recommend that you visit ISECOM's Web site at www.isecom.org to obtain and review the latest version of the *Open Source Security Testing Methodology Manual* before you begin your security testing of smart meters.

The six sections of ISECOM's *Open Source Security Testing Methodology Manual* are as follows[3]:

1. Information Security
2. Process Security
3. Internet Technology Security
4. Communications Security
5. Wireless Security
6. Physical Security

A majority of the analysis of ISECOM's OSSTMM will be focused on sections 3, 5, and 6, which are Internet Technology Security, Wireless Security, and Physical Security, respectively. We will summarize the other sections of OSSTMM, but encourage you to review them on your own.

In order to perform security testing in accordance with OSSTMM, each module contained in each section must be tested. However, modules that do not apply can simply be marked as such. ISECOM has provided an OSSTMM Data Sheet for performing OSSTMM compliant security testing; however for the purpose of this book, we will not be utilizing this documentation. This documentation is best used when performing actual testing against specific targets, rather than discussing the methodology and how to apply it to attack smart meters.

ISECOM's OSSTMM discusses the various approaches to perform security testing. Specifically, OSSTMM lists six common approaches to security testing ranging from Double Blind, where both the target and attacker are provided with no information before conducting the testing, to Tandem, where the target and attacker share information openly about the testing.[3] For the purpose of this book, we will discuss the OSSTMM in the context of a Double Blind approach to security testing. The selection of this approach was made, as it is the closest approach to that of a malicious attacker.

TIP

Although the discussion of ISECOM's OSSTMM and how it can be applied to attack smart meters are focused on the Double Blind approach, the authors of this book do not recommend either the smart meter manufacturers or the utility companies to utilize this approach when performing security testing of their smart meters. Although the Double Blind approach closely mimics an attack by an outsider with no or limited knowledge of the security controls of the smart devices, it is not the most efficient or effective approach to security testing. The authors of this book believe that the most efficient and most effective approach for the smart meter manufacturers or the utility companies to take is that of the Tandem approach to security testing. The Tandem approach to security testing is more efficient as information regarding the environment is openly shared between the testers and the targets, allowing for a better use of time. Similarly, the sharing of information will aid in the effectiveness of the security testing by allowing the testers to confirm the completeness of their scope and validate their assumptions. As a result of performing security testing using the Tandem approach, the smart meter manufacturers or utility companies will see a more complete and accurate report while, most likely, paying less for the security testing when compared with the other testing approaches, such as Double Blind.

To better understand how the *Open Source Security Testing Methodology Manual* can be applied to attacking the smart meters, let us review each of the applicable sections in depth.

Information Security

Within the Information Security section of OSSTMM resides eight modules. These eight modules are as follows[3]:

1. Posture assessment
2. Information integrity review
3. Intelligence survey
4. Internet document grinding
5. Human resources review
6. Competitive intelligence scouting
7. Privacy controls review
8. Information controls review

WARNING

When reviewing OSSTMM version 2.2, you may notice that the modules listed for each section do not match with the modules explained in detail under each section. This is because version 2.2 of the OSSTMM is meant as a change over from version 2.0 to version 3.0. Thus, the authors of this book recommend you to follow the applicable modules described in detail and complete the applicable tasks listed for each applicable module.

From a high level, the Information Security section of OSSTMM is focused on information gathering and validation. From the perspective of attacking smart meters, this would include obtaining and reviewing information about the particular make and model of smart meter you are targeting. Obvious choices for review would be the smart meter manufacturer's Web site, but also the utility company that installed and utilizes the smart meter.

For example, by simply reviewing Florida Power & Light's Questions and Answers section of their Web site, you can learn such information about their smart meters as,[4]

> *[the] technology is Internet Protocol (IP) based RF mesh. The RF capability means the meters communicate through radio frequency. Each meter is equipped with a full two-way 900MHz radio transmitter that sends and receives information to an access point which is also radio-equipped. The access point is the collection point for the meter information that is sent back into an FPL system. Each access point, which is typically mounted on a power pole, is the size of a shoe box and can handle communications to thousands of meters. New RF mesh technology expands the ability of a meter to communicate to an access point by allowing the signal to be relayed off of other meters to find a path and maintain the connection required for communications.*

The information gathering, evaluation, and verification that is discussed in the Information Security section of OSSTMM is fundamental to the success of any attack, and must be performed to understand and identify the attack vectors that will be utilized in the following sections.

TIP

Google can be a fantastic resource for obtaining information about any subject, including smart meters. Security researcher Johnny Long has published two editions of his Google Hacking for Penetration Testers books. In these books, Johnny discusses the techniques of how to utilize the power of Google to obtain information vital to any penetration test. *Google Hacking for Penetration Testers, Volume 2* (ISBN: 978-1-59749-176-1, Syngress) is available at: www. syngress.com/hacking-and-penetration-testing/Google-Hacking-for-Penetration-Testers.

Process Security Testing

The second section of ISECOM's *Open Source Security Testing Methodology Manual* focuses on testing the security of the processes of your target. The Process Security Testing section of the OSSTMM contains the following five modules[4]:

1. Posture Review
2. Request Testing
3. Reverse Request Testing
4. Guided Suggestion Testing
5. Trusted Persons Testing

The Process Security Testing section of ISECOM's OSSTMM covers what is traditionally known as "social engineering." Each of the five modules within the Process Security Testing section aims to obtain information from people through coercion or deception. In relating social engineering to attacking the smart meters, potential attacks include impersonating a utility company technician or consumer.

Valuable information, such as technical specifications or administrative or consumer credentials, may possibly be obtained through social engineering techniques. The modules contained within the Process Security Testing section of OSSTMM can validate the information obtained in the Information Security section, as well as provide valuable information that will be utilized in the Internet Technology Security Testing section.

Internet Technology Security Testing

A majority of the applicable modules to testing the security of smart meters are contained within OSSTMM's Internet Technology Security Testing section. We will review how some of the following 14 modules can be utilized to analyze the security of smart meters. Just as some of the OSSTMM's six high-level sections do not apply when testing the security of smart meters, some of the modules contained within the Internet Technology Security Testing section do not apply. This section of the OSSTMM contains the following 14 modules[4]:

1. Network Surveying
2. Port Scanning
3. Services Identification
4. System Identification
5. Vulnerability Research and Verification
6. Internet Application Testing
7. Router Testing
8. Trusted Systems Testing
9. Firewall Testing
10. Intrusion Detection System Testing
11. Containment Measures Testing
12. Password Cracking
13. Denial of Service Testing
14. Security Policy Review

Do not let the name of this section confuse you as to how it can be applied to attacking smart meters. Although the name suggests that this section may only be applicable to the Internet, its modules can be applied to internal networks as well. To better understand which modules of the Internet Technology Security Testing of OSSTMM apply to attacking the smart meters and how they can be utilized, let us review the applicable ones in more detail.

Network Surveying

The Network Surveying module of the Internet Technology Security Testing section focuses on the identification of target systems that are network accessible. In the case of smart meters, they will most likely be accessible to attackers through either wireless networks or home area networks. In either case, Network Surveying consists of obtaining information about the targets. This information gathering

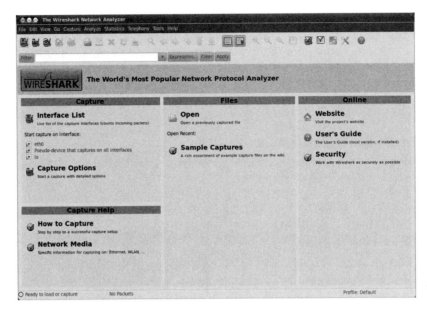

FIGURE 12.1

Wireshark network-sniffing tool.

can be performed by one of two ways: passively, by listening to traffic being transmitted across the network, or actively, by probing IP addresses for a response.

To passively identify targets, the Wireshark tool, as shown in Figure 12.1, can be utilized. Wireshark captures live traffic that is traversing any network and can provide deep inspection of hundreds of networking protocols.[5] To identify targets passively through Wireshark, simply create a list of the IP addresses to be captured by Wireshark. Wireshark is available for free at www.wireshark.org.

Conducting what is known as a ping sweep typically performs active target identification. Ping sweeps often utilize the Internet Control Message Protocol (ICMP) protocol to identify whether targets within specified network IP address ranges are active by analyzing their response. The Nmap security tool is often used to perform ping sweeps through its "–sP" switch. Nmap is freely available at www.nmap.org, along with a wealth of usage documentation.

Occasionally, ICMP traffic will be blocked between the attacker's system and the targets. In this case, Transmission Control Protocol (TCP) pings are often utilized. TCP pings are limited port scans that attempt to identify active hosts by seeing if they are running common services. Nmap is also the tool of choice for performing TCP pings.

Port Scanning

The next module covered in the Internet Technology Security Testing section of the OSSTMM discussed port scanning. Port Scanning consists of probing a target for responses on any of the 65,536 TCP and/or User Datagram Protocol (UDP) ports. Responses indicate that services are running on the associated port and may contain weaknesses that may ultimately allow access to the target.

As previously mentioned, the Nmap tool is the de facto port-scanning tool. TCP scans can be performed using TCP connect scans, which complete the TCP handshake, or through TCP SYN scans, which only utilize the SYN and SYN ACK parts of the TCP handshake.

The OSSTMM suggests that it is up to the discretion of the testing team to decide which of the 65,536 ports to scan.[5] The authors of this book recommend testing every port whenever possible, especially when dealing with smart devices. Otherwise, you may not identify services running on the targeted device that may contain weaknesses.

TIP

Nmap is a very powerful tool and can provide a considerable amount of information to security testers and attackers alike. However, if improperly configured, Nmap port scans can have adverse affects on network devices, such as firewalls, or targeted systems. Such adverse affects may include a temporary denial-of-service condition that is eliminated when your testing is completed, or a more permanent denial-of-service condition that requires the affected system to have services restarted or the entire system restarted. To better understand the details of how to properly use the Nmap tool, the authors of this book recommend Angela Orebaugh and Becky Pinkard's *Nmap in the Enterprise: Your Guide to Network Scanning* (ISBN: 978-1-59749-241-6, Syngress). It is available at: www.syngress. com/information-security-and-system-administrators/Nmap-in-the-Enterprise.

Services Identification and System Identification

Services Identification and System Identification are the third and fourth modules, respectively, listed in the Information Technology Security Testing section of the OSSTMM. The goal of these two sections is to enumerate the services running on the TCP or UDP ports that responded in the previous module, as well as to identify the underlying operating system of the target.

Both of these tasks can be performed utilizing the Nmap port-scanning tool. Specifically, issuing the –sV switch in your Nmap scan will have Nmap attempt to determine the version of the service running on the responding port. Figure 12.2 demonstrates the power of Nmap's version-detection capability. Rather than simply identifying that TCP port 443 is open on webserver.domain.com, Nmap has now told us that webserver.domain.com is running the Apache Web server, specifically version 2.2.8, as well as PHP and OpenSSL, complete with version information. This information can now be utilized to determine if known vulnerabilities exist in these versions of the running services.

In the case of the target used in Figure 12.2, webserver.domain.com, information regarding the operating system was also obtained because it was included in the version information for the Apache Web service. By adding the –O switch to your Nmap scan, you can obtain similar information regarding the operating system of the target. Just as an attacker would use the version information

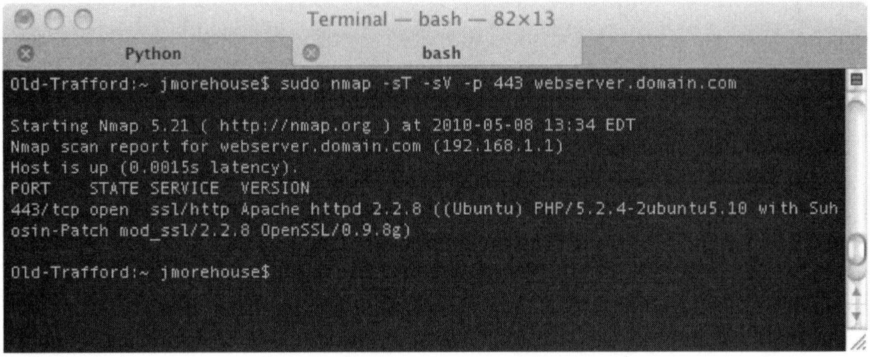

FIGURE 12.2

Nmap version detection output.

of the running services to identify vulnerabilities in the services, they would use the same approach to identify known vulnerabilities in the identified operating system.

Vulnerability Research and Verification

Once an attacker has identified the versions of the running services, as well as the operating system version of the target, he or she will perform the fifth module of the OSSTMM; Vulnerability Research and Verification. From a high level, this module consists of performing vulnerability identification and verification, both through a combination of automated and manual testing.

Vulnerability scanning consists of identifying known weaknesses in the target systems, and often performs the previously covered tasks of ping sweeps, port scans, and service/system identification. However, because we have already performed these tasks, we can tell our vulnerability-scanning tool what we already know to more efficiently attack our target.

A commonly used vulnerability-scanning tool is Tenable Network Security's Nessus, as shown in Figure 12.3. Nessus is freely available for home or personal use, but requires a $1,200 USD annual license for commercial use.[6] You can download a copy of Nessus from www.nessus.org.

Although Nessus is great for performing automated scanning to determine such weaknesses as an outdated version of Apache, manual testing should supplement automated scanning to identify weaknesses that may have otherwise been overlooked. An example of such a weakness could be the fact that the Apache Web server running on webserver.domain.com made its private SSL key available in its HTML document root through the carelessness of the system administrator. Unless Nessus contained a specific plug-in that attempted to identify such a weakness, it would not have identified the presence of the private SSL key.

OSSTMM states that automated vulnerability testing should be performed by at least two automated vulnerability scanners.[6] This is a statement that the authors of this book highly recommend, as the vulnerability coverage for each

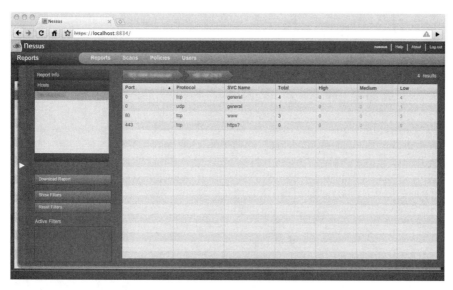

FIGURE 12.3

Nessus' Web interface.

vulnerability-scanning tool varies. In addition to performing multiple, automated vulnerability scans of the same target, manual vulnerability verification should be performed. Techniques to perform manual vulnerability verification vary greatly depending on the vulnerability, but examples of such verification either include using Telnet to observe the version of a specific service by connecting to it, or using an FTP client to connect to an anonymous FTP server.

In the process of attacking smart meters, Vulnerability Research and Verification is a critical step as it provides the potential entry points into the smart meters that will be exploited in a subsequent module.

NOTE

Like the majority of the tools mentioned in this chapter, Nessus can wreck havoc on targeted devices when not properly configured. There a number of published books that detail Nessus installations, deployments, and configurations, and the authors of this book highly recommend reading one of these books before using Nessus in any production environments. One such highly recommended book is Syngress' *Nessus Network Auditing, Second Edition* (ISBN: 978-1-59749-208-9) by Russ Rogers. It is available for purchase at www.syngress.com/special-interests/Nessus-Network-Auditing-Second-Edition.

Internet Application Testing

The previous section, "Vulnerability Research and Verification," traditionally identifies and verifies vulnerabilities within the services running on the target or smart meter. However, often vulnerability scanners do not include the capability to perform vulnerability identification and verification against Web applications. As more and more systems manufacturers are integrating security into their development life cycle, the number of running services available to an attacker is decreasing. This has shifted attackers to focus on the Web applications that are running on the target devices. In the case of smart meters, they may contain a Web application that allows consumers to view or configure usage information, or allow a technician to configure the device. The goal of this module is just the same as the previous module, only with a different scope.

Performing vulnerability identification and verification against Web applications is significantly more challenging than performing the same testing against running services. This is a result of the level of customization found within each Web application. It is rare that any Web application is exactly the same as another, and even in the case where two identical Web applications were found running, their backend infrastructure may be different. Because of this, the traditional approach to identifying vulnerabilities through the use of signature plug-ins is ineffective.

Although signature-based vulnerability scanning is ineffective on its own, it is still a component of identifying and verifying vulnerabilities in Web applications. However, manual testing plays a significantly larger role in the identification and verification of vulnerabilities in Web applications. In order to perform manually testing, a plethora of tools and techniques must be used. The Open Web Application Security Project (OWASP) has developed a Testing Guide for Web applications. It is available from OWASP at www.owasp.org/index.php/Category: OWASP_Testing_Project.

TIP

The ability to perform manual testing comes with experience in programming and security testing. Fortunately, there are many resources available for those interested in learning about and ultimately performing Web application security testing. The authors of this book highly recommend Steven Palmer's *Web Application Vulnerabilities: Detect, Exploit, Prevent* (ISBN: 978-1-59749-209-6), available from Syngress at www.syngress.com/hacking-and-penetration-testing/Web-Application-Vulnerabilities.

Password Cracking

The twelfth module contained within the Internet Technologies Security Testing section of OSSTMM relates to password cracking. In essence, password cracking involves attempting to identify valid credentials to a running service or Web application. Testing can be performed either by trying a precompiled list of passwords, known as a dictionary attack, or by trying every possible combination of a certain criteria (letters, numbers, special characters, and so on) known as brute-forcing.

When performing password cracking, be mindful that many services and Web applications implement account lockout functionality that either temporarily or

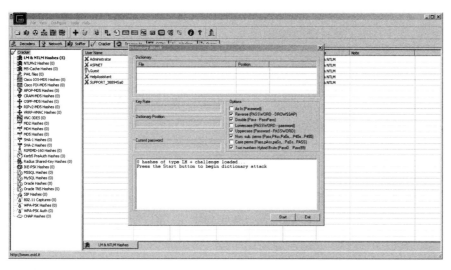

FIGURE 12.4

Cain & Abel password-cracking tool.

permanently disables an account if too many invalid password attempts are recorded during a certain time period.

A common tool to perform password cracking, through both dictionary and brute-force attacks, is Cain & Abel, shown in Figure 12.4. Cain & Abel is a Microsoft Windows tool and is freely available from www.oxid.it.

The Openwall Project maintains an extensive collection of wordlists to be used in dictionary attacks. A reduced version is freely available for download at www. Openwall.com/passwords/wordlists or a complete version is available through a variety of delivery options starting at $27.95 USD.[7]

Password cracking plays a significant role in attacking smart meters when presented with an authentication prompt. If an attacker can successfully obtain credentials to a smart meter, he or she may instantly gain complete access of the device, or may have an additional surface to perform the aforementioned security tests against.

Denial of Service Testing

The Denial of Service Testing module of the Internet Technologies Security Testing section of the OSSTMM focuses on identifying the weak points within the target infrastructure that could affect the availability of the target. In the case of smart meters, a number of weak points could exist on the device itself or in the underlying infrastructure. Testing for denial-of-service vulnerabilities in smart meters could include the use of the previously mentioned Wireshark and Nmap tools. For example, Wireshark could be used to determine the normal traffic patterns to and from the smart meter. The Nmap tool could then be used to gradually increase the traffic to the smart meter in an attempt to overwhelm the device itself or its underlying infrastructure.

If the goal of attackers were to simply deny service to a smart meter, it would be very easy for them to conduct such an attack when compared with attacks that attempt to compromise the confidentiality or integrity of the smart meter.

Exploit Testing

The modules list at the beginning of the OSSTMM mentions a module called Exploit Research and Verification under the Internet Technologies Security Testing section. However, in the detailed description of that section, there is no such module. Exploit Research and Verification has been rolled into the Vulnerability Research and Verification and Internet Application Testing modules.

The authors of this book thought it was prudent to call out exploit testing as a separate section because of its importance when attacking smart meters. All of the previous modules of the Internet Technologies Security Testing section of the OSSTMM have laid the groundwork to perform exploit testing. Exploit testing attempts to use the identified vulnerabilities and weaknesses to compromise the smart meter. Examples of exploit testing include using code to exploit a buffer overflow in a running service or using SQL Injection to access a command shell through an input validation weakness in a Web application.

As previously mentioned in Chapter 8, "Securing the Utility Companies," Metasploit is a freely available exploit tool that offers security testers and attackers alike a wealth of vulnerability exploits and payloads. Metasploit, shown in Figure 12.5, is available from Rapid7 at www.metasploit.com.

For a security tester, the ultimate goal is often the compromise of the target, whereas for an attacker, the same compromise of the smart meter may only be another step in their customized methodology to reach their ultimate goal.

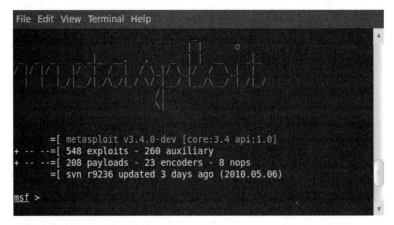

FIGURE 12.5

Metasploit vulnerability exploit tool.

> **WARNING**
>
> Of all of the tools discussed in this chapter, Metasploit has the biggest potential to adversely impact targeted systems. The authors of this book deem reading David Maynor's *Metasploit Toolkit for Penetration Testing, Exploit Development, and Vulnerability Research* (ISBN: 978-1-59749-074-0) as a prerequisite to using the Metasploit tool in a production environment. It is available from Syngress at www.syngress.com/hacking-and-penetration-testing/Metasploit-Toolkit-for-Penetration-Testing-Exploit-Development-and-Vulnerability-Research.

Communication Security Testing

The fourth section of ISECOM's OSSTMM covers the security testing of communications infrastructure. In particular, this section reviews the telephony network devices of the target through the following eight modules[7]:

1. Posture Review
2. PBX Review
3. Voicemail Testing
4. Fax Testing
5. Modem Survey
6. Remote Access Control Testing
7. Voice over IP Testing
8. X.25 Packet Switched Networks Testing

These modules, while important to include when evaluating the security of the Utility Companies, are not applicable to attacking the smart meters. Areas that may appear to be relevant overlap with those within the previous section, "Internet Technology Security Testing," and the next section, "Wireless Security Testing."

Wireless Security Testing

As wireless technologies are the primary method for communications between the smart meters and the utility companies, the modules contained within this section are critical to attacking the smart meters. As with the previous "Internet Technology Security Testing" section, not all of the following modules will apply to attacking the smart meters. The following 12 modules are included in the Wireless Security Testing section of ISECOM's OSSTMM[7]:

1. Posture Review
2. Electromagnetic Radiation (EMR) Testing
3. 802.11 Wireless Networks Testing
4. Bluetooth Networks Testing
5. Wireless Input Device Testing
6. Wireless Handheld Testing
7. Cordless Communications Testing
8. Wireless Surveillance Device Testing

9. Wireless Transaction Device Testing
10. Radio-frequency Identification (RFID) Testing
11. Infrared Testing
12. Privacy Review

To better understand which modules of the Wireless Security Testing of the OSSTMM apply to attacking the smart meters and how they can be utilized, let us review them in more detail.

802.11 Wireless Networks Testing

The third module of the Wireless Security Testing section of the OSSTMM relates to testing the security of any 802.11 based networks. Generally speaking, the goal of this module is to attempt to compromise the confidentiality, integrity, or availability of the data traversing any wireless networks.

Kismet is a common wireless sniffing tool that can be used to perform testing of 802.11 networks. In much the same way that Wireshark performs sniffing of wired networks, Kismet performs wireless network identification, including access point type, network name (SSID), connected clients, and implemented security (if any). It can also log packets for later review or integration into an encryption-breaking tool such as AirCrack-ng. Kismet, shown in Figure 12.6, is freely available for download at www.kismetwireless.net.

When reviewing the 802.11 Wireless Networks Testing module in the context of smart meters, you may find that the targeted smart meter does not utilize 802.11 wireless networks. Rather, it may utilize an 802.15.4 Wireless Network Protocol such as ZigBee. The same concepts that are discussed for 802.11 networks can be applied to 802.15.4 wireless networks. However, the hardware and software utilized for 802.15.4 networks may differ. For more information on testing the wireless security of 802.15.4, visit Travis Goodspeed's blog located at http://travisgoodspeed.blogspot.com. Travis has done a tremendous amount of work in the ZigBee space and has presented his findings through publications and

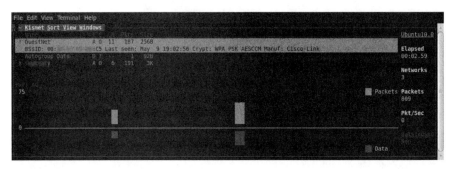

FIGURE 12.6

Kismet wireless sniffing tool.

conference presentations in an attempt to better secure devices utilizing 802.15.4 technologies, such as smart meters.

Bluetooth and RFID Security Testing

The Wireless Security Testing section of the OSSTMM contains two additional modules that discuss the security testing of Bluetooth and RFID wireless technologies. Although neither of these wireless technologies is widely used in current smart meters, the authors of this book suggest performing cursory testing to identify if either technology is in use on the targeted smart meter.

Kismet recently implemented functionality for discovering Bluetooth devices. Thus, Kismet could be used to perform discovery testing to determine if the targeted smart meter utilized Bluetooth technology. Identifying RFID technologies in use on the targeted smart meter is a bit more difficult. However, details on how to create your own RFID sniffing kit are available at http://rfid.marcboon.com.

NOTE

If you are interested in learning more about RFID security, the authors of this book recommend reading Frank Thornton and Paul Sanghera's *How To Cheat At Deploying & Securing RFID* (ISBN: 978-1-59749-230-0, Syngress). The book covers both attack and defense strategies for RFID technologies. It is available for purchase at www.syngress.com/information-security-and-system-administrators/How-to-Cheat-at-Deploying-and-Securing-RFID.

Physical Security Testing

The final section of ISECOM's *Open Source Security Testing Methodology Manual* covers testing the physical security of the target. With the utility companies aiming to deploy smart meters at each of their customers' locations, the physical security of smart meters is paramount in securing the smart grid. To evaluate the physical security posture of a target, OSSTMM includes the following seven modules within the Physical Security Testing section[7]:

1. Posture Review
2. Access Controls Testing
3. Perimeter Review
4. Monitoring Review
5. Alarm Response Review
6. Location Review
7. Environment Review

Just as certain modules of the Internet Technologies Security Testing and the Wireless Security Testing sections of the OSSTMM did not apply to attacking smart meters, the same applies to the aforementioned seven modules contained within the Physical Security Testing section. The modules contained within this section of the OSSTMM are written as if physical access to the target is not commonly allowed. However, as previously mentioned, this is not the case with smart meters. However, some parts of the Physical Security Testing modules can still apply to attacking smart meters.

The Access Control module of the Physical Security Testing section discusses how to test the access controls of a target. For attacking smart meters, this would include identifying any mechanisms that would detect the tampering of a smart meter and institute some type of alarm or trigger. Physical inspection of the device, as well as data mining on the Internet may be the two most effective way to evaluate the access controls of targeted smart meters.

In performing a test of the physical security of a smart meter, there may be monitoring controls in place that may compromise an attack. This module simply deals with identifying and monitoring solutions that may be observing the target, and determining how to defeat them. Examples would be a surveillance camera on a building's smart meter. Countermeasures to use when attacking the physical security of smart meter would include rendering the camera inoperable or masking your identity.

The Location Review module relates to identifying the weaknesses of the target as a result of its location. In the context of smart meters, this would simply involve determining if you could obtain physical access to the meter. As most meters are physically located on the sides of buildings, almost every attacker should encounter little to no controls preventing access to the smart meter.

NIST SPECIAL PUBLICATION 800-42: GUIDELINE ON NETWORK SECURITY TESTING

The National Institute of Standards and Technology (NIST) issued Special Publication 800-42: Guideline on Network Security Testing in October of 2003. Since then, security testers and attackers alike have utilized its methodology to evaluate the security of targeted devices. NIST 800-42 contains three high-level sections: Security Testing and the Systems Development Life Cycle, Security Testing Techniques, and Deployment Strategies for Security Testing.[8] For the purpose of attacking smart meters, we will review the "Security Testing Techniques" section in detail and discuss how it can be utilized to attack smart meters.

Security Testing Techniques

The Security Testing Techniques chapter, or Chapter 3, of NIST's Special Publication 800-42 contains the following sections[8]:

1. Roles and Responsibilities for Testing
2. Network Scanning
3. Vulnerability Scanning
4. Password Cracking

5. Log Reviews

6. File Integrity Checkers

7. Virus Detectors

8. War Dialing

9. Wireless LAN Testing ("War Driving")

10. Penetration Testing

11. Post-Testing Activities

12. General Information Security Principles

13. Summary Comparisons of Network Testing Techniques

Of the 13 sections of NIST 800-42's Security Testing Techniques chapter, not all apply when discussing on attacking smart meters. For the sections that do apply, let us review each of these categories in detail and describe how they relate to attacking smart meters. Comparisons and references to the previously discussed ISECOM's *Open Source Security Testing Methodology Manual* will be included in the following analysis, so the authors of this book highly recommend reviewing that section of this chapter before continuing.

Network Scanning

Section 3.2 of NIST 800-42 discusses how ping sweeps and port scans can be utilized to identify active hosts on targeted networks, as well as the network services operating on those hosts. Additionally, the section goes on to discuss operating system fingerprinting, which is equivalent to utilizing the –O switch when running Nmap.

The Network Scanning section of NIST 800-42 also explains how banner information can be utilized to identify the type of application that is running on an open port.[8] For example, Figure 12.7 demonstrates that Web servers often disclose information in what is known as a banner. Reading this banner information can help an attacker to determine if they are targeting an Apache Web server or a Microsoft Internet Information Services (IIS) Web server.

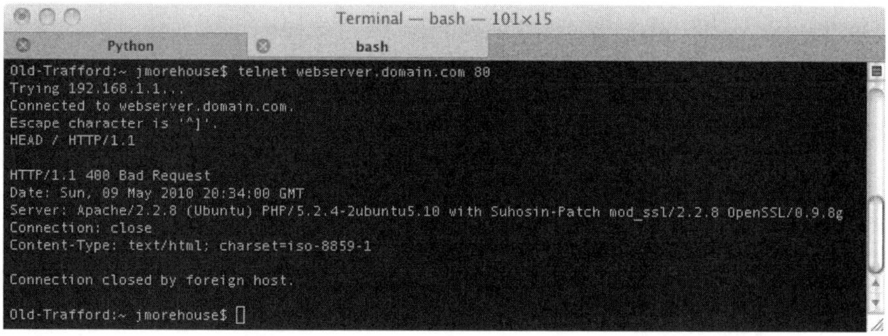

FIGURE 12.7

Apache Web server banner.

When relating the Network Scanning section of NIST 800-42 to attacking smart meters, it can be used by an attacker to identify targets, and determine their running services, application versions, and operating systems. This information can then be used by an attacker to customize their vulnerability-scanning tool(s), as well as refine their approach toward manual vulnerability identification and verification.

Vulnerability Scanning

The next section of NIST 800-42's third chapter covers the topic of vulnerability scanning. NIST reiterates the fact that vulnerability scanners can perform the previous steps of ping sweeps, port scans, and fingerprinting (both network service and operating system) and also discuss the different types of vulnerability scans (host and network based).[8]

From an attacker's point of view, the information valuable in section 3.3 of NIST 800-42 is the discussion on false-positives, their potential negative impact on hosts or networks being scanned, and the fact that vulnerability scanners tend to focus on well-known vulnerabilities and may overlook more obscure ones. Each of these discussions can be used by an attacker to refine his or her vulnerability identification and verification process.

First, to reduce the number of false-positives identified by an attacker's vulnerability scans, they can utilize different scanners. This was previously discussed by the OSSTMM in the Vulnerability Research and Verification section. Second, an attacker can attempt to minimize the impact of his or her vulnerability scans against the targets and the associated networks by using the Wireshark tool. Also previously discussed but this time in the OSSTMM's Denial of Service Testing section, an attacker can utilize the Wireshark tool to determine a normal traffic pattern and then throttle his or her vulnerability scans to stay as close as possible to the normal traffic volume. This may seem like a significant amount of work for little to no return; however, if the attacker's target is known to contain countermeasures that shut the device down when it is being targeted or if it is unstable, an attacker may only get one attempt to perform vulnerability scans. Finally, an attacker can perform manual research of the identified network services and operating system of the target to identify any vulnerability that was potentially missed by the attacker's automated vulnerability scans. This will help to reduce the false negatives that result from automated testing.

NIST 800-42 stresses the importance of vulnerability testing and timely patch management as a proactive technique to manage risk.[8] However, it can also be used by attackers to identify weaknesses that may result in the compromise of their targets, such as smart meters.

Password Cracking

Section 3.4 of NIST 800-42 describes the techniques used in cracking passwords. These techniques are similar to those covered in the Password Cracking section of the OSSTMM; however, several additional items are covered. Specifically, these items include obtaining passwords passively by network sniffing, and using hybrid-attacks to crack passwords.[8]

The first additional topic covered by NIST 800-42 related to password cracking is the use of network-sniffing tools to capture unencrypted passwords that traverse a network segment. From an attacker's point of view, they could utilize the Wireshark network-sniffing tool to capture unencrypted passwords traversing across the network. Although network sniffing across a switched network yields a significantly lower number of packets, sniffing wireless networks provides nearly every packet that traverses the wireless network. As previously mentioned in the 802.11 Wireless Security Testing section of the OSSTMM, Kismet can capture wireless packets that can later be viewed in tools such as Wireshark.

NIST 800-42 also introduces the password-cracking concept known as a hybrid attack.[8] This type of password cracking is based on using a wordlist and then adding characters to the word in the word list. For example, if a wordlist contained the word "yellow," a password-cracking tool that performed hybrid-attacks would test such passwords as "yellow1," "!yellow," and "!yellow@@." The previously mentioned Cain and Abel password-cracking tool, as shown in Figure 12.4, can perform hybrid attacks.

Each of these additional topics covered by NIST 800-42 can yield significant results for an attacker. Once an attacker has obtained valid credentials for a network service of, or the operating system running on a smart meter, he or she stands a significantly higher chance of being able to reach his or her goal, whatever that may be.

Wireless LAN Testing ("War Driving")

The ninth section of the third chapter of NIST 800-42 covers Wireless LAN Testing, with a focus on "war driving."[8] War Driving is the act of driving around neighborhoods, buildings, and offices looking for open or unencrypted wireless networks. Although this practice may not have a direct correlation to attacking a smart meter, it can be used to identify the station or access point that the smart meters communicate with. Once the base station or access point has been identified, almost all of the previously covered security testing techniques, from both NIST 800-42 and the OSSTMM, should be performed against the access point. If an attacker can compromise the device that it communicates with, the attacker may then be able to gain additional access to the smart meter.

Although the wireless networking tool, Kismet, has been previously discussed, NIST 800-42 discusses the use of Network Stumbler. Network Stumbler, shown in Figure 12.8, is a Microsoft Windows-based tool, much like Kismet, that performs access point identification. It does not contain all of features of Kismet, but is suitable for war driving activities.

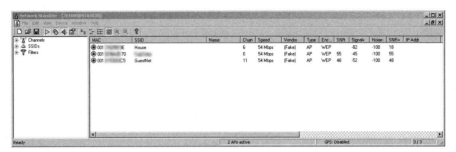

FIGURE 12.8

Network Stumbler wireless tool.

NOTE

Frank Thornton, Michael J Schearer, and Brad Haines authored *Kismet Hacking* (ISBN: 978-1-59749-117-4). This book focuses on performing wireless security testing using the Kismet tool. It also covers building Kismet drones, and mapping networks using GPS coordinates. Kismet Hacking is available from Syngress at www.syngress.com/hacking-and-penetration-testing/Kismet-Hacking.

Penetration Testing

The final section we will discuss in Chapter 3 of NIST 800-42 is section 3.10, Penetration Testing. From a high level, this section discusses the risks associated with penetration testing, as well common approaches to penetration testing,[8] Section 3.10 also discusses an often overlooked concept of penetration testing through NIST's Four Stage Penetration Testing Methodology.[8]

Read by the eyes of an attacker, the Penetration Testing section of NIST 800-42 can remind them of the importance of testing their exploit code before attempting to exploit actual smart meters. Much like we previously discussed during the Vulnerability Scanning section of NIST 800-42, penetration testing can have a significant impact on the target, and could result in the smart meter becoming unresponsive. To this end, an attacker must thoroughly test his or her exploit code on similar systems or devices before attempting it on smart meters. Otherwise, the attacker may have wasted his or her only opportunity to compromise the device.

NIST 800-42 presents its readers with two distinct approaches to penetration testing. The first approach, known as Blue Teaming, conducts penetration testing with prior knowledge of the target environment, as well as the consent of the organization responsible for targeted environment. The second approach, known as Red Teaming, conducts penetration testing without prior knowledge of the target environment and with limited knowledge (usually only upper management) of the testing within the targeted organization. Blue Teaming is equitable to

OSSTMM's Tandem approach, and Red Teaming is equitable to OSSTMM's Blind approach. An attackers approach will almost always most closely align with OSSTMM's Double Blind approach.

Finally, the Penetration Testing section of NIST 800-42 describes their Four Stage Penetration Testing Methodology. These four stages (planning, discovery, attack, and reporting) are similar to each of the larger methodologies outlined in this chapter. However, this specific methodology emphasizes that once an attacker has successfully compromised a vulnerable system, the methodology reverts to the discovery phase as the attacker determines if they can discover any additional information or systems that were previously inaccessible.

Attackers will definitely want to ensure that the utility companies or smart meter manufacturers are unaware of their testing activities. Similarly, attackers' security testing plan should incorporate additional discovery if and when they compromise the smart meter, as it may give them access to information and systems they had not originally thought would be available.

SUMMARY

Security testing can be a proactive practice of mature Information Security Program, or it can be part of an attackers plan to compromise a smart meter. Either way, both authorized and unauthorized security testing must follow a well-established methodology to be successful. Attackers can easily adopt either of the two methodologies described in this chapter when developing a plan to compromise smart meters. The utility companies and smart meter manufactures must follow similar methodologies in order to fully understand and uncover the threats that will come with providing each and every utility company customer with a smart meter. Otherwise, the utility companies will be gravely unprepared for the results of the successful compromise of their smart meters.

Endnotes

1. About Us [document on the Internet]. Institute for Security and Open Methodologies, www.isecom.org/about.shtml; [accessed 07.05.10].
2. OSSTMM – *Open Source Security Testing Methodology Manual* [document on the Internet]. Institute for Security and Open Methodologies, www.isecom.org/osstmm/; [accessed 07.05.10].
3. Herzog P. OSSTMM 2.2: *open-source security testing methodology manual*. Institute for Security and Open Methodologies; 2006.
4. FPL|AMI|How Advanced Electronic Meters Work [document on the Internet]. Florida Power & Light Company; www.fpl.com/ami/qa.shtml#2; 2010 [accessed 08.05.10].
5. About Wireshark [document on the Internet]. The Wireshark Foundation, www.wireshark.org/about.html; [accessed 08.05.10].

6. Nessus: The Network Vulnerability Scanner [document on the Internet]. Tenable Network Security; www.nessus.org/nessus; 2010 [accessed 08.05.10].

7. Wordlists and common passwords for password recovery [document on the Internet]. The Openwall Project, www.openwall.com/passwords/wordlists; [accessed 08.05.10].

8. Wack J, Tracy M, Souppaya M. NIST Special Publication 800-42: Guidelines on Network Security Testing. Gaithersburg (MD): National Institute of Standards and Technology; 2003.

Attacking Smart Devices

13

INFORMATION IN THIS CHAPTER

- Selecting a Target Smart Device
- Attacking a Smart Device

While smart meters are currently being rolled out to consumers, those interested in attacking smart meters are limited by their physical access to them. However, those targeting smart devices already have access to a plethora of devices that are only a click and credit card away. In Chapter 12, "Attacking Smart Meters," we reviewed two methodologies that an attacker might use when targeting smart meters. In this chapter, we will utilize ISECOM's *Open Source Security Testing Methodology Manual* to attack an actual smart device. While we will not disclose any particular vulnerabilities in the targeted smart device, we will examine, in detail, how to utilize the tools discussed in the previous chapter. Let the attacking begin.

NOTE

If you have jumped to this chapter hoping to dive right into attacking smart devices, the authors of this book highly recommend that you first review the previous chapter, "Attacking Smart Meters." Throughout this chapter we will be referencing information that was explained in detail in the previous chapter. However, if you are familiar with ISECOM's OSSTMM or NIST's Special Publication 800-42, then the previous chapter may just be a high-level review.

SELECTING A TARGET SMART DEVICE

Attackers targeting smart meters will be limited by those that are deployed in areas that they have ready access to. This is not the case with smart devices, as an attacker can simply order them off the Internet or pick them up at a local hardware store. In reviewing the available smart devices to target, an attacker has a wide range of devices to choose from. They can choose something as simple as Fujitsu's Smart Power Strip device (Figure 13.1) or as complex as Energy, Inc.'s Energy Detective 5000 (Figure 13.2).

FIGURE 13.1

Fujitsu's Smart Power Strip.

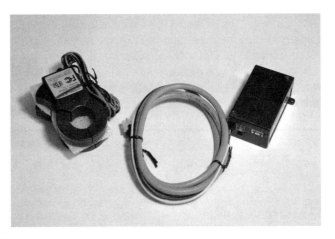

FIGURE 13.2

Energy, Inc.'s TED 5000 smart device.

Fujitsu's Smart Power Strip allows consumers to monitor the energy usage of devices connected to the power strip via a USB wireless transmitter that sends data across the user's home network.[1] The use of wireless network technology makes the Fujitsu Smart Power Strip an interesting target for an attacker; however, there are other devices that offer greater attack surfaces.

One such device is the aforementioned Energy Detective 5000, or TED 5000, by Energy, Inc., as shown in Figure 13.2. According to the Web site of Energy, Inc., the TED 5000 "is a simple, yet extremely accurate, home energy monitor that allows you to see electricity usage in real-time."[2]

From a high level, the TED 5000 is connected to your home's distribution panels and then it sends readings via power line communications (PLC) to a gateway device. This gateway device runs a Web server that presents the information for the user to monitor, as well as integrates with Google's Power Meter. You can learn more about the TED 5000 at www.theenergydetective.com.

For the purpose of this chapter, the TED 5000 was chosen as the targeted smart device because of its widespread deployment, availability, ease of installation, and attack surface (wireless, network services, and Web services).

> **TIP**
>
> While the TED 5000 is relatively simple to install, it requires basic understanding and familiarity with electrical work. The installation may require additional breakers to be installed in your home's electric panel and thus could cause serious injury or death if installed improperly. If you are not skilled at electrical work, the authors of this book recommend you hire a licensed electrician to install your TED 5000 for you.

ATTACKING A SMART DEVICE

Now that we have selected the TED 5000 as our targeted device, let us first review our plan of attack. In the coming sections, we will utilize ISECOM's OSSTMM methodology. Specifically, we will focus on the Process Security Testing section of the OSSTMM, highlighting the following applicable modules:

- Network Surveying
- Port Scanning
- Services Identification and System Identification
- Vulnerability Research and Verification
- Internet Application Testing
- Password Cracking
- Denial-of-Service Testing
- Exploit Testing

For each of the modules listed above, we will utilize open-source tools to perform the testing. If you want to pause here before continuing to make sure you have all of the covered tools, we will utilize the following:

- Wireshark – www.wireshark.org
- Nmap – www.nmap.org
- Nessus – www.nessus.org
- w3af – http://w3af.sourceforge.net
- Bruter – http://sourceforge.net/projects/worawita/
- Metasploit – www.metasploit.com

These tools do not represent the only tools that can be used to perform the testing described in the OSSTMM modules. There are dozens of alternatives, both commercial and open source that can be used as replacements.

TOOLS

In developing the content for this chapter, the authors of this book utilized multiple systems and operating systems, including Apple's Snow Leopard, Microsoft's Windows 7, and Ubuntu 10.04 (Lucid Lynx). While having access to all three of these operating systems is the recommended approach, there is an easier way to quickly access a majority of the aforementioned tools – BackTrack. BackTrack is a Linux-based operating system that can be run completely from a Live DVD, a VMware image, or can be installed like any other Linux distribution.[3] One of the significant advantages of utilizing BackTrack, besides having a portable penetration testing arsenal in your DVD case, is that included tools are preconfigured to run within the BackTrack environment. This means little to no configuration, which is often a deterrent for those who have little experience with Linux. BackTrack is freely available from www.backtrack-linux.org.

Network Surveying

The *Network Surveying* module aims to identify targets for further inspection. In the case of attacking the TED 5000, we simply want to identify its IP address. This can be accomplished by two ways, as discussed in the previous chapter:

- Passively – Utilizing the Wireshark tool to capture network traffic and manually identify the TED 5000
- Actively – Utilizing Nmap to perform ping sweeps to locate the TED 5000's response

First, let us look at how we would identify the IP address of the TED 5000 passively using Wireshark. In order for this passive identification to work, your testing system must reside on the same network as the targeted device. For the purpose of this chapter, our testing system was connected to the TED 5000 via a hub. Figure 13.3 shows a packet capture of communications between 192.168.210.1 and 192.168.210.5. Looking at the line that says "Ethernet II, SRC: CompalIn_ef:14:04 (00:1e:ec:ef:14:04), Dst: Energy_21:2d:65 (00:25:2f:21:2d:65)" we can learn the following:

- The TED 5000 has a MAC address of 00:25:2f:21:2d:65.
- The TED 5000 has an IP address of 192.168.210.5.

We know this because the MAC address in the conversation is registered to Energy, Inc., as provided by Wireshark, and its associated IP address, 192.168.210.5, is listed as the destination in the line "Internet Protocol, Src: 192.168.210.1 (192.168.210.1), Dst: 192.168.210.5 (192.168.210.5)" as also shown in Figure 13.3.

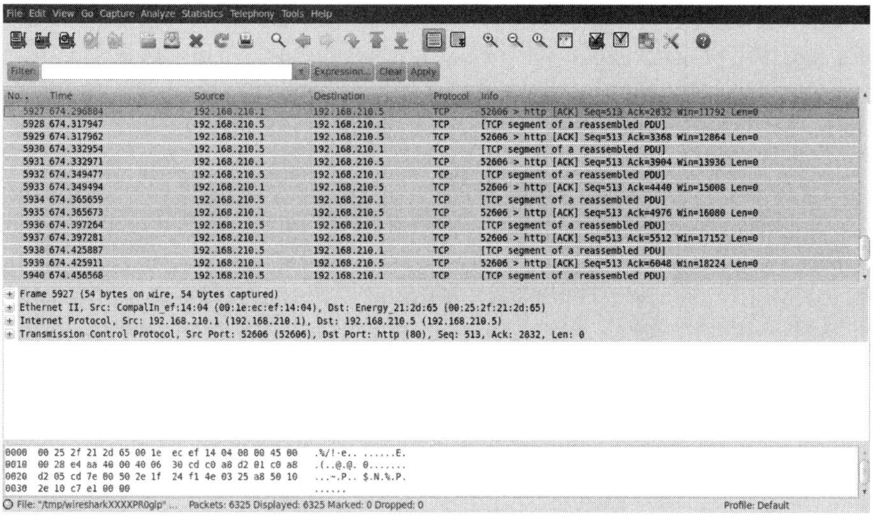

FIGURE 13.3

Screenshot of Wireshark packet capture identifying the TED 5000.

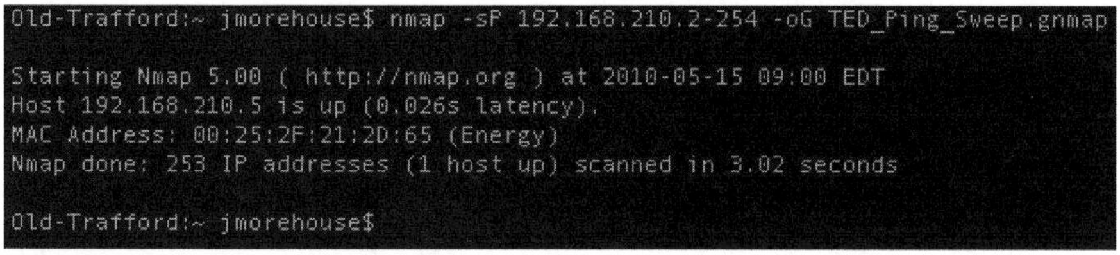

FIGURE 13.4

Screenshot of Nmap ping sweep results identifying the TED 5000.

If you are unable to passively capture packets using Wireshark, for example because you are not on the same network, you can actively identify the TED 5000 using Nmap's ping sweep capability. Figure 13.4 demonstrates how to perform a ping sweep using Nmap to identify target systems. By issuing the -sP switch when using Nmap, you can perform ping sweeps that will return active target's IP and MAC addresses. Figure 13.4 shows that a MAC address registered to Energy (Energy, Inc.) is alive on IP address of 192.168.210.5.

At this point we have completed the objective of the *Network Surveying* module. We have identified our target, the TED 5000 Smart Device, with an IP address of 192.168.210.5 and a MAC address of 00:25:2F:21:2D:65. This information will be used throughout the rest of the modules, so it is important to write it down.

Port Scanning

The objective of the *Port Scanning* module of the Process Security Testing section of ISECOM's OSSTMM is to identify the services that are running on the target (TED 5000). To accomplish this, we will utilize Nmap to perform a port scan of our targeted smart device. Figure 13.5 shows the syntax used to identify all open TCP ports on the TED 5000 Smart Device.

The following switches were used when running Nmap to identify the services running on the TED 5000:

- **-n** – This switch tells Nmap not to perform DNS resolution. This was added simply because there was not a DNS record for the TED 5000 on the network utilized for testing. Omitting this switch will have Nmap to perform DNS resolution for active hosts.
- **-sS** – This switch tells Nmap to perform what is known as a SYN scan. SYN scans only perform a partial TCP handshake with the target. SYN scans are often used to increase the speed of a port scan and lessen the impact on the target.
- **-p-** – This switch tells Nmap to identify any responding ports on 65,535 TCP ports on the target. While performing complete TCP port scans takes significantly longer than performing TCP port scans against a subset of ports, for example 1-1024, the authors of this book highly recommend it as it will provide you with more complete results.
- **-oG** – This switch tells Nmap to output its results to a file that is in a greppable format. Greppable formatted files are useful for searching within multiple output files. Other common Nmap outputs are Normal (oN) and XML (oX) formats. To output the results in the three major formats at the same time, use the –oA flag.

As shown in Figure 13.5 by the highlighted text, the TED 5000 Smart Device responded on two TCP ports, 80 and 443. These ports are associated with Web

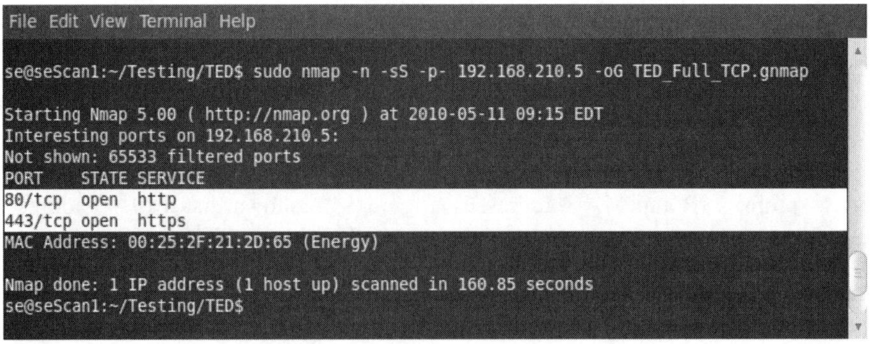

```
File Edit View Terminal Help

se@seScan1:~/Testing/TED$ sudo nmap -n -sS -p- 192.168.210.5 -oG TED_Full_TCP.gnmap

Starting Nmap 5.00 ( http://nmap.org ) at 2010-05-11 09:15 EDT
Interesting ports on 192.168.210.5:
Not shown: 65533 filtered ports
PORT    STATE SERVICE
80/tcp  open  http
443/tcp open  https
MAC Address: 00:25:2F:21:2D:65 (Energy)

Nmap done: 1 IP address (1 host up) scanned in 160.85 seconds
se@seScan1:~/Testing/TED$
```

FIGURE 13.5

Screenshot of Nmap TCP port scan of the TED 5000.

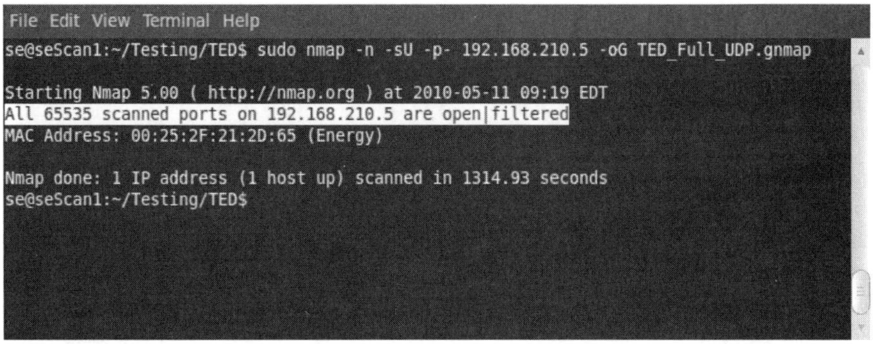

```
File Edit View Terminal Help
se@seScan1:~/Testing/TED$ sudo nmap -n -sU -p- 192.168.210.5 -oG TED_Full_UDP.gnmap

Starting Nmap 5.00 ( http://nmap.org ) at 2010-05-11 09:19 EDT
All 65535 scanned ports on 192.168.210.5 are open|filtered
MAC Address: 00:25:2F:21:2D:65 (Energy)

Nmap done: 1 IP address (1 host up) scanned in 1314.93 seconds
se@seScan1:~/Testing/TED$
```

FIGURE 13.6

Screenshot of Nmap UDP port scan of the TED 5000.

servers, with TCP port 80 commonly used for HTTP and TCP port 443 commonly used for HTTPS.

TIP

If you identify ports on targeted devices that you are not familiar with, there are a number of resources on the Internet that list the services commonly associated with TCP and UDP ports. One of these is Internet Assigned Numbers Authority's (IANA) Port Numbers located at www.iana.org/assignments/port-numbers.

By simply switching the -sS switch to -sU, Nmap performs a complete (65,535 ports) UDP port scan against the targeted device. Figure 13.6 shows that the TED 5000 Smart Device did not respond on any UDP port.

Alternatively, the TCP and UDP scans can be combined into one command. While this scan will take a very long time to complete, it does eliminate the need to watch for when the TCP scan finishes.

The results shown in Figures 13.5 and 13.6 show that the TED 5000 has a limited footprint of running services. This limited footprint reduces the potential attack vectors for the device. Despite this, by simply performing the aforementioned Nmap TCP and UDP port scans, this module of the Process Security Testing section of the OSSTMM is complete.

Services Identification and System Identification

The objective of the *Services Identification and System Identification* module of the Process Security Testing section of ISECOM's OSSTMM is to identify the services that are running on the TCP and UDP ports that responded during the *Port Scanning* module. For example, in the *Port Scanning* module we learned that the TED 5000 Smart Device is running services on TCP ports 80 and 443. While these ports most commonly are associated with a Web server, the *Services Identification and System Identification* modules attempt to determine WHAT Web server (i.e. Apache or Internet Information Services) is running on WHAT operating system (Red Hat Linux or Microsoft Windows 2008 R2).

Nmap can be used to identify the services and the operating system of the targeted device. Several new switches were used to identify the services and operating systems. Since only TCP ports responded, assume that we used the -sS switch not the -sU switch. The new switches used were

- **-sV** – This switch tells Nmap to perform version detection of the services running on the open ports.
- **-p 21-25,80,443** – This switch tells Nmap to scan the TCP ports 21 (FTP), 22 (SSH), 23 (Telnet), 24 (any private mail system), 25 (SMTP), 80 (HTTP), and 443 (HTTPS). While only TCP ports 80 and 443 responded to our initial TCP port scan in the *Port Scanning* module, we asked Nmap to look for TCP ports 21 through 25 so that it could identify the closed ports. When performing identification of operating system, Nmap looks for responses and compares them to a database of known responses. Both open and closed responses are used, so by having Nmap evaluate the closed responses for TCP ports 21 through 25, we increased the likelihood that it will identify the target's operating system.
- **-O** – This switch tells Nmap to attempt to identify the target's operating system based on the responses to the aforementioned scanned TCP ports.

Figure 13.7 shows the results of our Nmap version scan. As you can see, Nmap was unable to identify the services running on either TCP port 80 or TCP

FIGURE 13.7

Screenshot of Nmap service and operating system detection results.

port 443. This is because it does not have a signature for the TED 5000's response in its database.

Likewise, Nmap was unable to identify the operating system running on the targeted device. While this may seem like a waste of time, it is a valuable part of enumerating your target. Plus, all is not lost as Nessus, which will be used in the *Vulnerability Research and Verification* module, also attempts to identify the services running and the operating system.

Vulnerability Research and Verification

The *Vulnerability Research and Verification* module of ISECOM's OSSTMM's Process Security Testing section aims to identify vulnerabilities on the services running on the TED 5000. This module shares a lot of the same underlying objectives as the *Internet Application Testing* module, which is discussed next. However, this module focuses on identifying vulnerabilities in services available via the network, whereas the *Internet Application Testing* module focuses on identifying vulnerabilities in what are traditionally known as Web applications.

The process of identifying vulnerabilities in targeted systems involves both manual and automated testing. Since the only services running on the TED 5000 were Web services, manual vulnerability research and verification will be covered in detail in the next module.

To perform vulnerability research and verification, the Nessus Vulnerability Scanning tool was used. While setting up Nessus takes more time than simply issuing switches to Nmap, actually running Nessus is fairly simple. If you need further assistance in installing Nessus, the Nessus documentation provides step-by-step instructions for installing Nessus and creating a user to log in the Web interface.

NOTE

For the purpose of this module, Nessus, version 4.2.2 was used. Prior to Nessus, version 4.2, Nessus consisted of a server that performed the vulnerability testing and a client that connected to the server to issue commands. Since version 4.2, Nessus has implemented a Web interface that handles what was previously performed via the Nessus client. For those of you who like the client/server model better, Nessus 4.2.2 still supports the Nessus 4 client. However, we utilized the Web interface of Nessus 4.2.2 for the purpose of this book.

First, we logged into the Nessus server running on our Ubuntu 10.04 (Lucid Lynx) system, as shown in Figure 13.8. Figure 13.8 shows that the Professional Feed for Nessus was used during this experiment. The Nessus Professional Feed is required when running Nessus for commercial uses, and at the time this chapter was written, it was available from Tenable for US $1,200. Tenable also provides a personal-use license that is freely available. You can read more about Nessus' licensing model at www.nessus.org/products/professional-feed.

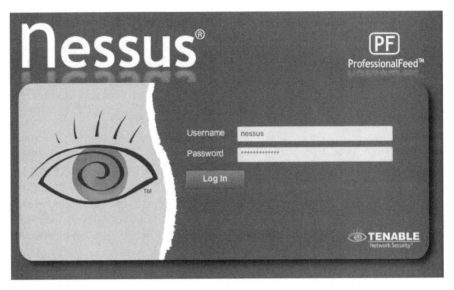

FIGURE 13.8

Nessus Web interface login screen.

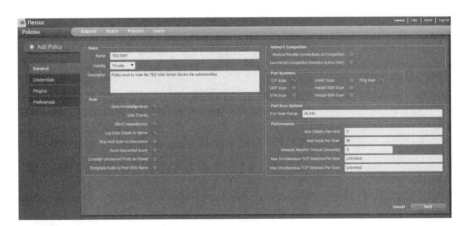

FIGURE 13.9

Nessus scan policy configuration.

After logging into Nessus, a unique scan policy was created for the target, the TED 5000. Scan policies are configurations that Nessus uses to run vulnerability scans. The TED 5000 Smart Device scan policy was created by clicking on the **Policies** tab on the top of the screen. Figure 13.9 shows the options selected for the TED 5000 Smart Device scan policy.

Several of the policy settings were changed from the default settings and the following list describes why. These settings were

- **Name** – This setting is simply used for the unique identifier for this scan policy. You can set this to any value you would like.
- **Description** – This is an optional setting for your own use. Remembering what a specific policy was/is used for can be difficult when you have multiple scan policies.
- **Save Knowledge Base** – This setting saves the information regarding your scan to the Nessus server. This information can be useful in troubleshooting or if you encounter any issues during your scan.
- **Log Scan Details to Server** – This setting is similar to the Save Knowledge Base setting as it logs details about your scan to the Nessus log files. This information can again be useful in troubleshooting any issues or monitoring the status of your scan (if the new progress bar is not behaving normally).
- **Port Scanners** – As the TED 5000 only responded to TCP ports, we unchecked all the other scanners. The Ping Host setting was left as we wanted to ensure the host was still alive prior to performing our vulnerability scan.
- **Port Scan Options** – We changed this setting from Nessus' default ports to only the TCP ports we previously identified using Nmap in the *Port Scanning* module. Reducing the number of ports scanned decreases the duration of vulnerability scans. Only change this setting if you have previously performed port scans, using Nmap or an alternative port scanner, or change this setting to 0-65535 if you would like to perform complete port scans.

Once the scan policy was created for the TED 5000 Smart Device, the scan was set up by clicking on the **Scan** tab at the top. Figure 13.10 shows the settings used for the Nessus scan of the targeted device.

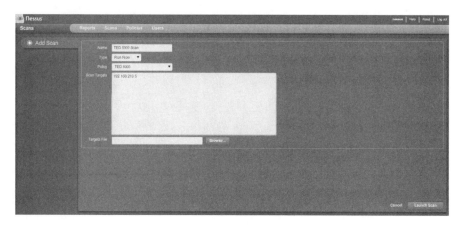

FIGURE 13.10

Nessus scan settings.

As you can see by reviewing Figure 13.10, since most of your configuration is completed in the scan policy, there are few options when configuring a scan. Below are the settings that were used for this Nessus scan of the TED 5000 Smart Device:

- **Name** – This setting is simply used for the unique identifier for this scan. You can set this to any value you would like. Note that this will be the name of the report in the Reports tab once the scan has completed.
- **Type** – This setting allows you to either run the scan now or schedule the scan for later. For the purpose of this test, the scan was run immediately.
- **Policy** – This setting is the scan policy Nessus will use when performing the scan. The TED 5000 policy that was previously created in the Policies tab was selected.
- **Scan Targets** – This setting is where the IP address of the TED 5000 Smart Device is entered. Nessus also accepts network ranges, host names, and DNS names. If you have a precompiled list of targets, you can use the Targets File setting instead of the Scan Targets setting.

Once the scan was configured, click the **Launch Scan** button to let Nessus do its thing. Figure 13.11 shows Nessus's new progress bar. As Nessus is performing the vulnerability tests, it updates the status of the scan with the percentage complete, as well as the number of High, Medium, and Low vulnerabilities, along with the number of open ports. You will notice that Nessus only identified two open ports on the TED 5000 Smart Device because we configured the TED 5000 scan policy to test only TCP ports 80 and 443.

When Nessus completes a vulnerability scan, it moves the scan from the Scans tab to the Reports tab. To view the results of the scan, simply click on the **Reports** tab and then double-click on the name of the scan you set when creating

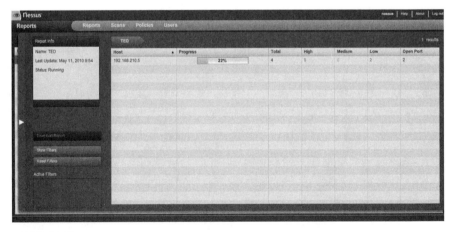

FIGURE 13.11

Nessus vulnerability scan progress.

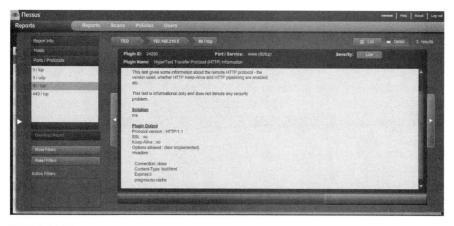

FIGURE 13.12

Nessus vulnerability scan results.

the scan. Figure 13.12 shows the information Nessus discovered for the service running on TCP port 80 (HTTP).

After completing the Nessus vulnerability scan of the TED 5000 Smart Device, the results were reviewed and Nessus was unable to identify any vulnerabilities with a medium- or high-risk classification. Thus, manual testing or automated Internet Application Testing will be necessary to identify an entry point into the targeted device.

Internet Application Testing

Much like the objective of the Vulnerability Research and Verification module, the objective of the Internet Application Testing module of ISECOM's OSSTMM is to identify weaknesses in the Web applications and technologies of the targeted device. To accomplish this objective, a combination of manual and automated testing will be used.

To perform manual testing of the targeted Smart Device, a Web browser was used. The following Web browsers were considered to be part of the toolkit:

- **Microsoft Internet Explorer** – Available for only the Microsoft Windows Operating System from www.microsoft.com/windows/internet-explorer
- **Google Chrome** – Available for most operating systems (Microsoft Windows, Apple OSX, and Linux) from www.google.com/chrome
- **Mozilla Firefox** – Available for most operating systems (Microsoft Windows, Apple OSX, and Linux) from www.getfirefox.com

To start the automated testing portion of the *Internet Application Testing* module of the OSSTMM, we simply opened up Google Chrome's Web browser and entered the TED 5000 Smart Device's URL, http://192.168.210.5. Figure 13.13 shows that when attempting to access the TED 5000's Web interface, it was password-protected.

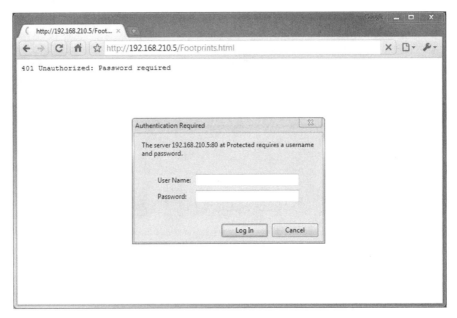

FIGURE 13.13

TED 5000 password-protected Web interface.

In order to gain access to the TED 5000's Web interface, we would have to obtain valid credentials or brute-force the password. We cover both these methods of obtaining credentials to the TED 5000's Web interface in the subsequent *Password Cracking* module. For the purpose of this module, we will assume that we have obtained credentials to the TED 5000's Web interface.

Now that we have access to the TED 5000's Web interface, we needed to get an understanding of the technologies it used. Figure 13.14 shows the TED 5000's main page that provides a majority of the information its users would be looking for.

At first glance, it would appear that the TED 5000 is utilizing Adobe's Flash technology to serve this information, but upon closer inspection, we found that this was not the case. Using Google Chrome's Inspect Element feature (right-click on the element you want to inspect), we determined that the TED 5000 was presenting information through JavaScript. Figure 13.15 shows that the Real-Time KW Usage reading of 3.043 kW was presented via a HTML code and not via an Adobe Flash object as originally thought.

While there are ways to test Adobe Flash Web applications, such as SWF Scan (https://h30406.www3.hp.com/campaigns/2009/wwcampaign/1-5TUVE/index.php?key=swf), the fact that the TED 5000 used JavaScript allowed us to use the more common Web Application Attack and Audit Framework (w3af) tool.

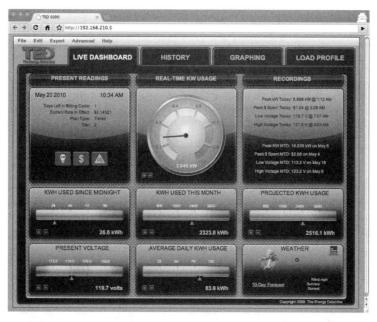

FIGURE 13.14

TED 5000's main page.

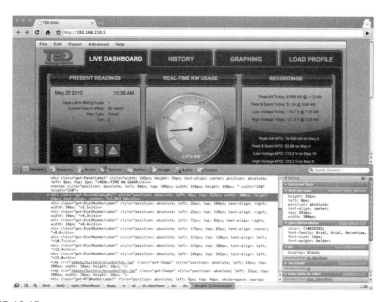

FIGURE 13.15

Google Chrome's inspect element feature.

TOOLS

Andrés Riancho's Web Application Attack and Audit Framework, or w3af for short, is an open-source Web application tool that provides a framework for identifying vulnerabilities in Web applications.[4] W3af also provides attack, or penetration testing, capabilities for discovered vulnerabilities. The tool can be utilized to perform both automated and manual vulnerability identification and exploitations and comes with a number of preconfigured scan policies, including one for the Open Web Application Security Project's (OWASP) Top 10. You can learn more about w3af and download a copy for yourself from http://w3af.sourceforge.net.

Now that we have learned the technologies used by the TED 5000's Web interface, we can utilize w3af to crawl, or spider, the targeted device's Web server. The goal of spidering the Web server is to create an index of the available pages on the Web site and then test them individually for vulnerabilities. Fortunately, w3af contains a preconfigured scan policy called Sitemap that crawls the target site. Figure 13.16 shows how to have w3af crawl the TED 5000 Smart Device.

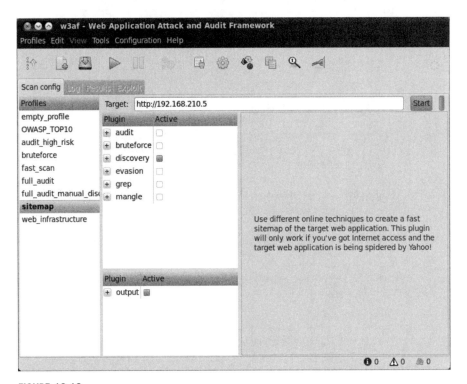

FIGURE 13.16

W3af sitemap feature.

Once we completed a scan of the TED 5000 Smart Device using w3af's Sitemap scan policy, we reviewed the results to identify pages to manually evaluate. Since a majority of the TED 5000's pages are static in nature, our manual evaluation of the pages identified by the Sitemap policy scan reviewed no vulnerabilities.

The next step in performing Internet Application Testing using w3af was to utilize the tools' built-in OWASP Top 10 scan policy. If you will remember from the preceding chapter, we discussed how that the OWASP Top 10 was a great tool to use when attempting to identify vulnerabilities. Thus, the authors of this book welcome the inclusion of the OWASP Top 10 built-in scan policy to w3af. You will notice that Figure 13.17, which shows the plug-ins that are selected for the OWASP Top 10 scan policy, shows that the Discovery plug-in is checked. This was the same plug-in that was used for the previous Sitemap scan policy. We performed the separate Sitemap policy scan because often times the OWASP Top 10 scan can take a significant amount of time to complete. In an effort to be more efficient, completing the Sitemap policy scan allows you to perform manual inspection of the identified pages while w3af performs the OWASP Top 10 policy scan.

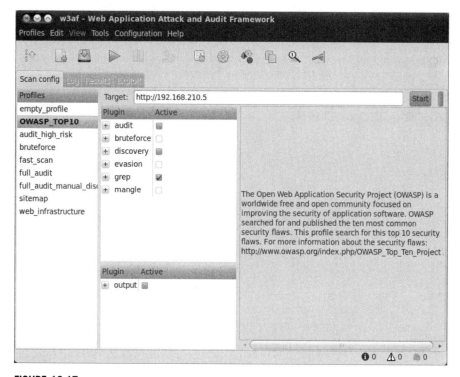

FIGURE 13.17

W3af OWASP top 10 policy scan.

As w3af conducts the OWASP Top 10 policy scan, you will see a progress meter along with log information, as shown in Figure 13.18. W3af will also flag vulnerabilities as they are identified, both in the Results section, as shown in Figure 13.19, and in the Log section, as shown in Figure 13.18.

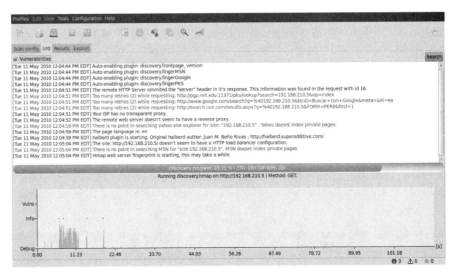

FIGURE 13.18

W3af scan progress.

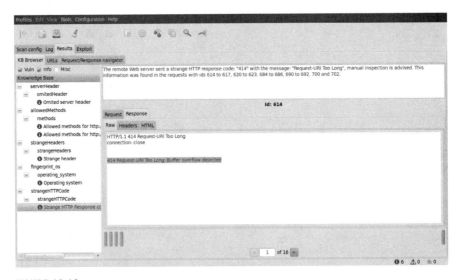

FIGURE 13.19

W3af scan results.

Once the scan was completed, we reviewed the results by simply clicking on the **Results** tab of w3af. While reviewing the results, we noticed one possibly interesting result, as highlighted in Figure 13.19. W3af flagged a potential buffer overflow vulnerability on the TED 5000 Smart Device because the Web server responded to several requests with a HTTP response code of "414"and the message of "Request-URI Too Long." At first glance, this vulnerability appears to be just the type of break an attacker would be looking for. However, we needed to validate its existence.

In order to validate the potential buffer overflow on the TED 5000 Smart Device's Web interface, we researched the 414 Request-URI Too Long Web server message. As a result of our research, we determined that this was a false positive. However, this potential vulnerability demonstrated how an attacker may utilize the *Internet Application Testing* module of ISECOM's OSSTMM's Process Security Testing section to potentially compromise as smart device.

Password Cracking

The *Password Cracking* module of ISECOM's OSSTMM aims to obtain credentials to password-protected targets. As previously mentioned in the *Internet Application Testing* module, the TED 5000 Smart Device's Web interface was protected by a log-in and a password. Figure 13.13 shows this protection. In much the same way that we identified the TED 5000's IP address, there are passive and active attacks that can result in obtaining valid credentials to the TED 5000's Web interface. For the purpose of this module, we will use the Wireshark sniffing tool for our passive attack and the Bruter brute-force password tool for our active attack.

Utilizing Wireshark to obtain log-in credentials to a Web site or other network service can be very effective under the right circumstances. Just like in the *Network Surveying* module, for Wireshark to be effective, you must be on the same network as either the client logging into the target device or the target itself. In switched network environments, even if you are on the same network, you still may not be able to view the packets that contain the log-in credentials. However, the ideal network to be sniffing would be a wireless one, such as those at an airport or a coffee shop. Likewise, for the passive attack to be effective, the log-in credentials must be sent as is unencrypted or encrypted with an encryption scheme with known flaws. As shown in Figure 13.13, the authentication prompt presented to users attempting to access the TED 5000's Web interface will be obfuscated in the weak Base64 encoding used for basic authentication. Let us now look at how we used the Wireshark tool to obtain the log-in credentials for the TED 5000's Web interface.

Using Wireshark's filtering capability, we first filtered our packet capture to show only the packets sent to or from the TED 5000's IP address, 192.168.210.5. This can be accomplished by setting a filter of "ip.addr==192.168.210.5." Then, we browsed the packets looking for HTTP protocol packets. You could set an additional filter for only the HTTP protocol packets sent to or from the TED 5000 Smart Device, but since our packet capture was of limited size, simply using the sort feature and manually reviewing the HTTP protocol packets worked for us.

Figure 13.20 shows the packet capture information that includes the Base64 encoded credentials being sent from the client to the TED 5000's Web interface. The decoded packet contains "Authorization: Basic YWRtaW46Wj FNYjMz." The information panel of Wireshark clearly shows that the packet contained authorization information, as shown by the highlighted text in Figure 13.20. Now that we know the Base64 encoded log-in and password, you could utilize your favorite encoder/decoder to obtain the plain text version of the log-in and password, as shown in Figure 13.21, Wireshark already did this for us. By simply clicking on the arrow next to the Authorization information in the information panel of Wireshark, we now know that credentials for the TED 5000's Web interface are admin / Z1gb33.

Now that we obtained the credentials to the TED 5000's Web interface via a passive attack, let us review how we used the Bruter password cracking tool to

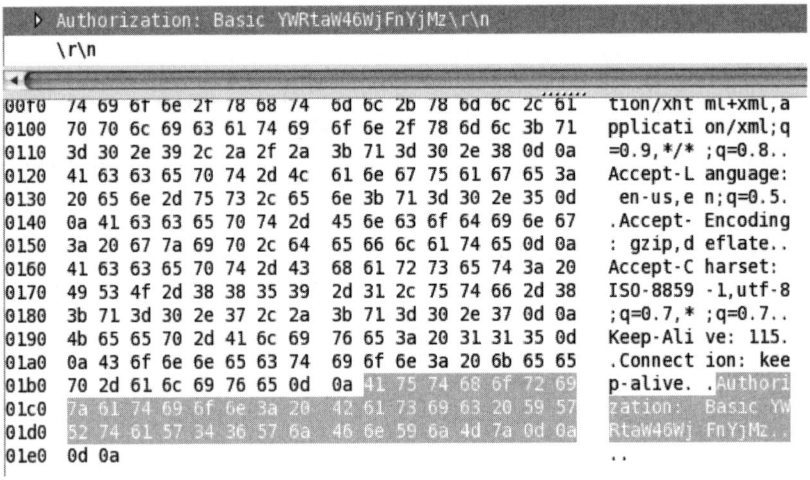

FIGURE 13.20

Wireshark packet capture.

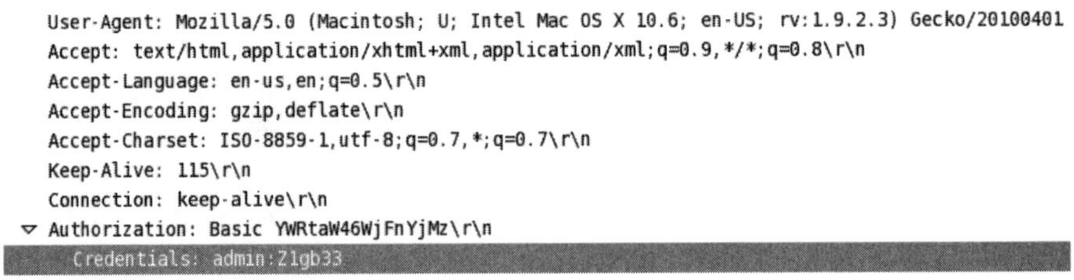

FIGURE 13.21

Wireshark Base64 decoded credentials.

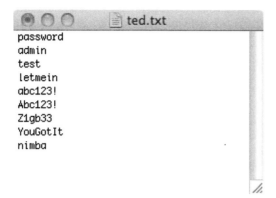

FIGURE 13.22

Sample dictionary file.

obtain the same credentials via an active attack. For Bruter to successfully obtain valid credentials for the target system, you must successfully identify the log-in account name and the associated password. Usually, the default log-in account name can be obtained by viewing the targeted device's documentation. For the purpose of this module, we used the log-in account name of the admin.

Bruter allows you to perform both brute-force and dictionary-based attacks against HTTP Basic Authentication, the scheme used to protect the TED 5000's Web interface. In testing, we created a simple dictionary file of common passwords to try, as shown in Figure 13.22.

> **NOTE**
>
> For demonstration purposes, and as we were the ones who configured the TED 5000 Smart Device, we made sure that the actual password was contained in our dictionary file. For more robust dictionary files, review the Section "Password Cracking" in the preceding chapter.

To use Bruter, we simply entered the IP address of the TED 5000's Web interface, 192.168.210.5, the protocol (HTTP Basic), the user (admin); selected the dictionary option; and browsed to our dictionary text file (ted.txt). Then, we simply clicked the **Start** button, and a few seconds later we were presented with the password for the admin account on the TED 5000's Web interface. Figure 13.23 shows our results and the valid credentials to access the targeted device's Web interface.

Once we obtained valid credentials to the TED 5000's Web interface, we were able to perform the aforementioned testing included in the *Internet Application Testing* module. Password Cracking, unlike the other modules of ISECOM's OSSTMM Process Security Testing section, may need to be performed often and may be out of order when compared to the other modules.

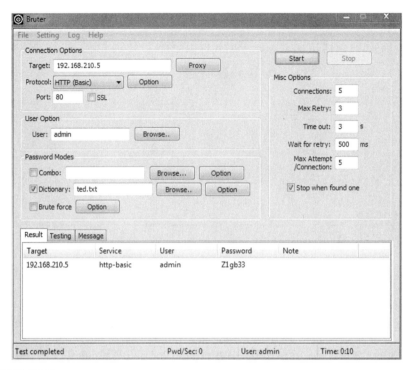

FIGURE 13.23

Bruter results.

WARNING

More than likely you will have to use active attacks when trying to obtain valid credentials for services or applications. Be mindful that the account(s) you are attempting to brute-force or attack via a dictionary list may have an account lockout threshold for invalid attempts. You can attempt to throttle your testing via the number of attempts per minute or the total number of attempts over a period, but if the account(s) you are targeting disable the account permanently, instead of only for a limited period such as 15 minutes, you will be unable to continue testing those accounts.

Denial-of-Service Testing

The objective of the *Denial-of-Service Testing* module of the Process Security Testing section of ISECOM's OSSTMM is to identify whether the targeted device is vulnerable to Denial-of-Service attacks. While a Denial-of-Service attack will most likely have a greater impact on a smart meter than on a smart device, depending on how the smart device is utilized by a consumer, a successful Denial-of-Service attack could have significant implications (think blackout). However, a Denial-of-Service attack against our targeted smart device, the TED 5000, would simply result in the loss of power monitoring for the duration of the attack.

Regardless of the impact of a Denial-of-Service attack, vulnerabilities scanners provide a wealth of plug-ins that check for these types of vulnerabilities. However, as running these plug-ins may very well result in an unresponsive target, they must be explicitly enabled. This can be accomplished by unchecking the **Safe Checks** setting in your Nessus scan policy, as shown in Figure 13.9.

If you plan on performing Denial-of-Service vulnerability checks against your targeted smart device, be sure you are aware of the consequences. Otherwise, you may end up with an inoperable device or lose valuable data. Consider yourself warned.

Exploit Testing

The final module of the Process Security Testing section of ISECOM's OSSTMM that we utilized for the purpose of this chapter was the *Exploit Testing* module. While Nessus did not identify any vulnerability that could be exploited, and the one w3af potential vulnerability was a false positive, there was little reason to attempt to exploit the TED 5000 Smart Device. However, we decided to run all of the exploits provided in the Metasploit tool against the TED 5000 Smart Device in an attempt to demonstrate how to perform Exploit Testing. One applicable detail from our previous Nessus results indicated that the TED 5000 Smart Device was running the BSD operating system.

To determine the exploits that Metasploit contains for a certain service, such as Apache, start the Metasploit console and type "search apache." Figure 13.24 shows the available Auxiliary modules, Exploits, and Payloads for the Apache service.

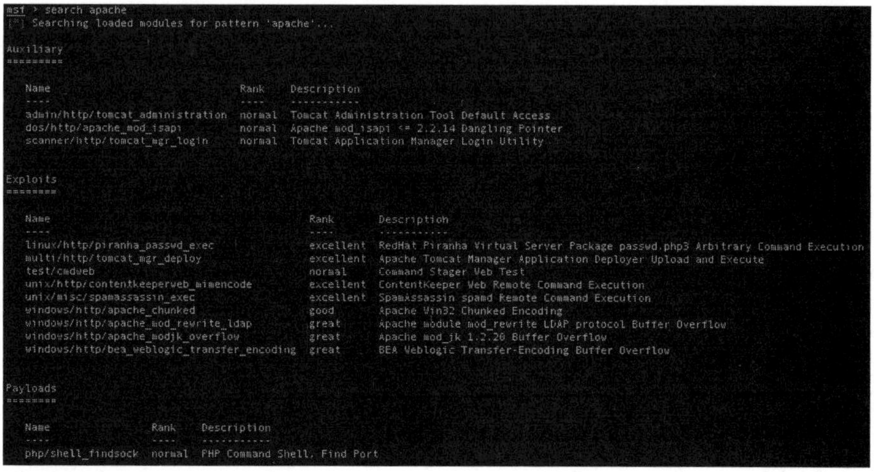

FIGURE 13.24

Metasploit Apache modules.

In reviewing the resulting modules, we realized that Metasploit only contained exploits for two Apache vulnerabilities for the UNIX operating system. However, both these vulnerabilities were for plug-ins not installed or utilized by the TED 5000 Smart Device. At this point, it was apparent that the TED 5000 Smart Device was not going to be compromised via Exploit Testing. However, Exploit Testing is the culmination of the OSSTMM, and successfully exploiting vulnerabilities can allow attackers to perform subsequent attacks until they attain their ultimate objective.

SUMMARY

In Chapter 12, "Attacking Smart Meters," we discussed the common methodologies used to perform security testing. In this chapter, we applied ISECOM's OSSTMM methodology to attack smart devices. Much like smart meters, smart devices will be subject to those with access to them. However, unlike smart meters, the current availability of smart devices is widespread. While the successful compromise of a smart device will most likely have significantly less impact than a successful compromise of a smart meter, this does not preclude smart device manufacturers from performing security testing devices. If certain smart devices became ubiquitous, they will most certainly find themselves in the sights of attackers and curious consumers alike. If these smart devices had not been previously subjected to security testing and had their vulnerabilities remediated, smart device users may find themselves in for unintended consequences.

Endnotes

1. Lilly P. Fujitsu Develops Smart Power Strip, Monitors Power Use [document on the Internet], Maximum PC;www.maximumpc.com/article/news/fujitsu_develops_smart_power_strip_monitors_power_use; 2010 [accessed 19.05.10].
2. What is Ted? [document on the Internet], Energy, Inc.;www.theenergydetective.com/about-ted; 2010 [accessed 19.05.10].
3. BackTrack Linux [document on the Internet], BackTrack Linux; www.backtrack-linux.org; 2010 [accessed 19.05.10].
4. w3af – Web Application Attack and Audit Framework [document on the Internet], Andrés Riancho; http://w3af.sourceforge.net; [accessed 20.05.10].

What's Next?

INFORMATION IN THIS CHAPTER

- Timeline
- What Should Consumers Expect?
- What Should Smart Grid Technology Vendors Expect?
- What Should Utility Companies Expect?
- What Should Security Professionals Expect and What Do They Predict?
- Smart Grid Community

Implementing a smart grid will not happen overnight, and once a smart grid is in use, it will continue to change and be updated to support new technologies and functionality. This chapter discusses what consumers, technology vendors, and utility companies should expect to see in the near future. In addition, this chapter discusses what security professionals are predicting for the smart grid and how to stay current with the movement to secure the smart grid.

TIMELINE

The deployment of smart grid infrastructure has been accelerated by initiatives across the world. In particular, projects that deploy smart meters and their supporting advanced metering infrastructure (AMI) have increased significantly in the past few years. The Smart Metering Project Team at the Energy Retail Association (www.energy-retail.org.uk/smartmeters.html) in the United Kingdom have maintained a map of current AMI and automatic meter reading (AMR) projects across the world, which is displayed in Figure 14.1. For a more detailed look, Figure 14.2 depicts current AMI and AMR projects in North America.

As illustrated in Figures 14.1 and 14.2, there are many smart-grid-related projects, most of which involve the deployment of smart meters, that are currently planned or in the process of being implemented. In March 2010, the Edison Foundation estimated that 60 million smart meters are currently being deployed in the United States.[2] So if you live in the United States, a smart meter may already be installed in your home.

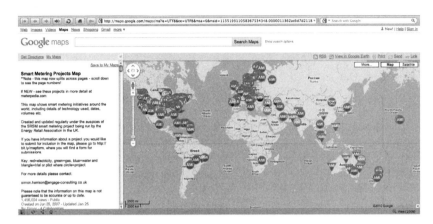

FIGURE 14.1

SRSM Smart Metering Project and Google maps covering the World.[1]

FIGURE 14.2

SRSM Smart Metering Project and Google maps covering North America.[1]

WHAT SHOULD CONSUMERS EXPECT?

Consumers have been promised that the smart grid will bring many improvements to their daily lives. Smaller electric bills, less frequent and shorter power outages, and more immediate access to energy usage information are just some of the promises made to consumers. In order to fulfill these promises, several new technologies will be invading consumers' homes and businesses including:

- Smart devices
- Smart meters

- Home area network
- Electric vehicles
- Personal power plants

Smart Devices

For consumers, the more visible components of the smart grid will include the smart devices that reside in people's kitchens, living rooms, bedrooms, and offices. Mechanical appliances will now include digital components once reserved for personal computers and office workstations. Appliances at home and office now have built-in processing capabilities and communication abilities to improve energy efficiency and ease of use.

Smart Appliances in Home

In addition to the smart devices discussed in Chapter 13, "Attacking Smart Devices," consumers can expect to see their traditional devices, such as refrigerators, dishwashers, heaters, washing machines and dryers, and water heaters replaced with their smart counterparts. As an example, General Electric's (GE) smart water heater is displayed in Figure 14.3. GE's smart water heater has the capability to be connected to a smart meter, which could allow either the utility company or the consumer to change the operating mode to an energy saving mode in order to decrease the power consumption.[3] This is designed to save the consumers' money and prevent power outages during peak-demand times.

Other smart consumer appliances, such as dishwashers and air conditioners, will also have similar network interfaces that allow consumers and utility companies to manage their energy consumption through either a smart meter or a third-party interface. It is safe to assume that most new appliances, ranging from power strips to dishwashers, will be built with some form of communications technology to remotely control the appliance. With this new level of connectivity, consumers will be able to manage their home appliances whether they are at home or anywhere in the world.

NOTE

Why is a book about security discussing washing machines and water heaters? New technologies bring new risk, and in a smart grid world, numerous devices that were once isolated will be connected to an information network. By adding this new level of connectivity, the devices will be introduced to the risk of a remote attack. Any node in a network should be considered a potential attack injection point. As such, even washing machines and water heaters will need to be secured appropriately in a smart grid.

Smart Appliances in Office

Businesses will also be introduced to new technologies that utilize the functionality of smart grids. Data centers running hundreds or thousands of computers, switches,

FIGURE 14.3

GE smart water heater.[4]

routers, and other network devices, along with battery backups and heating, ventilating, and air conditioning (HVAC) systems draw massive amounts of energy. Thus, energy usage can be a huge component of a company's budget. With the detailed energy usage information available in a smart grid, data centers should be able to identify inefficiencies in electrical usage to reduce energy-related costs. The Department of Energy is one organization that is currently performing research, as part of the Energy Smart Data Center project, to improve the efficiency of data center cooling, power generation, conversion, and distribution.[5] More information on these efforts can be viewed at http://esdc.pnl.gov/.

Facilities management will also be able to take advantage of the remote management capabilities of smart devices. Now in many buildings, lights are turned off automatically at a certain time, and air conditioning or heating is turned off over long holiday weekends when no one is in the building. While this once may have been a complex operation, smart devices will allow this to be as simple as clicking a few buttons in a Web application.

Businesses are already trying to save on energy costs through technical initiatives, such as virtualization initiatives that reduce the number of physical servers running in an environment. Additionally, companies such as Hewlett-Packard (HP – www.hp.com) are starting to sell servers with built-in sensors that can detect energy waste and compensate to improve energy efficiency.[6]

Smart Meters

As illustrated in the section "Timeline," millions of smart meters are being deployed all across the world and consumers should expect that trend to continue. From the consumers' perspective, the new meters will currently provide real-time energy usage information and limited control over smart devices. In the near future, as more smart devices become available, smart meters will be used as the consumers' control center for most devices within homes and businesses.

It is thought that viewing how much energy each device consumes will help consumers choose to purchase more energy efficient devices and turning off devices when not in use. Unfortunately, just turning off the devices does not completely eliminate energy waste. Even when most devices are either turned off or in standby mode, they will still draw power. The energy used by these devices while turned off or in standby mode is commonly referred to as vampire energy waste. As an example, the vampire energy waste of an average plasma television is estimated to cost consumers $165.00 per year.[7] For more examples, Table 14.1 lists the estimated energy usage of several common devices while in standby mode in homes and businesses. The third column in Table 14.1 lists the average watts (W), which is an energy measurement (joules) that the device draws per second.[8] The fourth column of Table 14.1 lists the average energy consumption in kilowatt-hours per year if the device is left in standby mode the entire year.[8] The last column lists the average cost of the device's energy waste if the device were left in standby mode for the entire year, which is based on the United States' residential national average electricity cost of 10.72 cents per kilowatt-hour (as of February 2010).[9]

The amount of power drawn by these devices in standby mode or when powered off is significantly lower than when they are turned on, and individually, the numbers listed in Table 14.1 may not seem significant. However, the average American home has 40 devices constantly drawing power.[11] When the energy waste for those 40 devices is combined for a single American, the numbers begin to appear more significant. Considering there are millions of homes in America, billions of watts of energy per year are wasted when these devices are not even being used. It is estimated that almost 10 percent of residential electricity use is vampire energy waste,[11] which equates to Americans spending about $4 billion on wasted electricity each year.[7]

Table 14.1 Vampire energy cost estimates[10]

Product	Mode	Average (W)	Annual average (kW-h/year)	Average annual cost ($)
Air conditioner	Powered off	0.9	0.81	0.09
Central furnace heating	Powered off	4.21	37.89	4.06
Gas range	Ready mode	1.13	10.17	1.09
Garage door opener	Ready mode	4.48	40.32	4.32
Low-voltage landscape	Ready mode	1.13	10.17	1.09
Cordless power tool	Ready mode and completely charged	8.34	75.06	8.05
Irrigation timer	Powered off	2.75	24.75	2.65
Irrigation timer	Ready mode	2.84	25.56	2.74
Coffeemaker	Powered off	1.14	10.26	1.10
Microwave ovens	Ready mode and door closed	3.08	27.72	2.97
Microwave ovens	Ready mode and door open	25.79	232.11	24.88
Surge protector	Powered off	1.05	9.45	1.01
Mobile phone charger	Connected to fully charged phone	2.24	20.16	2.16
Mobile phone charger	Phone not connected	0.26	2.34	0.25
CRT computer monitor	Powered off	0.8	7.2	0.77
CRT computer monitor	Sleep mode	12.14	109.26	11.71
LCD computer monitor	Powered off	1.13	10.17	1.09
LCD computer monitor	Sleep mode	1.38	12.42	1.33
Desktop computer	Powered off	2.84	25.56	2.74
Desktop computer	Sleep mode	21.13	190.17	20.39
Notebook computer	Powered off	8.9	80.1	8.59
Notebook computer	Sleep mode	15.77	141.93	15.21
Notebook computer	Power supply only	4.42	39.78	4.26
Computer speakers	Powered on, but no sound	4.12	37.08	3.97
Computer speakers	Powered off	1.79	16.11	1.73
USB hub	Powered off	1.44	12.96	1.39
DSL modem	Powered off	1.37	12.33	1.32
Cable modem	Powered off	3.84	34.56	3.70
Cable modem	Standby mode	3.85	34.65	3.71
Inkjet printer and fax	Powered off	5.31	47.79	5.12
Laser printer and fax	Ready mode	6.42	57.78	6.19
Inkjet multifunction device	Powered off	5.26	47.34	5.07

(Continued)

Table 14.1 Vampire energy cost estimates[10]—cont'd

Product	Mode	Average (W)	Annual average (kW-h/year)	Average annual cost ($)
Laser multifunction device	Powered off	3.12	28.08	3.01
Inkjet printer	Powered off	1.26	11.34	1.22
Laser printer	Powered off	1.58	14.22	1.52
Flatbed scanner	Powered off	2.48	22.32	2.39
Copier	Powered off	1.49	13.41	1.44
DVR set-top box	Powered on, but not recording	37.64	338.76	36.32
DVR set-top box	Powered off	36.68	330.12	35.39
Digital cable with DVR set-top box	TV powered off and DVR not recording	44.63	401.67	43.06
Digital cable with DVR set-top box	Powered off by remote control	43.46	391.14	41.93
Digital cable set-top box	TV powered off	24.65	221.85	23.78
Digital cable set-top box	Powered off by remote control	17.83	160.47	17.20
Digital cable set-top box	Powered off by switch	17.5	157.5	16.88
Satellite with DVR set-top box	TV powered off and DVR not recording	28.35	255.15	27.35
Satellite with DVR set-top box	Powered off by remote control	27.8	250.2	26.82
Satellite set-top box	TV powered off	15.95	143.55	15.39
Satellite set-top box	Powered off by remote control	15.66	140.94	15.11
Satellite set-top box	Powered off by switch	15.47	139.23	14.93
CRT television	Powered off by remote control	3.06	27.54	2.95
CRT television	Powered off by switch	2.88	25.92	2.78
Rear projection television	Powered off by remote control	6.97	62.73	6.72
Rear projection television	Powered off by switch	6.6	59.4	6.37
Television/VCR	Powered off with remote control	5.15	46.35	4.97

(Continued)

Table 14.1 Vampire energy cost estimates[10]—*cont'd*

Product	Mode	Average (W)	Annual average (kW-h/year)	Average annual cost ($)
Television/VCR	Powered off by switch	5.99	53.91	5.78
AM/FM Tuner	Powered on, but not playing	9.48	85.32	9.15
AM/FM Tuner	Powered off	1.12	10.08	1.08
Amplifier	Powered on, but not playing	33.99	305.91	32.79
Amplifier	Powered off	0.27	2.43	0.26
CD player	Powered on, but not playing	8.62	77.58	8.32
CD player	Powered off	5.04	45.36	4.86
DVD recorder	Powered off	0.75	6.75	0.72
DVD player	Powered on, but not playing	7.54	67.86	7.27
DVD player	Powered off	1.55	13.95	1.50
DVD/VCR	Powered on, but not playing	13.51	121.59	13.03
DVD/VCR	Powered off	5.04	45.36	4.86
Game console	Powered off	1.01	9.09	0.97
Game console	Ready mode	23.34	210.06	22.52
Musical instruments	Powered off	2.82	25.38	2.72
Audio receiver	Powered on, but not playing	37.61	338.49	36.29
Audio receiver	Powered off	2.92	26.28	2.82
Subwoofer	Powered on, but not playing	10.7	96.3	10.32

TIP

A common joke in the security industry is that a computer is only secure when it is turned off and burned to small pieces. Many people turn off their computers at the end of the day because of this advice provided by countless blogs. By going one step further and unplugging the computers and new smart devices, consumers could significantly reduce the amount of energy wasted and prevent their electronics from being attacked, for at least a few hours.

Variable Pricing

Most consumers in the United States currently pay a fixed rate for electricity. So, a price is set per kilowatt-hour and their bill is calculated using the set rate for every kilowatt-hour used. However, utility companies pay a variable rate for energy in the wholesale market, where the price is based on the time and present demand. Smart meters will provide utility companies with the functionality to apply this variable rate model, or time-of-use model, to consumers. The variable pricing model has risen from the issue of peak-demand times, which are times during the day when power demand from the electric grid is at its highest level. There are two basic strategies to dealing with the increasing demand during these peak-demand times. The first option is to build more power plants to generate more energy to meet the demand during the peak-demand times. This option is of course costly and creates significant waste during the nonpeak demand times. Predicting how much energy demand will exist at a given moment is nearly impossible. As a result, power plants usually generate a larger energy supply than the existing demand. So when there is less demand, the excess energy is currently wasted. Storing this excess energy for future use is currently being researched and may play a large role in the future smart grid, but until these large-scale batteries are deployed, the energy will be wasted. Thus, building more power plants will only increase energy waste during the nonpeak demand times.

The second option is to reduce the demand during the peak-demand times. One such method is to convince consumers to perform energy intensive operations, such as running the dishwasher or clothes dryer, during the nonpeak demand times. So, for example, instead of running the dishwasher at 6:00 P.M., a consumer would schedule his or her smart dishwasher to start running at 2:00 A.M. when the demand for power is less. Some people may be convinced to alter their dishwashing schedule for environmental reasons. However, most people will need further motivation to change their habits, which will most likely be in the form of time-of-use pricing. If a consumer knows that energy costs twice as much at 6:00 P.M. than at 2:00 A.M., then it is thought that the consumer will be more likely to run their dishwasher at 2:00 A.M.

EPIC FAIL

It would seem that consumers are getting a good deal. They receive more control over their electricity consumption and the potential for a smaller electric bill. However, not every consumer has been thrilled with the rollout of the new smart meters. For example, consider the Pacific Gas and Electric Company (PG&E –www.pge.com/) smart meter project in California where customers have submitted almost 1,000 complaints to regulators.[12] The customer complaints state that the bills are inaccurate and significantly higher than the bills they received with the previous, traditional meters.[12] According to California State Senator Dean Florez, "This is a revolt. The Tea Party has nothing on smart meters in the Central Valley."[12]

PG&E is not the only utility company with customers complaining about smart meters. Oncor, which services parts of Texas, has received a similar number of complaints regarding higher-than-usual electric bills.[13] According to Ree Wattner, her electric bill jumped from about 1,500 kW-h to about 4,400 kW-h after a smart meter was installed in her home.[14] In

(Continued)

(Continued)

response, Wattner has cofounded the Smart Utility Reform Citizens (www.smarturcitizens.com) consumers group that blames the higher electric bills on smart meters.

In addition to angry customers forming groups and filing complaints with the local public utility commissions, some customers have taken to filing lawsuits against the utility companies. One such lawsuit accuses Oncor of committing fraud, which has turned into a class action lawsuit, and PG&E has a similar lawsuit pending against them.[15] Even if the utility companies win the lawsuits, some angry customers may seek to damage the utility companies in other ways that could turn into potential security threats.

PG&E and Oncor have stated that unusual weather and recent rate increases were the reason for the higher electrical bills, not faulty smart meters.[13] However, Oncor did state that up to 1 percent of smart meters may have been installed incorrectly due to human error.[13] As a result of the installation error, between 3,800 and 7,600 people could receive inaccurate electric bills that are higher than usual.[13] Regardless of the reason, Oncor and PG&E now have a considerable number of angry customers that may impede the adoption of the smart grid and who may become security threats.

In addition, some utility companies are offering cycling programs that would allow the utility company to cycle off certain appliances during peak-demand times.[16] Essentially, the utility company provides the customer with monetary incentives for the ability to briefly turn off certain appliances, such as air conditioners, during peak-demand times. The utility company performs the cycling operations by sending a command to either the smart device or smart thermostat. Hopefully, the smart device or thermostat will also receive the command to turn back on or have a built-in function to automatically turn back on after a certain amount of time has passed. Otherwise, a few hot summer days could lead to customer backlash against these programs.

Many smart grid marketing campaigns have used time-of-use pricing and cycling programs as the basis for convincing consumers that smart grids will reduce their electric bill. Of course, this all relies on consumers accepting the new devices, schedules, and price plans. For those consumers who do accept the new technologies, the risk posed by cyber threats will continue to increase. As these consumers begin to rely more on connected appliances, a successful cyber attack will be even more devastating.

Home Area Network

A communications network will need to be set up in consumers' homes and businesses to support the required communication between the smart meters and the smart devices. This network has been commonly labeled the Home Area Network (HAN). As standard protocols for the HAN continue to be debated and refined, the HAN may take many different forms.

Some smart devices and smart meters have been designed to connect to the consumers' existing home or business network. These devices rely on the consumers having a broadband Internet connection to transmit data and commands between the utility company, third-party service providers, and the smart meter and devices. For example, Yello Strom developed and sells smart meters to their customers that utilize the customers' existing broadband Internet connection. While this eliminates the need to set up a wireless network to transmit data between home and utility substations, there are significant security risks with taking this approach. Most consumers' home networks, especially wireless networks, are still configured insecurely using encryption protocols with known weaknesses and default passwords.

As an example, consider the Verizon FiOS wireless routers that are configured by default to use Wired Equivalent Privacy (WEP) encryption. In addition to the many known weaknesses with WEP, Verizon sometimes uses a program to calculate the WEP key based on the wireless network service set identifier (SSID). While this approach seems better than using the same WEP encryption key on every Verizon FiOS router, it does not really improve the security of these wireless networks. The algorithm Verizon uses is publicly known and does not incorporate randomness into the key generation, which is critical to creating a secure encryption key. As a result, several people have created easy-to-use Verizon WEP key calculators.[17] A description of the key generation algorithm and a JavaScript version of the calculator can be found at http://xkyle.com/2009/03/03/verizon-fios-wireless-key-calculator/. The calculator only needs the SSID of the wireless network in order to calculate the default WEP key. Thus, an attacker would only need to identify the name of the consumer's wireless network and within seconds be able to connect to the consumer's wireless network.

WARNING

Consumer-managed networks should not be considered secure, and trust relationships should not be set up between utility networks and HANs. The Verizon default WEP calculator should serve as an example for this warning. To state the obvious, most consumers are not security professionals, and in general, they do not spend time to properly secure their home networks. Further default security controls, which need no configuration from users, should be built into the smart devices and applications to ensure the confidentiality and integrity of data transmitted across the HAN.

So, who is responsible for the HAN? If the smart devices and smart meter rely on the consumers network and the consumer network is breached, is the breach also considered to be a breach of the utility company, or third-party service provider? If so, does the breach fall under the numerous breach and privacy laws that the utility company would need to comply with? The answers to these questions will likely play out in the judicial systems of countries over the next 20 years.

Electric Vehicles

With high gasoline prices likely to continue, consumers may turn to alternative fuel vehicles to replace their current gasoline-powered vehicles. Currently, there is not a large selection of electric vehicles available; however, some companies have either released or are developing plug-in electric vehicles (PEV) including

- Nissan Leaf – http://nissanusa.com/leaf-electric-car
- Chevy Volt – www.chevrolet.com/pages/open/default/future/volt.do
- Tesla Roadster and Model S – www.teslamotors.com/

PEVs could either be the solution to storing excess electricity in the smart grid or cause massive power outages in the electric grid. PEVs store electricity in a large battery and use the energy for fuel, as opposed to traditional vehicles that use gasoline. One potential benefit to a nation using PEVs is the capability of the smart grid to extract energy from PEVs during peak-demand times.[18] The idea is to charge the PEVs' batteries during nonpeak demand times, when energy supply is more than demand. Thus, the excess energy supply would be stored in the PEVs, which would reduce the energy waste created during nonpeak demand times.

Unfortunately, that is just the ideal scenario in which PEVs will only need to recharge during nonpeak demand times. Consider the more likely scenario in which PEVs do need to recharge during peak-demand times. In 2007, there were over 254 million registered passenger vehicles in the United States.[19] If only a quarter of 254 million vehicles became PEVs, the burden on the electric grid could be crippling. Millions of PEVs charging during peak-demand times may strain the electric grid too much, causing a massive distributed denial of service (DDoS) against the electric grid.

Personal Power Plant

George Westinghouse's centralized power generation vision is starting to fade into a more hybrid approach to power generation. While large power plants still exist and will likely remain for at least the next century, distributed power generation technology is starting to become a viable option for many consumers. Relatively cheap solar panels and wind power generators, coupled with government rebate incentives, have influenced consumers to begin installing power-generating capabilities in their own homes.

In the current vision of the smart grid, consumers will also have the ability to sell excess electricity back to the utility companies. The ability to sell electricity back to the utility companies will certainly attract some entrepreneurial types; however, it will also attract the fraudulent types who will seek to manipulate the data sent back to the utility company.

Privacy

One of the major consumer concerns facing the adoption of the smart grid is privacy. As discussed in Chapter 2, "Threats and Impacts: Consumers," smart meters and smart devices will be collecting massive amounts of data and transmitting this data through the smart grid. Concerns for the security of their information may lead some people to live off the grid, but this will most likely be a small number. Of more, concern are the people who will go great lengths to prevent being connected to the smart grid. As an example, consider the Bakersfield, California, man who plans to fight the PG&E installation of a smart meter at his home. Due to privacy concerns, he has locked up his existing meter and made the following statement to a reporter: "If they show up they are going to have to go through me to get at it. It will take a court order and a whole bunch of police officers. PG&E needs to be stopped in their tracks here."[20] While this represents an extreme position, it may be a signal to utility companies to protect their workers' safety when they try to install smart meters in people's homes.

While not to the extreme of putting up a physical fight, other consumers and legal experts have agreed with the position that smart meters could violate the Fourth Amendment to the United States constitution, which guarantees citizens the right to privacy. As discussed in Chapter 2, analysis of energy usage data from smart meters would allow the utility company, or any other organization with access to the data, to determine what appliances you are using and map out your lifestyle within your home. Some consumers in California have claimed this to be corporate intrusion and a violation of rights.[20] However, this could also allow government agencies to view your activities inside your home, which could be unconstitutional. According to Attorney Lee Tien with the Electronic Frontier Foundation (EFF –www.eff.org/), "It's really very clear, both under the Constitution, the 4th Amendment, the privacy of the home is really the most important value,"[20] and "Inside your home is where the government isn't supposed to intrude without some kind of a warrant usually. And yet when this data is flowing freely outside your home, then the information gets outside that protected boundary and you start to have a problem."[20] This could lead to future lawsuits against the utility companies and government agencies if there are incidents where people believe their privacy is being violated, which could slow down or even reverse the adoption of smart grid technologies.

WHAT SHOULD SMART GRID TECHNOLOGY VENDORS EXPECT?

Technology vendors should expect an initial boom for their products and services. There is a lot of money, excitement, and curiosity in the energy industry, from both utility companies and consumers. Utility companies will need to purchase smart meters, network devices, and services from technology vendors. Some early adopting consumers will immediately replace their existing, inefficient appliances with new smart appliances, and the remaining consumers will gradually replace their appliances as the old appliances break down.

Technology service providers will also be met with scepticism though. As discussed in the section "What Should Consumers Expect," some consumers are resisting the new devices from technology providers. Although other technology service providers are being tasked to validate the accuracy of new devices,[13] a backlash may occur against these new devices when security breaches occur and consumers' privacy is violated. Technology service providers will need to be able to defend the security posture of their products to calm the critics.

While some consumers will be initially excited to try out the new devices to save money on their electric bills, others will be excited to both play with and hack the new devices. Technology vendors should assume that people will find vulnerabilities in these devices, and recent history shows it is not a matter of if but only a matter of when vulnerabilities are exposed in these systems as well. Rather than viewing these people in an adversarial manner, technology vendors should actively work with those people to promote responsible disclosure of the identified vulnerabilities. Otherwise, the technology vendors risk the fate of being specifically targeted for their adversarial relationship to the security community, which could turn to malicious attacks.

WHAT SHOULD UTILITY COMPANIES EXPECT?

Utility companies have also been promised that the smart grid will bring many improvements to their operations. New technology will help utility companies reduce energy waste, perform more accurate billing, increase the stability of the electric grid, and reduce operating costs. The question for this book, though, is will the smart grid bring a more secure electric grid?

Reducing Energy Demand to Reduce Costs and Security

While government incentives will help pay for some of the costs, utility companies will need to make a major investment up front to achieve the goals of the smart grid. However, the benefits will be reaped for decades to come. In the section "Smart Meters," it was noted that about 10 percent of the residential energy consumed in the United States is wasted through vampire energy waste. If that 10 percent was eliminated through more efficient appliances and better-informed consumers, utility companies could potentially shut down and retire multiple aging power plants without having to replace them in the near future. Retiring the power plants could save the utility companies money as well as eliminate the need to secure those power plants. Thus, the number of facilities and systems to secure would be reduced.

With the introduction of two-way communication between the smart meter and the utility company, physical visits to consumers' homes and businesses will significantly decrease. Physical visits to perform maintenance and other various tasks will still be required; however, the requirement for utility workers to physically read the electric meters will be virtually eliminated.

Reducing the number of physical visits will reduce the operational costs for utility companies. Utility companies currently spend significant amounts of money on gas and vehicles for the utility workers to read consumers' meters, which is just one reason utility companies are rapidly deploying AMI. Implementing the two-way communication functionality involved in AMI will certainly introduce risk to the utility company; however, there is one hidden security benefit. Utility company workers will not need to leave the physical protective boundary of their offices to read the meters and more importantly, they will not need to take utility company electronic devices that store sensitive information outside this physical protective boundary. As a result, the risk of mobile device theft will decrease.

Reducing the physical visits will also increase the safety for utility workers. While dogs and other pets have been a nuisance of utility workers for decades, utility workers have faced serious threats from consumers. As described in the section "Privacy," making visits to the consumers' homes can turn into dangerous situations for utility company workers. Utility companies do not always make popular decisions, and some consumers have taken their anger out on utility company employees, which has resulted in the physical injuries to the employees.[21] In other cases, some consumers have mistaken the employees for robbers and tried to defend their houses with deadly weapons.[21]

Diagnosing Problems Faster

Smart grid implementations will most likely include advanced sensor networks that will report potential problems in the electric grid. One such technology that could be employed in smart grids are SynchroPhasors in combination with phasor measurement units (PMUs), which record grid measurements at about 30 observations per second.[22] The North American SynchroPhasor Initiative (NASPI –www. naspi.org/) is working to advance the deployment of SynchroPhasors and PMUs in the electric grid, which includes the following:

- Networked phasor measurement devices
- Phasor data sharing
- Applications for
  - Wide-area monitoring
  - Real-time operations
  - Power system planning
  - Forensic analysis of grid disturbances[22]

Information sharing is critical to utilizing the full potential of a wide-area sensor network. As a result, the network architecture of a wide-area sensor network would include multiple utility companies and how they communicate with each other and the different components in a deployment. SynchroPhasors and their supporting infrastructure, as well as any other sensor infrastructure, require a supporting network infrastructure and applications to transmit, analyze, and present the data in a human readable format. Sensors, devices, supporting network infrastructure, and applications will all need to be secured or they risk becoming potential injection points for attacks. The good news is that securing networks, applications, and systems should be nothing new. Traditional security controls will apply to new sensor devices. For example, changing default passwords, disabling unnecessary services, and implementing a patch management process to apply firmware updates will all apply to these new devices.

Beyond Electricity

The electric grid is receiving the most attention for transforming into a smart grid; however, other utilities including natural gas and water are going through their own transformations. The smart gas and water grids will be very similar to the smart electric grid and most of the content found in this book applies to all three smart grid types. Smart meters, metering infrastructure, and applications will be deployed and enable utilities as well as consumers to intelligently manage their usage of all utility types. In addition, advanced sensor networks will be deployed to assist utilities in finding water and gas leaks faster and remotely correct potential issues before they become problems. Just as with the smart electric grid, each new device and supporting infrastructure will need to be secured to avoid local or potential national catastrophes. The security concepts discussed throughout this book will apply to these utility types as well.

An All Encompassing Smart Grid

Due to how similar the infrastructure is for electricity, gas, and water in smart grids, some cities are combining the three into one smart grid. As an example, the city of Tallahassee, FL is creating a smart grid for electric, gas, and water utilities. All three will operate on the same network that transmits data from consumers to utility companies and allows consumers to schedule smart devices to operate during off-peak hours.[23]

This seems like a logical choice since the utility companies will be able to utilize the same network, meter, and other devices that will reduce the costs associated with deploying smart grids. This will also reduce the number of devices that need to be installed in consumers' homes and businesses and potentially combine all their usage data into one location. Thus, instead of requiring consumers to check three different Web sites for their electricity, gas, and water energy usage information, they could just check one Web site.

Reese Goad, Tallahassee's director of utility business and customer service, describes the approach of a single network and a single smart meter per consumer as "Having all three systems under one umbrella, we'll be able to tell them the total cost of utility services, and view in real time the amount of utility services they're using."[23] On the other hand, a security professional may call this a single point of failure. If an attacker were to successfully execute an attack against this single network, consumers could be without all utilities. A backup, or redundant network, would be nice to have in this situation; however, budgetary concerns leading to risk acceptance could easily prevail in the design phases for these smart grids. In addition, combining all three utilities into one smart meter will provide a single point of attack for potential attackers. With remote shutoff capabilities built into smart meters, an attacker could potentially turn off electricity, gas, and water by attacking the single smart meter.

Curiosity Attacks

As with the technology service providers, utility companies should expect an initial increase in attacks. By installing new devices in homes, some consumers will be curious to see how the devices work and what they can do with the devices. Electricity theft has long plagued utility companies, and some consumers will attempt to use cyber attacks in order to perform electricity theft. Unfortunately, curiosity and minor theft will not be the only causes for attacks. As discussed in the next section, utility companies will need to be prepared to face attacks from organized crimes, organized hacking groups, terrorist groups, and foreign governments.

WHAT SHOULD SECURITY PROFESSIONALS EXPECT AND WHAT DO THEY PREDICT?

Currently, there is a lot of rhetoric for securing the smart grid. Governments consider it to be a matter of national security and most marketing material states that a smart grid will improve the security of the existing electric grid. However, most security professionals realize there are many threats to smart grid technologies and that old security vulnerabilities will be present in new technologies. Security professionals, as well as other government officials, predict that these vulnerabilities will be present and exploited in smart grids across the world.

Security versus Functionality

As in most situations, security professionals should expect a healthy debate when arguing for security to not be secondary to functionality. Security has been mentioned as one of the primary goals for smart grids; however, there will be situations when security controls directly conflict with the implementation of other goals for the smart grid. In these situations, management will need to make the ultimate decision. The security department will be responsible for ensuring that management understands the risk associated with the new functionality so that management can make an educated decision. Assuming management decides the new functionality is worth the risk, the security department will then be responsible for developing compensating controls that mitigate the risk associated with the new functionality.

Making the Argument

Speaking in terms of theoretical doomsday scenarios will not sway most executives. If you are responsible for presenting the risk to management, a quantitative analysis of the real cost of a breach backed by statistics and mandatory regulations will make the best argument. Most states in the United States have breach notification laws that require organizations to disclose when personally identifiable information has been disclosed. Thus, finding statistics and real-world examples to present to management will not be difficult. As an example, the Privacy Rights Clearinghouse maintains a list of the publicly disclosed breaches involving personally identifiable information (PII) since 2005, which they call the Chronology of Data Breaches. The list can be viewed at www. privacyrights.org/ar/chrondatabreaches.htm. In addition, the Open Security Foundation maintains a database and has a mailing list for breaches involving PII. More information on the Open Security Foundation DatalossDB database and mailing list can be found at http://datalossdb.org/.

In addition to the costs associated with investigations, lawsuits, and remediating a vulnerability after a breach has occurred, compliance with mandatory regulations is a powerful argument to use when discussing risk with management. In Chapter 6, "Public and Private Companies," compliance with NERC CIP reliability standards is discussed along with the repercussions of noncompliance. Under Section 215 of the Federal Power Act, NERC has the authority to fine United States entities up to $1 million per day.[24] While NERC CIP compliance will not help in every situation, it should help security professionals achieve a minimum baseline of security within their organization.

Risk Acceptance

When an organization has deemed the remediation of a vulnerability to be too costly, the organization may decide to just accept the risk. Risk acceptance, also known as risk acknowledgement, and some other similar terms are commonly used in the compliance world when an audit or risk assessment has identified a vulnerability. For example, let's consider a critical business application called FlicksJavaApp, which was written in the Java programming language. In order to run a Java application, a user must have a Java Runtime Environment (JRE) installed on his/her computer. As the Java programming language and its application programming interface (API) evolve, legacy objects and functions become unsupported as newer ones replace them. Thus, if FlicksJavaApp relies on the legacy functions that are no longer supported by the latest version of the JRE, then updating the JRE installed on the users' computers will cause FlicksJavaApp to stop executing correctly. Since FlicksJavaApp is a critical business application that is required for the organization to operate, the organization needs to decide to either spend the resources to recode FlicksJavaApp to use the updated JRE or accept the risk of running an outdated version of the JRE that is susceptible to vulnerabilities. While the remediations may be costly, security professionals should advise their organizations to only accept the risk as a last resort option.

> ## EPIC FAIL
>
> Accepting risk may seem like an easy solution for managements, as it tends to cut costs in the current budget. However, worst-case scenarios have happened to organizations that have accepted risk in the past. Consider the BP (www.bp.com) oil spill in the Gulf of Mexico, where many risk exceptions were accepted and granted by BP, its partners, and government regulators. For example, BP engineers decided to use a risky set of pipes and casings for lining the well in place on the ocean floor that violated BP's own safety policies. The decision to go forward with the risk components could only be allowed if BP management decided to accept the risk.[25] In addition, regulators granted an exception that delayed mandatory testing of a blowout preventer weeks before the rig explosion occurred.[25]
>
> BP's own engineers expressed concern over the safety violations; however, the BP oil drilling project was under financial stress since a 43-day delay had cost the company more than $21 million.[25] Leasing the oil rig was costing BP $500,000 per day,[25] so BP management was under pressure to get the project back on track. While the risk acceptance saved the company delays and millions of dollars in the near term, risk acceptance is now costing BP billions of dollars. As of June 19, 2010, BP stated they have paid out $104 million in claims to residents along the Gulf Coast.[26] With motivation following a meeting with the President of the United States, BP has also set up a $20 billion fund to pay out additional expected claims.[27] As a result of accepting the risk, 11 people lost their lives, BP will end up paying billions, and from April 19 to June 10, 2010 their stock price has dropped almost 50 percent.[28]

Security Devices

While the majority of new smart grid technologies will seek to increase the functionality of the smart grid, devices that are dedicated to securing the smart grid will most likely follow as well. These security devices may include the following:

- Antivirus for smart meters and devices
- Host-based intrusion detection and prevention for smart meters and devices
- Firewalls for smart meters and devices
- Encryption for low-power devices
- Physical tamper prevention

Security professionals will be responsible for determining the extent to which these products help mitigate risk in their organizations and whether they are worth the investment.

Visions of Gloom and Doom

Potential threats to the smart grid are discussed in Chapter 2, "Threats and Impacts: Consumers," and Chapter 3, "Threats and Impacts: Utility Companies and Beyond"; however, these were for the most part still hypothetical. In the next 10 years though, security professionals and national security experts predict these threats will move from hypothetical to actual.

Mike McConnell, who recently retired as the chief of national intelligence and oversaw the Central Intelligence Agency (CIA – www.cia.gov), Defense Intelligence Agency (DIA – www.dia.mil), and National Security Agency (NSA – www.nsa.gov) did an interview with Steve Kroft of CBS News (www.cbsnews. com) and discussed the possibility of a cyber attack against the United States' critical infrastructure.[29] In the interview, McConnell states that if he wanted to inflict significant damage to the United States, he would attack the electric grid on either coast and attempt to propagate the attack throughout the country's electric grid to cause widespread power outages.[29] More importantly though, McConnell believes that militaries and organized crimes across the world have the ability of performing this type of an attack against the electric grid.[29]

A cyber attack that cripples the country is commonly referred to as a Cyber Pearl Harbor, and McConnell is not the only person who believes that a Cyber Pearl Harbor attack will involve the electric grid. Many security professionals have voiced their concern over the security of the smart grid and the inherent risk with making the electric grid more accessible. Instead of launching missiles and executing surgical strikes with special operations forces, the next war could be initiated with a cyber attack to destroy a nation's critical infrastructure.

SMART GRID COMMUNITY

Whether you are a security professional with 10 years of experience or have no experience and are just interested in the smart grid security, the smart grid community has amassed a wealth of information and resources. Information about the latest developments can be obtained from resources including

- Conferences
- Agencies and groups
- News sites and blogs

Conferences

Smart-grid- and security-related conferences will provide details on the latest threats, vulnerabilities, and exploits for smart-grid-related technologies. Table 14.2 lists some of the relevant conferences in which smart grid security is discussed. The conferences listed in Table 14.2 represent a small sample of the hundreds of smart-grid- and security-related conferences that occur throughout the year and across the world. The good news is that there are most likely conferences that occur within your geographic area.

Agencies and Groups

Numerous government agencies and industry and community groups are performing research, discussing, and providing information about smart grid security. If you are looking to get involved, some of these organizations are looking for

Table 14.2 Smart grid and security conferences

Conference	URL
Applied Security Conferences: CanSecWest, PacSec, EUSecWest	http://cansecwest.com http://pacsec.jp http://eusecwest.com
Black Hat	http://blackhat.com
DEFCON	http://defcon.org
Hackers to Hackers	www.h2hc.com.br/index.php
National Smart Grid Conference	www.nationalsmartgridconference.com
OWASP AppSec Conferences	www.owasp.org/index.php/Category: OWASP_AppSec_Conference
RSA	www.rsaconference.com
SCADA and Process Control Summit	www.sans.org/scada-security-summit-2010/
SecTor	www.sector.ca/
Shmoocon	www.shmoocon.org
Smart Grid Cyber Security Summit	www.smartgridsecuritysummit.com
Smart Grid Summit	http://smart-grid.tmcnet.com
SOURCE Conferences	www.sourceconference.com/
ToorCon	www.toorcon.org
WiMob	http://conferences.computer.org/wimob2010/

volunteers. For example, the National Institute of Standards and Technology release draft versions of their publications for public comment. Throughout this book, many of these organizations have already been mentioned, but for convenience Table 14.3 lists out a sample of a few relevant agencies and groups. These should only serve as a starting point to find the organization that best matches your interest and skill set.

Information Sharing

In the security world, sharing information can be an oxymoron. As a security professional, your job is to protect your organization's sensitive information from being disclosed and is most likely against your organization's security policies. However, discussing risk, threats, and successful attacks can help other organizations prevent the same attack from succeeding in other organizations. Sharing lessons learned from accomplishments and failures has the potential to benefit both your organization and the smart grid community alike.

Issuing press releases or openly discussing internal security-related topics with members of the press is probably not the best approach though. Thankfully, more discrete resources do exist and some are mentioned in Table 14.3. Specifically, ES-IAC is a member-only communication channel that promotes the discussion of security-related topics within the electricity sector. The goal of ES-IAC is to provide a channel for collaboration between the members of the electricity sector to better address threats to the security of the electric grid.[30]

Table 14.3 Smart grid oriented agencies and groups

Organization	URL
Electric Power Research Institute (EPRI)	www.epri.com/
Electricity Sector – Information Sharing and Analysis Center (ES-IAC)	www.esisac.com/
GridWise Alliance	www.gridwise.org/
IEEE Smart Grid	http://smartgrid.ieee.org/
National Association of Regulatory Utility Commissioners (NARUC)	www.naruc.org
National Institute of Standards and Technology (NIST)	www.nist.gov/smartgrid/
North American Electric Reliability Corporation (NERC)	www.nerc.com/
Open Web Application Security Project (OWASP)	www.owasp.org/
Smart Grid Australia Alliance	www.smartgridaustralia.com.au/
Smart Grid Consumer Collaborative	www.smartgridcc.org/
Smart Grids European Union	www.smartgrids.eu/
United States Department of Energy (DOE)	www.oe.energy.gov/smartgrid.htm
United States Federal Energy Regulatory Commission (FERC)	www.ferc.gov/industries/electric/indus-act/smart-grid.asp
UtiliSec	http://osgug.ucaiug.org/utilisec/default.aspx

Standards Development

The agencies and groups listed in Table 14.3 will continue to develop more standards for smart grids. Standards will need to be created for every new technology introduced into smart grids as well as for assessing new technologies. Global collaboration will be needed in order to create the best possible security standards that address the unique challenges that different geographic locations face. Fortunately, some countries have begun to work together already. For example, Japan and the United States have agreed to explore joint smart grid projects in Okinawa and Hawaii. These islands share common climates and dependence on traditional fuel types, which makes the collaboration between the two countries a logical choice.[31] The two countries have agreed to cooperate over smart grid technology that should improve the electric grid on the two islands.[31] Unfortunately, since the security of electric grids is considered a matter of national security, multinational collaboration will most likely be limited.

Blogs, News Web Sites, and RSS Feeds

The mainstream news will cover the larger stories regarding smart grid security. For daily updates and more technical analysis, readers should regularly view blogs and news Web sites related to smart grid security and technology. If you are reading

Table 14.4 Security and technology blogs and news Web sites

Name	URL
CSO Online	www.csoonline.com
The DOD Energy Blog	http://dodenergy.blogspot.com/
earth2tech	http://earth2tech.com/
European Energy Review	www.europeanenergyreview.eu
Engadget	www.engadget.com
Greentech Media	www.greentechmedia.com
NTS Smart Grid Blog	http://smartgrid.testing-blog.com/
Smart Grid News	www.smartgridnews.com
SC Magazine	http://scmagazine.com
The Smart Grid Security Blog	http://smartgridsecurity.blogspot.com/
Transmission and Distribution World	http://tdworld.com/
Unfettered Blog	http://community.controlglobal.com/unfettered

this book, then there is a good chance that you already have your favorite blogs and news Web sites, which are already in your RSS feed. However, if you are new to the industry or security in general, then the Web sites listed in Table 14.4, as well as the Web sites mentioned in Tables 14.2 and 14.3, provide a gentle approach to technology and security.

SUMMARY

The future is bright for the electric grid, as well as for other utilities. Upgrading the infrastructure with new technologies will provide utilities and consumers with functionality and benefits that Thomas Edison, George Westinghouse, and Nikola Tesla could have never imagined. However, some security professionals have sounded the alarm.

Ultimately, it will take a concerted effort between federal governments, state and local governments, utility companies, technology companies, and vigilant consumers to achieve a secure smart grid. Each will play a critical role in securing smart grids all across the world. Without the proper security controls in place, the threats to the smart grid will be realized, and the vision for the smart grid will never achieve reality.

Endnotes

1. http://maps.google.com/maps/ms?ie=UTF8&oe=UTF8&msa=0&msid=11551931105836-7534348.0000011362ac6d7d21187; [accessed 29.05.10].

2. Wood L. The Edison Foundation Institute for Electric Efficiency. Consumers are the key to future smart energy management [document on the Internet]. www.edisonfoundation.net/iee/issueBriefs/Wood_SantaFe_March10.pdf; 2010 [accessed 29.05.10].

3. Bryan C. Clarity Digital Group LLC d/b/a Examiner.com. GE adopts Zigbee protocols for smart appliance products [document on the Internet]. www.examiner.com/x-43343-Energy-Policy-Examiner~y2010m6d5-GE-adopts-Zigbee-protocols-for-smart-appliance-products; 2010 [accessed 21.06.10].

4. General Electric Company. Geospring hybrid water heater [document on the Internet]. www.geappliances.com/heat-pump-hot-water-heater/electric-water-heater-features.htm; 2010 [accessed 20.06.10].

5. U.S. Department of Energy Pacific Northwest National Laboratory. PNNL: Energy Smart Data Center (ESDC): Cooling Supercomputers [document on the Internet]. http://esdc.pnl.gov/; 2010 [02.06.10].

6. Hewlett-Packard. HP Data Center Smart Grid [document on the Internet]. http://h18000.www1.hp.com/products/solutions/converged/datacenter-smartgrid.html; 2010 [accessed 02.06.10].

7. Raphael JR. PC World. Unplug for Dollars: Stop 'Vampire Power' Waste [document on the Internet]. www.pcworld.com/article/153245/unplug_for_dollars_stop_vampire_power_waste.html; 2008 [accessed 03.06.10].

8. U.S. Department of Energy Lawrence Berkeley National Laboratory. Standby power : FAQs [document on the Internet]. http://standby.lbl.gov/faq.html; 2010 [accessed 03.06.10].

9. U.S. Energy Information Administration. Average retail price of electricity to ultimate customers by end-use sector, by state [document on the Internet]. www.eia.doe.gov/electricity/epm/table5_6_b.html; 2010 [accessed 03.06.10].

10. U.S. Department of Energy Lawrence Berkeley National Laboratory. Standby power summary table [document on the Internet]. http://standby.lbl.gov/summary-table.html; 2010 [accessed 03.06.10].

11. U.S. Department of Energy Lawrence Berkeley National Laboratory. Standby power [document on the Internet]. http://standby.lbl.gov/; 2010 [03.06.10].

12. Sakamoto K. KRON 4 The Bay Area's News Station. PG&E Under Fire for 'Smart Meter' Program [document on the Internet]. www.kron.com/News/ArticleView/tabid/298/smid/1126/ArticleID/5800/reftab/64/t/PGE%20Under%20Fire%20for%20Smart%20Meter%20Program/Default.aspx; 2010 [accessed 05.06.10].

13. Tweed K. Greentech Media. Oncor Reacts to Smart Meter Anger [document on the Internet]. www.greentechmedia.com/articles/read/oncor-reacts-to-smart-meter-anger/2010 [accessed 05.06.10].

14. Souder E. The Dallas Morning News. Couple sues Oncor over smart meter [document on the Internet]. http://energyandenvironmentblog.dallasnews.com/archives/2010/03/couple-sues-oncor-over-smart-m.html; 2010 [05.06.10].

15. Tweed K. Greentech Media. Oncor sued for fraud over smart meters [document on the Internet]. www.greentechmedia.com/articles/read/oncor-sued-for-fraud-over-smart-meters; 2010 [05.06.10].

16. Baltimore Gas and Electric Company. Save energy and get BGE Bill credits with peak-rewards [document on the Internet]. http://peakrewards.bgesmartenergy.com/what-is-peakrewards; 2010 [04.06.10].

17. Anderson K. Verizon FiOS Wireless Key Calculator [document on the Internet]. http://xkyle.com/2009/03/03/verizon-fios-wireless-key-calculator; 2009 [accessed 24.06.10].

18. National Institute of Standards and Technology. NIST Special Publication 1108: NIST Framework and Roadmap for Smart Grid Interoperability Standards, Release 1.0 [document on the Internet]. www.nist.gov/public_affairs/releases/upload/smartgrid_interoperability_final.pdf; 2010 [accessed 06.06.10].

19. Research and Innovative Technology Administration Bureau of Transportation Statistics. Table 1-11: Number of U.S. Aircraft, Vehicles, Vessels, and Other Conveyances [document on the Internet]. www.bts.gov/publications/national_transportation_statistics/html/table_01_11.html; 2010 [accessed 06.05.10].

20. Werner A. CBS LOCAL. PG&E Smart Meter 'Rebellion' Growing [document on the Internet]. Anna http://cbs5.com/local/pge.smart.meters.2.1555294.html; 2010 [accessed 07.06.10].

21. Ishola B. The Dallas Morning News. Incidents put two Oncor employees in danger [document on the Internet]. www.dallasnews.com/sharedcontent/dws/news/localnews/crime/stories/DN-oncor_19met.ART0.State.Edition1.4c13eef.html; 2009 [accessed 14.06.10].

22. North American SynchroPhasor Initiative. North American SynchroPhasor Initiative (NASPI) Home Page [document on the Internet]. www.naspi.org/; 2010 [16.06.10].

23. Nichols R. Government Technology. Tallahassee Preps Nation's First Smart Grid That Fuses Electricity, Gas and Water Utilities [document on the Internet]. www.govtech.com/gt/751021?topic=290184; 2010 [accessed 15.06.10].

24. Ziegler K. North American Electric Reliability Corporation. Press Release NERC, FERC, FPL Reach Agreement on Reliability Enhancements [document on the Internet]. 2009 www.nerc.com/fileUploads/File/PressReleases/PR_100809_FPL.pdf; 2009 [accessed 19.06.10].

25. Urbina I. Cleveland Live, Inc. Conflicts in management, exceptions to safety rules seen leading up to BP disaster [document on the Internet]. www.cleveland.com/nation/index.ssf/2010/06/conflicts_in_management_except.html 2010 [accessed 20.06.10].

26. BP p.l.c. BP Claim Payments Exceed $100 Million [document on the Internet]. www.bp.com/genericarticle.do?categoryId=2012968&contentId=7063000; 2010 [accessed 20.06.10].

27. BP p.l.c. BP Establishes $20 Billion Claims Fund for Deepwater Horizon Spill and Outlines Dividend Decisions [document on the Internet]. www.bp.com/genericarticle.do?categoryId=2012968&contentId=7062966; 2010 [accessed 19.06.10].

28. Pepitone J. Cable News Network. BP shares recover after reassurance [document on the Internet]. http://money.cnn.com/2010/06/10/news/companies/BP_stock/index.htm; 2010 [accessed 10.06.10].

29. Messick G, Kroft S. CBS Interactive Inc. Cyber War: Sabotaging the System [document on the Internet]. /www.cbsnews.com/stories/2010/06/10/60minutes/main6568387.shtml?utm_source=feedburner&utm_medium=feed&utm_campaign=Feed:+CBSNewsInvestigates+(CBS+News+Investigates); 2010 [accessed 10.06.10].

30. North American Electric Reliability Corporation. Information Sharing and Analysis Center for the Electricity Sector [document on the Internet]. /www.esisac.com; 2010 [24.06.10].

31. Kyodo News. Japan, U.S. to explore smart grid joint project in Okinawa, Hawaii [document on the Internet]. www.japantoday.com/category/technology/view/japan-us-to-explore-smart-grid-joint-project-in-okinawa-hawaii; 2010 [24.06.10].

Index

Page numbers in *italics* indicate figures and tables

A

Access control, 148
Accidental threats, 27–28
Advanced metering infrastructure (AMI), 13–14
American Recovery and Reinvestment Act
    (ARRA) of 2009, 50–53
AMR. *see* Automatic meter reading
Apache Web server, 227, *227*
Application attacks
    compiled code applications, 134–135
    life-imitating art, 121
    non-Web applications, 135
    Web applications
        for corporate operations, 122–123
        custom Web application code, 126–131
        for smart grid operations, 123–126
        trade tools, 131–133, 135
        Web server software, 133
ARRA. *see* American Recovery and Reinvestment
    Act of 2009
Asset management, 147
Aurora vulnerability, 24
Authentication controls, 208–209
Automatic meter reading (AMR)
    data collection technologies
        handheld devices, 6
        notebook computers, 6
    data transport technologies
        hybrid models, 8
        power line communication, 7
        wireless networks, 6–7
    network topologies, 8
Availability
    consumer targets, 40–41
    market manipulation, 43–44
    national security targets, 44–47
        domestic, 44–45
        international, 45
        precursor to war, 47
    organizational targets, 41–42
    vertical targets, 42–43

B

Bluetooth, 138
Breach notification laws, 69
Bruter, 253, *254*

Bureaucracy and politics, 70
Business continuity management, 149

C

Cain & Abel password-cracking tool, 221, *221*
California Public Utility Commission, 74–75
Carbon footprint, 17
Cellular networks, 138
Clear-text protocols, *175*
Code and command signing, 155
Code signing, 181–182
Colorado Court of Appeals, 81
Communication security testing, 223
Communications and operations management, 148
Compiled code applications, 134–135
Compliance, 149–150
    vs. security, 104–105
Computer installations, 151–152
Confidentiality
    consumer privacy, 36–37
        consumption data, 37
        PII, 36–37
    proprietary information, 37–38
Configuration hardening, 158
Consumer attacks
    functionality undermines security, 167
    Microsoft Hohm and Google PowerMeter,
        167–169
        persistent authentication, 168–169
        single sign-on, 168
    with smart devices, 169–170
Consumer privacy, 36–37
    consumption data, 37
    personally identifiable information, 36–37
Consumer threats, 19–20
    financial impacts, 31–32
    intelligent consumers, 13
    likelihood of attack, 32
    power availability
        emergency services, 31
        mobility, 31
        personal availability, 30–31
    privacy impacts, 29–30
    vulnerability impacts, 28
        see also Individual and organizational
        threats; Naturally occuring threats
Critical business applications, 151

Critical cyber asset identification–CIP-002, 87–88

Cross-site scripting attacks, 130, *130*

Current smart grid technologies
AMI security, 55–56
NASPI security, 56
wireless network security, 56

Custom Web application code, 126–131

Cyber security standards, 60–61

Cyber vulnerability assessment, 96

D

Daisy-chaining trust, 171–172

Data access, 172–173
data classification, 172–173
data segmentation, 173

Data collection technologies
handheld devices, 6
notebook computers, 6

Data transport technologies
hybrid models, 8
power line communication, 7
wireless networks, 6–7

Default deny firewall rules, 155

Denial of service testing, 219–222

Department of Energy (DOE)
current smart grid technologies
AMI security, 55–56
NASPI security, 56
wireless network security, 56
lack of deployment, 56
legacy electric grid technologies, 54–55
recommendations, 53

Deregulation, 4–5

DHS National Infrastructure Protection Plan (DHS NIPP), 66–67

Digital signature, 182

Disaster recovery–CIP-009, 98–99

Disk encryption, 187

Distribution networks, 2

DOE. *see* Department of Energy

Domestic terrorism, 44–45

E

ECPA. *see* Electronic Communications Privacy Act

800-42 NIST security testing techniques, 226–231
network scanning, 227–228
password cracking, 228–229
penetration testing, 230–231
vulnerability scanning, 228
wireless LAN testing, 229–230

802.11 Wireless network testing, 224–225

Electric grids
definition of, 1–2
deregulation, 4–5
topologies, 2–4

Electric vehicles, 267–268

Electricity theft, 17

Electromagnetic interference, 62

Electromagnetic pulse (EMP), 61, 62

Electronic Communications Privacy Act (ECPA) of 1986, 68

Electronic security
critical cyber asset identification, 87–88
disaster recovery, 98–99
electronic security protection, 90–93
incident reporting and response planning, 96–98
security management controls, 88–90
system security management, 94–96

Electronic security perimeter, 86

Electronic security protection–CIP-005, 90–93

EISA. *see* Energy and Independence Security Act

E-mail attacks, 183–184

EMP. *see* Electromagnetic pulse

Encryption, 156

End user environment, 152

Energy and Independence Security Act (EISA) of 2007, 50

Energy Conservation Responsibility Act, 14

Energy Policy Act of 2005, Section 1251, 39

Exploit testing, 220–223

Extortion, 43

Extortive malware. *see* Ransomware

F

Facebook, 199–202
PICOwatts, 199–200
SmartSync, 200–201
WattsUp, 201–202

Federal Energy Regulatory Commission (FERC)
Mandatory reliability standards, 56–57
Smart grid policy, 57

FlicksJavaApp, 274

FOA. *see* Funding Opportunity Announcement

Forensics, 190–191

Fujitsu's Smart Power Strip, 234, *234*

Funding Opportunity Announcement (FOA), 53

G

General attack methodology, 127

Google Chrome, 245

H

Hackers, 23–25
    nonmalicious motives, 24
    personal gain, 24–25
    security testing, 24
    vengeance and vindictiveness, 25
HAN. *see* Home Area Network
Handheld devices, 6
Handset attacks, 183
Heartland Payment Systems, 104, 105
HMI. *see* Human machine interface
Home Area Network (HAN), 266–267
Honeypots, 156
Human machine interface (HMI), 12
Human resources security, 147
Hurricanes, 21–22

I

Idaho National Laboratory (INL) document
    current smart grid technologies
        AMI security, 55–56
        NASPI security, 56
        wireless network security, 56
    legacy electric grid technologies, 54–55
Identity controls, 208
Illinois Power Agency Act, SB 1592, 75
Incident reporting and response
    planning–CIP-008, 96–98
Individual and organizational threats
    government
        illegal activity, 27
        warfare, 26–27
    hackers, 23–25
        nonmalicious motives, 24
        personal gain, 24–25
        security testing, 24
        vengeance and vindictiveness, 25
    smart thieves and stalkers, 22–23
    terrorism, 25–26
        eco-terrorism, 26
    utility companies
        accidental threats, 27–28
        intentional attacks, 28
        load shedding, 28
Information security, 213–214
Information Security Forum (ISF), 150–151
    see also Standard of Good Practice (SoGP)
Information security incident management, 149
Information sharing controls, 209
Information systems acquisition, development, and
    maintenance, 148–149
Injection attacks, 128

INL document. *see* Idaho National Laboratory
    document
Integrated two-way communication, 10–12
Integrity
    sensor data manipulation, 38–40
    service fraud
        net metering, 39
    service theft, 38–39
Intelligent consumer, 13
Intentional attacks, 28
Internal security assessment, 115–116
International Organization for Standardization/
    International Electrotechnical Commission
    (ISO/IEC), 144
Internet application testing, 219–220, 245–251
Internet technology security testing
    denial of service testing, 221–222
    exploit testing, 222–223
    Internet application testing, 219–220
    network surveying, 215–216
    password cracking, 220–221
    port scanning, 216–217
    services identification and system
        identification, 217–218
    vulnerability research and verification, 218–219
ISF. *see* Information Security Forum
ISO/IEC. *see* International Organization for
    Standardization/International
    Electrotechnical Commission
ISO/IEC 27000 standards, 144–152
ISO/IEC 27002 standards guidelines
    access control, 148
    asset management, 147
    business continuity management, 149
    communications and operations management, 148
    compliance, 149–150
    human resources security, 147
    information security incident management, 149
    information systems acquisition, development,
        and maintenance, 148–149
    organization of information security, 147
    physical and environment security, 147–148
    risk assessment, 146
    security policy, 146–147

K

Karmetasploit, 137–138
Kismet wireless sniffing tool, 224, *224*

L

Legacy electric grid technologies, 54–55
Legacy systems, 120

Likelihood of attack, 32
Load shedding, 28
Logging and monitoring, 158–159
Looped topology, 4, *5*

M

Malicious Web sites, 184
Maryland Public Service Commission, 75
Mechanical appliances, 259
Mesh grid topology, 3, *4*
Mesh network AMR topology, 8
Metasploit Framework, open-source testing tool, 157
Metasploit vulnerability exploit tool, 222, *222*
Meter tampering, 17
Microsoft Hohm and Google PowerMeter, 167–169
    persistent authentication, 168–169
    single sign-on, 168
Microsoft Internet Explorer, 245
Mobile applications, 179–180
    encryption, 192
    security controls, 191–192
Mobile device security
    best-practice guides, 186
    disk encryption, 187
    education, 191
    forensics, 190–191
    recovery, 190
    screen locking, 188–189
    secure syncing, 187
    traditional security controls, 187
    wiping device, 190
Mobile platforms, 180
Motivation
    security assessment, 111–112
    vulnerability assessment *vs.* penetration test,
        110–111
Mozilla Firefox, 245

N

NASPI security. *see* North American
    SynchroPhasor Initiative security
National Association of Regulatory Utility
    Commissioner (NARUC), 76–78
National Institute of Standards and Technology
    (NIST), 226–231
Naturally occurring threats, 20–22
    weather and other natural disasters, 21–22
NERC. *see* North American Reliability Corporation
NERC Critical Infrastructure Protection (CIP)
        Standards
    electronic security

critical cyber asset identification–CIP-002,
        87–88
    disaster recovery–CIP-009, 98–99
    electronic security protection–CIP-005, 90–93
    incident reporting and response
        planning–CIP-008, 96–98
    security management controls–CIP-003, 88–90
    system security management–CIP-007, 94–96
physical and personnel security
    personnel and training–CIP-004, 100–101
    physical security of critical cyber
        assets–CIP-006, 102–103
Nessus, 218, *219, 242, 243, 244, 245*
Net metering, 39
Network access, 173–174
    monitoring, 174
    segmentation, 174
Network attacks
    methodologies standards, 114
    network security assessment
        discovery, 116–117
        penetration, 117–119
        reconnaissance, 114–116
        vulnerability identification, 117
Network scanning, 227–228
Network security assessment
    discovery, 116–117
    penetration, 117–119
    reconnaissance, 114–116
    vulnerability identification, 117
Network security testing tools, *115*
Network stumbler wireless tool, 229, *230*
Network surveying, 215–216, 236–237
Network topologies
    mesh network AMR topology, 8
    star network AMR topology, 8
Networking controls, 209
NIST. *see* National Institute of Standards and
        Technology
NIST SP 1108, 58
    cyber security standards, 60–61
    cyber security strategy and requirements, 62–66
    electromagnetic disturbances, 61
    electromagnetic interference, 62
    Priority Action Plans (PAPs), 61
    smart grid information networks, 59
NISTIR-7628
    high-level security requirements, 64–66
    risk assessment, 63–64
    standards and requirements assessment, 66
Nmap, 240, *240*

North American Electric Reliability Corporation
(NERC), 57
North American SynchroPhasor Initiative (NASPI)
security, 56
Notebook computers, 6

O

Oklahoma City bombing of 1995, 45, *46*
Open Source Security Testing Methodology
Manual (OSSTM), 211–226
communication security testing, 223
information security, 213–214
Internet technology security testing, 215–223
physical security testing, 225–226
process security testing, 214–215
wireless security testing
12 modules, 223
802.11 wireless networks testing, 224–225
Bluetooth and RFID security testing, 225
Open Web Application Security Project
(OWASP), 192
Organization of information security, 147
OSSTM. *see* Open Source Security Testing
Methodology Manual
OWASP. *see* Open Web Application
Security Project

P

PAPs. *see* Priority Action Plans
Passive testing, 114
Password cracking, 220–221, 228–229, 251–254
Patch management, 27–28
Payment Card Industry Data Security Standard
(PCI DSS), 104–105, 162
Penetration test, 110
Penetration testing, 157, 230–231
Perimeter security controls, 119
Personal Information Protection and Electronic
Documents Act (PIPEDA), 69
Personal power plant, 268
Personally identifiable information (PII), 29, 36–37
Personnel and training–CIP-004, 100–101
Physical and environment security, 147–148
Physical and personnel security
personnel and training–CIP-004, 100–101
physical security of critical cyber
assets–CIP-006, 102–103
Physical attacks, 139–140, 184–186
Physical security of critical cyber
assets–CIP-006, 102–103
Physical security testing, 225–226

PICOwatts, 199–200
PII. *see* Personally identifiable information
PIPEDA. *see* Personal Information Protection and
Electronic Documents Act
PLC. *see* Power line communication
Politics, 70, 83
Port scanning, 216–217, 238–239
Power line communication (PLC), 7
Priority Action Plans (PAPs), 61
Process security testing, 214–215
Proprietary information, 37–38
PSEXEC module, 118
Public Utility Commission (PUC)
of California, 74–75
of Colorado, 78–79
of Texas, 79–80

R

Radial grid topology, 3, *3*
Ransomware, 25
Renewable energy sources, 9–10, 17
Risk acceptance, 274–275
Risk assessment, 146

S

SAS 70. *see* Statement on Auditing Standards No. 70
SCADA systems. *see* Supervisory Control and
Data Acquisition systems
Script kiddies, 40
SDLC. *see* System development lifecycle
Sector-Specific Plans (SSP), 67
Security assessments, 111
Security education, 82–83
Security laws
Breach notification laws, 69
Electronic Communications Privacy Act of
1986, 68
The Identity Theft Enforcement and Restitution
Act of 2008, 67–68
Personal Information Protection and Electronic
Documents Act, 69
Security management, 151
Security management controls–CIP-003, 88–90
Security policy, 146–147
Security professionals
security devices, 275
security *vs.* functionality, 273–275
visions of gloom and doom, 275–276
Security testing tools
for compiled code applications, *135*
for Web applications, *132*

Security testing tools (*Cont.*)
    wireless, *137*
Segmentation, 154–155
Sensing and measurement technologies, 12
    see also Smart meter
Sensor data manipulation, 39–40
Service fraud
    net metering, 39
    service theft, 38–39
Service theft, 38–39
Services identification and system identification,
    217–218, 239–241
Short Message Service (SMS), 183
SGIG Program. *see* Smart Grid Investment
    Grant Program
SGIP-CSWG. *see* Smart Grid Interoperability
    Group-Cyber Security Working Group
Smart consumer appliances
    in home, 259
    in office, 259–261
"Smart Grid, Smart City" initiative, 14
Smart grid community
    agencies and groups, 276–278, *278*
        information sharing, 277
        standards development, 278
    conferences, 276, *277*
    blogs, news Web sites, and RSS feeds,
        278–279, *279*
Smart grid information networks, 59
Smart Grid Interoperability Group-Cyber Security
    Working Group (SGIP-CSWG)
    high-level security requirements,
        64–66
    risk assessment, 63–64
    standards and requirements assessment, 66
Smart Grid Investment Grant Program (SGIG), 53
Smart grid Social Networking Security Checklist
    authentication controls, 208–209
    identity controls, 208
    information sharing controls, 209
    networking controls, 209
    usage controls, 209
    before you begin, 207
Smart grid technology vendors, 269–270
Smart grids
    basic diagram, *11*
    components
        advanced components, 12
        advanced control methods, 12
        applications of smart grid technology, 13
        improved interfaces and decision
           support, 12–13

integrated two-way communication, 10–12
    sensing and measurement technologies, 12
    definitions, 10
    goals of, 8
    international initiatives
        Australia, 14
        Canada, 14–15
        China, 15
        Europe, 15
    reliability justification, 9
    renewable energy sources, 9–10
    vs. security features, 16
        affordability, 17
        carbon footprint, 17
        reliability, 16–17
        renewable energy sources, 17
    waste justification, 9
Smart meter, 12, *13*, 261–266
SmartGrids Platform, 15
SmartSync, 200–201
SMS. *see* Short Message Service
Social engineering attacks, 138–139
Social networking sites. *see* Facebook; Twitter
Social networking threats, 203–207
    information disclosure, 204–207
SoGP. *see* Standard of Good Practice
Source code review, 157
Sponsoring security, 70
SSP. *see* Sector-Specific Plans
Stalker, 23
Standard of Good Practice (SoGP),
    150–151
    computer installations, 151–152
    critical business applications, 151
    end user environment, 152
    networks, 152
    security management, 151
    systems development, 152
Star network AMR topology, 8
State Courts
    Colorado Court of Appeals, 81
    privacy implications, 81
State laws
    California Public Utility Commission,
        74–75
    Illinois Power Agency Act, SB 1592, 75
    mandated security, 75
    Maryland Public Service Commission, 75
State regulatory bodies
    Colorado PUC, 78–79
    future planning, 80–81
    NARUC, 76–78

PUC of Texas, 79–80
Web sites, 78–77
Statement on Auditing Standards No. 70
(SAS 70), 176
"Strengthened Smart Grid" initiative, 15
Strong authentication, 158
Structured Query Language (SQL) injection, 37
Supervisory Control and Data Acquisition
(SCADA) systems, 54, 119–120
Syncing, 187
System attacks
legacy systems, 120
SCADA systems, 119–120
System development lifecycle (SDLC), 80
System security management–CIP-007, 94–96
Systems development, 152

T

Technical practices, smart grids
code and command signing, 155
configuration hardening, 158
default deny firewall rules, 155
encryption, 156
honeypots, 156
logging and monitoring, 158–159
penetration testing, 157
segmentation, 154–155
source code review, 157
strong authentication, 158
threat modeling, 153–154
vulnerability management, 156
TED 5000 smart device, 234, 235
Denial of service testing, 219–220
exploit testing, 220–221
Internet application testing, 245–251
network surveying, 236–237
password cracking, 251–254
port scanning, 238–239
services identification and system
identification, 239–241
vulnerability research and verification,
241–245
The Identity Theft Enforcement and Restitution
Act of 2008, 67–68
Third-party access security
assessing, 175–176
data access, 172–173
data classification, 172–173
data segmentation, 173
network access, 173–174
monitoring, 174
segmentation, 174

transport security, 174–175
trust, 171–172
Third-party service providers
attacking, 170
billing, 161–162
access for payment processors, 162, 163
compliance, 162
consumer interfaces, 162–165
energy consumption applications,
163–164, 164
smart devices management, 164–165
device support, 166, 166–167
Third-party services, 30
Threat modeling, 153–154
Timeline, 257
Transmission networks, 2
TrueCrypt tool, 187
Trust
application developers and consumers,
180–182
utility companies and third-party service
providers, 171–172
Twitter
definition, 195, 196
smart meter and broadband integration, 199
Tweet-a-Watt, 198–199
tweeting energy usage, 196–197

U

U.S. Federal Government laws
American Recovery and Reinvestment Act of
2009, 50–53
Energy and Independence Security Act of
2007, 50
Usage controls, 209
Utility companies
accidental threats, 27–28
availability
consumer targets, 40–41
market manipulation, 43–44
national security target, 44–47
organizational targets, 41–42
vertical targets, 42–43
beyond electricity, 272–273
confidentiality
consumer privacy, 36–37
proprietary information, 37–38
curiosity attacks, 273
faster diagnosis, 271–272
integrity
sensor data manipulation, 39–40
service fraud, 38

Utility companies (*Cont.*)
  intentional attacks, 28
  load shedding, 28
  to reduce costs and security, 270–271

V

Variable pricing, 264–266
Vulnerability assessment, 110
Vulnerability management, 156
Vulnerability research and verification,
    218–219, 241–245
Vulnerability scanners, 117
Vulnerability scanning, 218, 228
Vulnerable network device driver, 39

W

w3af, *248, 249, 250*
War dialing testing tools, *120*
War driving, 229–230
WattsUp, 201–202

Web applications attacks
  for corporate operations, 122–123
  custom Web application code, 126–131
  for smart grid operations, 123–126
  trade tools, 131–133, 135
  Web server software, 133
Wi-Fi networks, 138
Wired Equivalent Privacy (WEP) encryption, 267
Wireless attacks, 135–138
  Bluetooth, 138
  cellular networks, 138
  Wi-Fi networks, 138
  wireless clients, 127
Wireless clients, 127
Wireless LAN testing, 229–230
Wireless networks, 6–7
Wireless security testing
  12 modules, 223
  802.11 Wireless Network Testing, 224–225
  Bluetooth and RFID security testing, 225
Wireshark network-sniffing tool, 216, *216*